P9-AGO-796

WILLIAM GOYEN

A *Study of the Short Fiction*

Also available in Twayne's Studies in Short Fiction Series

Twayne's Studies in Short Fiction

Gordon Weaver, General Editor
Oklahoma State University

William Goyen
Photograph courtesy of Mrs. Charles P. Goyen

WILLIAM GOYEN

—————— *A Study of the Short Fiction* ——

Reginald Gibbons
Northwestern University

TWAYNE PUBLISHERS • BOSTON
A Division of G. K. Hall & Co.

Twayne's Studies in Short Fiction Series, No. 20

Copyright 1991 by G. K. Hall & Co.
All rights reserved.
Published by Twayne Publishers
A division of G. K. Hall & Co.
70 Lincoln Street
Boston, Massachusetts 02111

Copyediting supervised by Barbara Sutton.
Book design by Janet Z. Reynolds.
Book production by Gabrielle B. McDonald.
Typeset in 10/12 Caslon by Compset, Inc. of Beverly, Massachusetts.

First published 1991.
10 9 8 7 6 5 4 3 2 1

The paper used in this publication meets the minimum requirements
of American National Standard for Information Sciences—Permanence
of Paper for Printed Library Materials, ANSI Z39.48-1984. ∞™

Printed and bound in the United States of America.

Library of Congress Cataloging-in-Publication Data
Gibbons, Reginald.
    William Goyen : a study of the short fiction / Reginald Gibbons.
        p.   cm.—(Twayne's studies in short fiction ; no. 20)
    Includes bibliographical references and index.
    ISBN 0-8057-8308-3 (alk. paper)
        1. Goyen, William—Criticism and interpretation.   2. Short story.
    I. Title.   II. Series.
    PS3513.097Z68   1991
    813′ .54—dc20   90-48707
                                                                            CIP

To Doris Roberts

Contents

Preface

William Goyen was one of the most original and brilliant writers of
short fiction that American culture has produced in our time. If his
work is not as well known as that of some of his glittering contemporaries, this fact has to do more with the power of literary fashion than
with the value of Goyen's writing. One proof of the injustice of this
disparity lies in the high reputation of Goyen's work outside the United
States, where more of his books are in print than within our own
boundaries, where his translators have included the most distinguished
of this century, and where the most thoroughgoing critical studies have
been written. This volume is an attempt to give the reader a grounding
in the general contours of Goyen's short fiction and to point out the
particular qualities that mark it as utterly original.

I begin with a brief sketch of Goyen's formation as an artist, which
is of the greatest importance in understanding his work. In the subsequent chapters, the analyses of individual stories are not grouped together but rather appear in connection with topics of general relevance
to Goyen's particular character as a writer of fiction: the special element of Goyen's fiction that he called the "teller-listener situation,"
his themes, and his last work. The rationale for proceeding in this way
is to equip the reader to read any Goyen story, whether it is analyzed
in this volume or not, with an attentiveness to Goyen's characteristic
fictional technique, his artistic originality, and his themes.

Even Goyen's novels seem closer to the intensity and compression
of the short story than to the extended scope of long narratives. *The
House of Breath* and *Come, the Restorer,* particularly, are composed of
linked sections, like the quilt medallions Goyen refers to in both the
interviews reprinted in this volume. Goyen presented a section of his
novel *In a Farther Country* as a story in his *Selected Writings;* and his novel
The Fair Sister is an amplification of what Goyen first wrote as a short
story, "Savata, My Fair Sister." In studying Goyen's stories, we
thus study not only one major portion of his life's work but also that
portion which underlies the other major portion, his novels (whereas

studying the novels would not help us so much to understand the stories.)

All of Goyen's stories show his highly distinctive style and fictional method—his readily recognizable artistic signature. Readers who admire his work tend not to be halfhearted about it but to be enthusiastic and devoted. There is a certain quality in this work that is uncommon in American fiction of the second half of this century, and for lack of a better word, it might be called "inspiring." I mean this term in both the figurative and the literal senses. There is, indeed, much wrestling with deep and unanswerable questions of *spirit* in Goyen's fiction—with genuine mysteries of life—and for many readers Goyen's way of expressing this struggle, once they have discovered it, becomes a part of their "equipment for living" (which is Kenneth Burke's definition of literature). And because Goyen was concerned artistically with perfecting the fictional technique of storytelling in his own, highly original way, his work is also "inspiring" in the sense that it is really meant to be spoken by the human voice, to be read aloud, and more than once, for it aims to create in language a kind of musical score for the voice that will bring in breath and expel it in Goyen's rhythms and cadences. Goyen's work participates in a human *social* reality—one person speaking to another, and that other person listening; it does not encourage us, when we are reading it, to experience ourselves as isolated individual minds. That is, Goyen's short stories create for us the vivid illusion of there being two persons present when we are reading—and I don't mean the characters in the story; I mean, rather, to acknowledge the striking intimacy and presence of those voices who so often speak to us when we read Goyen's fiction.

I hope this book will help to introduce more readers to an extraordinary writer. I believe that some of Goyen's stories, from the early "Ghost and Flesh, Water and Dirt" to the late "Arthur Bond," are among the most original, memorable, and important by any writer we have. Goyen's complete stories will be published in the not-so-distant future, as will a selection of his letters; gradually American critical attention will turn in his direction; and the mastery and uniqueness of his work, especially the short stories and his novels *The House of Breath* and *Arcadio*, will become the common property of all those who read.

I would like to thank Patrice Repusseau for his excellent studies of Goyen and, although we have never met, for his critical companionship, for I have been spurred on and moved by his untiring work as translator and critic of Goyen's fiction; Robert Phillips, for his long devotion and many labors on behalf of Goyen and Goyen's work; Robert S. Nelsen, for his very acute suggestions when this book was in manuscript; Gwenan Wilbur, who prepared the index; and Kate Chaltain, who helped with the preparation of the manuscript.

Acknowledgments

Quotations for Goyen's work and letters copyright © by Doris Roberts and the Charles William Goyen Trust and are reprinted by permission. All rights reserved. Goyen's letters to Margo Jones are held in the Margo Jones Collection of the Dallas Public Library.

"Interview with William Goyen" by Robert Phillips, *Writers-at-Work*, vol. 6, ed. George Plimpton. © 1984 by the *Paris Review*, Inc. All rights reserved. Reprinted by permission of Viking Penguin, Inc., a division of Penguin Books USA, Inc.

Interview with William Goyen by Reginald Gibbons. © 1983 by *TriQuarterly* magazine, a publication of Northwestern University. Reprinted by permission.

Essay by Lyman Grant on William Goyen first published in the *Texas Observer*. © 1983 by the *Texas Observer*. Reprinted by permission of the author.

Introduction to William Goyen, *Had I a Hundred Mouths*, by Joyce Carol Oates. © 1989 by Joyce Carol Oates. Reprinted by permission of the author and Clarkson N. Potter.

"Ghost and Flesh: William Goyen's Patterns of the Invisible and of the Visible" by Robert Phillips. © 1979 by Robert Phillips. Reprinted by permission of the author.

Essay on William Goyen by James Korges, *Contemporary Novelists*, ed. James Vinson. © 1982 by St. Martin's Press. Reprinted by permission.

Part 1

THE SHORT FICTION

Goyen's Formation as an Artist

Goyen's Life

William Goyen was born in Trinity, a small town in East Texas, in 1915. His father was of a Mississippi family whose itinerant work in the forests and sawmills of the East Texas lumber industry are suggested in his short story "Old Wildwood"; his mother was a native of Trinity, and her family counted Texans for several generations back. Goyen's mother's family was more settled than his father's, and her father was the postmaster of Trinity. Trinity was very small, with fewer than a thousand inhabitants, about half white and half black.[1] Goyen's early childhood was lived in this small-town and family realm of talk and storytelling, and in such a realm there is perhaps a keener sense of the possibilities of story in every person's life. That is, the desire to hear and tell stories perhaps calls one's attention to the narrative possibilities in the lives around one. In Goyen's first novel, *The House of Breath* (1950), and in a number of his stories, such as "Pore Perrie" (from his first collection, *Ghost and Flesh*, 1952), one sees a vivid presentation of the atmosphere of storytelling, especially the telling of sad or even tragic stories of lives wounded or haunted by accident and by mysteries of temperament. Although two of Goyen's early stories, "The White Rooster" and "Tapioca Surprise," are humorous despite their underlying darkness, and indeed there is often in Goyen, even at his bleakest, a possibility of laughter, he is nonetheless a writer whose imagination turns often to the loss of love, to loneliness, to grief.

This tendency may in part follow from his own experience of loss and of loneliness. When Goyen was still a boy, he was uprooted from his familiar surroundings when his parents left their small-town household and moved to Shreveport, Louisiana, and then soon afterward back to Texas, this time to Houston. The child's painful longing for that house they left behind, and the gathering of relatives, is the spark from which Goyen kindled the fire of his visionary first novel, *The House of Breath*, years later.

The move also altered his sense of the surrounding world: at the time of Goyen's birth, the entire state of Texas had about four million inhabitants; much of the state, especially in the thickly wooded lands of East Texas, was still wilderness, although it was less wild than it had been for his grandfather. In "Old Wildwood," the narrator's grandfather says of that time in Texas, "Twas all wildwood then, son, but so soon gone."[2]

Transplanted to the city, Goyen was aware from early youth of his personal loss of a natural realm, and he became aware as he matured of the larger loss to which his was parallel—the despoliation of nature by the timber and oil companies. Goyen's melancholy awareness of ecological destruction, which surfaces in the story "Bridge of Music, River of Sand" and in Goyen's last major work, the short novel *Arcadio* (1983), seems to have arisen quite naturally from his earliest experience. As he said in an interview, "I grew up in the fields, by a river and trees. My family were all poor, and their job was to cut down those trees at a nearby peckerwood sawmill. I just lived in terror of there being no more woods, no more river, and sure enough there aren't many woods, and the river that I loved is nothing; it's dry and gone. . . . The destruction of nature is very personal to me, and the greed which does it is enraging."[3]

So the move from Trinity to Houston would have been not only from one landscape to another but also from rural isolation and small-town institutions to what was by comparison a true city at a pitch of commercial fervor for new business and the quick dollar. From a reading of Goyen's work one can sense that this first great loss—of his family home and his natural home—made a remarkable and ineradicable impression on him.

Goyen came of age in a realm of rapid changes, fresh starts by immigrants arriving in Texas from other American states and from abroad, bringing with them extreme hopes and finding brash success and bitter disappointments. The atmosphere in the 1920s and 1930s was a typically American combination of marvels and possibilities, failures and crushing practical realities and injustices. The young Goyen realized that his father was not one of the energetic boomtown men, not one of those to ride the wave of real estate development and new industry, and thus something of a failure. At the same time, Goyen disliked the successful businessmen his father failed to emulate. The natural desire to please his father was thus frustrated in Goyen by his inability to admire his father, as well as by his father's incomprehension of Goyen's artistic interests.[4]

As an adult and an artist, Goyen seems to have looked back at his early childhood not only as the unrecoverable realm of profound sense impressions and pure feeling that it is for most children but also as a lost place to which he could not find his way back even geographically. In many passing phrases of his work one hears a tone of baffled wonder at the impossibility of satisfying this desire to return to the first place: the traveler is lost, and the place no longer exists.

Not only was Goyen physically removed from his familiar home by his father's decision to leave Trinity, or alienated by the changes wrought on the East Texas landscape by the oil and timber industries; he was also torn from a certain linguistic environment, a certain time of language—that is, his maturing sense of language both initiated his literary ability and began to separate him from the matrix of language in which he had been formed. Indeed, in addition to Goyen's sense of his own language as an individual, shaped and influenced by forces both literary and personal after his childhood, the language of Texas itself was changing. In Goyen's lifetime the population of Texas became far more urbanized, its rural folkways receded further into the past, and its financial prosperity, beginning with World War II, remade the culture of small town and city alike. Goyen's Trinity was Edenic, and while Houston scarcely appears in his stories (although with its city high school, its city hall and library, its Rice Institute, its Cotton Exchange, and its neighborhoods, it was the scene of Goyen's youth and young manhood), much of his work is set in unnamed small towns. The city was a rapidly growing, segregated, already-oil-rich town, with a few comparatively grand buildings and a cultural life typical of a backwater commercial center—visits from touring theater companies, opera, orchestral music and ballet, and other performers, who would seem to the young Goyen to have come from another world and who departed for it again after their performances.

What Goyen particularly noticed and felt was the lostness of the small-town people transplanted to the city. In the story "Zamour, or A Tale of Inheritance," for example, he writes:

> This was a time when people from small towns and farms were migrating to bigger towns and small cities, the time of change in Texas. Princis and Mr. Simpson moved into a small frame house in a neighborhood on Hines Street in Houston. The block of houses, called the Neighborhood by those living there, was inhabited by migrants from little towns, and a few were even from Red River County. These people had changed their style of living and slid into the pattern of the city. But oddly enough—for one would have thought

she would be the first to change—Princis Lester did not alter, but from the day she settled there went on living as if she were still in Red River County. Something in Red River County kept her. (*CS*, 187)

Small as it was then, Houston was gigantic compared with the nine hundred souls of Trinity. "What caught me up so early and made me feel that I had to be a voice for it was the sense of exile, misplacement, the poverty, spiritual and material, of city living, the growing hell of automobiles, the loss of open nature of woods and rivers, the simple lyric yearning of people out of place. . . . Houston in those early days seemed to me a place of the half-lost and the estranged, even the persecuted," Goyen wrote many years later (*WYWA*, 3). Even allowing for the writer's unavoidable coloration of his early memories by the nostalgic lens of his reflective age, when he had found these themes fully and could manipulate them more deliberately in his fiction, it is quite certain that Goyen himself felt "half-lost and . . . estranged." In his stories the reader encounters a number of young men in this condition, wandering or wounded or both, who feel, as Goyen wrote in "Old Wildwood," "cruelly left alone in the whole world" and "orphaned" despite their having parents (*CS*, 147). "I was infused with such a sense of a lost country," Goyen wrote of himself, "with such a feeling of being foreign and alien and transferred, against my will, that the city of Houston represented a kind of internment" (*WYWA*, 4).

This feeling of being orphaned was also rooted in familial and psychological situations more intimate than the geographical displacement. Goyen received a B.A. and an M.A. from Rice Institute, and although he was a good student with a gift for languages, during these years he confirmed in himself an artistic more than a scholarly temperament. As he related in his sixties, he had originally wanted to study the piano, and because of his father's disapproval had enrolled secretly in the Houston Conservatory of Music with the help of his mother; he made a cardboard keyboard and, hidden in a corner of the house, played on it works by Chopin that only he could hear. But he was discovered by his father, who could not comprehend his son's interest in music and who prevented him from continuing. Later, when Goyen was a freshman at Rice, his father would drive him to the college entry gate and drop him off there every day for his classes, but the young Goyen would wait until the car was out of sight and then cross Main Street, at that time quite far from downtown, into wooded Herman Park, and while away the day there daydreaming and writing. "As I learned and grew and matured," Goyen later wrote, "I saw my peers training for commerce in a growing city of opportunity; I felt estranged" (*WYWA*, 8).

Thus Goyen felt apart from his own family and from most of his age-mates. As the outward realm in which he lived, Houston was of great negative importance in his formation as a person and an artist, because the atmosphere of the city, so bent on frenzied business growth, was filled with the same attitudes and values that inside his family were oppressing Goyen. The father's small-mindedness about his son's performing ambitions was a reflection of the prevailing attitudes of the place. By the time Goyen began college, these attitudes had already not only quashed his desire to study piano but also done the same to his desire to study voice and dance. Goyen's early refusal to attend his college classes came from his having identified the school with the values of father and business world, of those "peers training for commerce in a growing city of opportunity."

But in his second year Goyen discovered that Rice also offered the opportunity to immerse himself in the college theater, to attend concerts and ballets in the city, to participate in a creative writing club, to study literature. Goyen became a passionate reader and student of languages and devoured poetry and fiction in English, French, Spanish, and German. He was extremely active in student theater, writing, acting, and participating in other ways. And he found a sympathetic English professor, George Williams, who recognized his talents as a writer and encouraged him. Goyen stayed at Rice for a master's degree, writing a thesis on the Elizabethan stage, and then embarked for the University of Iowa to pursue a doctorate. Already he had written fiction, drama, and poetry, increasing his mastery of this last-discovered art form, which he could carry on secretly without anyone hearing him practice and into which he could, in a way, pour his other artistic hopes by writing about people like the "dancer, singer, fantastico" he could not himself become.

During his college years Goyen appears to have been a brooding, passionate, self-involved young man. He felt committed already to an artistic career; he found a few friends who shared similar aspirations with a similar intensity, and he spent much time with them; he seems to have had a number of passionate relationships and was known as a handsome, unwittingly seductive young man to whom women were very attracted. He was already preoccupied with the artistic themes that would dominate his life's work (one theme present from the beginning is the emotional violence and dizziness of the erotic), and in many ways one can see that, quite unsurprisingly, just as there is a recognizable stylistic signature in his every piece of fiction, right from the beginning of his career, so the young Goyen was in some ways already recognizably the artist (although not yet in control of his powers) that he would be throughout his career. (Other themes present from the beginning of Goyen's writing are the presence of the past, exile, the deformed and the outcast, and the destruction of nature.)

Iowa was not the place for him; after three months he abruptly returned to Texas, unable to remain away, as yet. He taught briefly at the University of Houston, but then World War II wrenched him decisively out of Texas and into the U.S. Navy for four and a half years, much of that time spent on an aircraft carrier. During this period he continued to write, his most important work being the earliest drafts of what would become his extraordinary first novel, *The House of Breath*. When he returned to Texas it was only long enough to gather his things. With Walter Berns, a shipmate with whom he had begun a collaborative novel (never finished), he set off by car from Texas for San Francisco, a city he had visited and liked while in the navy. He thought that there he might find it congenial to write. But Goyen and Berns were so struck by the landscape of northern New Mexico that they stopped.

By chance, while working as a waiter, Goyen met Frieda Lawrence, D.H. Lawrence's widow, who lived near Taos. She gave him and Berns three acres of land, and there they lived in relative isolation for several years on and off in a tiny adobe house the two of them built with the help of three Native American men. There Goyen worked on stories and *The House of Breath*. The unusual and beautiful landscape of northern New Mexico, echoing with the spiritual traditions of the Pueblo Indians, reinforced Goyen's already-intense feelings about nature and his strong sense of an opposition between the unfettered life of the soul and the dragging claims of the material life of the body. He had come to hate the crassness of the business world—*that* sort of materialism. But as he matured as a writer he also brought into his fiction the conflict between the body, especially as it feels erotic hunger, and the soul, as it desires a love free of physical torment.

While his war experience rarely appears as an overt subject in any of his work (except in a minor way in the story "Ghost and Flesh, Water and Dirt," which treats an extraordinary range of themes in a very brief space, from tragedy and grief to erotic passion and joy), there are notable connections among many of Goyen's works through the imagery of water—from, for example, the river in the *The House of Breath*, and all that takes place in it, to the short stories "Old Wildwood," "The Rescue," and "Bridge of Music, River of Sand." Water as a kind of amniotic fluid of earliest experience and water as a medium of erotic experience join these stories with passages in other works. While in Goyen's work, experience of water is usually the source of reverie and is used to evoke the greatest heights of feeling, there is also something threatening about the water (as in Otey's drowning in *The House of Breath* or Nick Natowski's in "Ghost and Flesh, Water and Dirt"). His time at sea, which he described as deeply traumatic—frightening, tedious, isolated, and the cause of seasickness—seems to have formed, to some extent, the way in which he utilizes water in his fiction. Likewise, the pollution and destruction of Texas rivers and the aridity of the New Mexico desert must in part have shaped this artistic preoccupation with water.

While in New Mexico, Goyen met many writers and artists who lived nearby or had traveled to see Frieda Lawrence, among them the English poet Stephen Spender. That these years were vitally important to Goyen is indicated by the autobiographical project he left unfinished at his death, for it was to be called *Six Women* and consisted of six sections, each devoted to a woman whose influence on him had, he felt, been decisive. Three of the six were women of New Mexico—Frieda Lawrence, Mabel Dodge Luhan, and Dorothy Brett. Among and between them—forceful personalities all—Goyen found his first artistic companionship and welcome patronage as he sought to begin his writing career.

Goyen accepted Spender's invitation to visit him in London. Spender was much impressed by Goyen, especially by Goyen's struggle to define his own aesthetic, independently of literary and commercial fashion. In a 1949 essay, Spender discussed the case of a commercial magazine editor's having altered Goyen's first published story, presumably to suit the attitudes of the magazine's readers; the full version of "The White Rooster" was published in Cyril Connolly's magazine *Horizon*, along with Spender's essay. And it was in Spender's house that Goyen finished the novel, which was published as *The House of Breath* in 1950; his first volume of stories, *Ghost and Flesh*, was published two years later.

Goyen's experience of Europe (over many years) is reflected in his stories in two ways, both as subject matter (as in "Old Wildwood" or

"The Texas Principessa") and as an elating validation of the grandeur Goyen found in the very humble Texas locales and life experiences behind his fiction. *The House of Breath* includes a passage in the opening chapter that, in representing the young Goyen's undoubted excitement at seeing the art treasures of Europe, turns his wonder into an invocation of the local Texas backwoods: "Yet on the walls of my brain, frescoes: the kneeling balletic Angel holding a wand of vineleaves, announcing; the agony in the garden; two naked lovers turned out; and over the dome of my brain Creations and Damnations, Judgments, Hells and Paradises (we are carriers of lives and legends—who knows the unseen frescoes on the private walls of the skull?)."[5]

When the novel was published, it received much praise, and with Guggenheim grants two years in a row, Goyen returned to live in Europe. Between 1948 and 1957, Goyen gravitated to London, Rome, and New York. Although he returned periodically to New Mexico and thought of it as his new home, he was leaving it behind for New York. New York City was the next stage of his ongoing, voluntary, and yet painful exile from Texas.

The pain was not only of homesickness but also, after his initial great success, of disappointment. Although his first two books won him considerable acclaim and the Guggenheim grants, his next works were not so welcomed by reviewers, and by the mid-1960s Goyen felt keenly his inability to earn his living as a writer. His writing life was less productive and he was drinking too much. In 1966 he took a position as an editor at McGraw-Hill, working there until 1971. This obligation drew him even further from his writing, and for about eleven years in all, he said, he scarcely wrote. (Yet while working at McGraw-Hill and indeed for the rest of his life, Goyen was known for the generosity of attention and the practical help he offered to younger writers.)

When the big city appears in Goyen's short fiction, as in "The Horse and the Day Moth" and "There Are Ravens to Feed Us," from his second collection, *The Faces of Blood Kindred* (1960), it is associated with artistic stagnation, an oppressiveness of the multitude, a fatigue with life. This author of journeying and exile (whose personal stationery in the 1970s bore the image of a roadrunner) experienced the most devastating of all his exiles in this long period of estrangement from his own artistic vocation. During his New York period, he was, to be sure, among a striking group of literary friends and acquaintances, in the United States or abroad, most notably Katherine Anne Porter, with whom he had a troubled love affair, and Carson McCullers, Truman

Capote, and others. Katherine Anne Porter and Margo Jones, an innovative theater director who was known in New York, although she worked in Texas, are two more of Goyen's *Six Women*. But Goyen's participation in literary life—which included a fair amount of itinerancy as he sought to write now here, now there—was no substitute for the *home* from which his personal and artistic development had estranged him. And his excessive drinking—so common a problem among American writers—impaired his artistic powers and his personal resolve. To some extent his New York period brought him success in another realm, the theater, for which he wrote several plays. These more than any other aspect of his work seem to have sustained him through this time of disappointment and silence as a fiction writer. It was also in the theater that he met Doris Roberts, a Broadway actress; they were married in 1963. Looking back on their life together, he and she would later speak of how much each learned, as artists, from the other. Given these genuine resources, it is perhaps not entirely surprising that Goyen was able to arise admirably from this period of personal stagnation. In 1974 he published his novel *Come, the Restorer*, and in 1975 his *Collected Stories*. In 1976, after he stopped drinking (he was never to drink alcohol again), he wrote a new story, "Precious Door"—only his second story after a publishing silence of thirteen years. This story, like a door into a realm of intense and fertile creativity, led him into the remarkable last period of his writing, from 1976 until his death in 1983. During this time he wrote the new stories that were collected in the posthumous 1984 volume *Had I a Hundred Mouths* (which also contains a selection of his earlier short fiction), the short novel *Arcadio* (1983), and several autobiographical essays. He also began work on a novella, "Leander"; returned to work on his autobiography, *Six Women*; revived and revised some of his earliest uncollected or unpublished stories; and proposed to his publisher another novel based on the Greek myth of Philoctetes. But he did not live long enough to finish any of these projects. The general outline of this period of late creativity suggests that Goyen continued to find the roots of much of his fiction in his earliest experience in Texas, both in terms of the kinds of characters and situations he wrote about and in terms of his way of writing—his characteristic storytelling method.

Moments or periods of illness define several important phases of Goyen's life and undoubtedly influenced his exploration of certain themes. Subject to seizures as a child, Goyen must early have felt a keen sense of being different from other children. Illness during and immediately after the war—especially his chronic seasickness while serving on an aircraft carrier—contributed not only to this sense of differentness but also to the sensitivity in his fiction to human relations founded on, or carried on through, illness or hurt, as in the unpublished novel *Half a Look of Cain*, which Goyen had completed by 1954 but which appeared in print only partially, in the form of several short stories, two of which are focused on a male nurse. After Goyen began to recover from it in 1976, his alcoholism issued in the late story "Where's Esther?" And the work of his last years was much affected by his final illness, lymphoma. His moving essay "Recovering" (published posthumously in *TriQuarterly* magazine, no. 58, 1983) and the emphasis on reconciliation in such late stories as "Precious Door" and "Tongues of Men and of Angels," as well as his last novel, *Arcadio*, speak of his experience of writing while ill. Goyen's understanding of illness and of creativity was profound and represents not a simple struggle of the one against the other, of the artist against his physical decline, but rather a probing of weakness or wound within which one discovers strength.

Goyen's Artistic Project

Some critics have called Goyen a southern writer, a regional writer. Goyen never rejected or minimized the importance of his upbringing among a people given to talking and telling stories, but as he says in the interviews reprinted in part 2 of this volume, it is not a particular historical or regional speech that he sought to reproduce or suggest in his work, however accurately he did wish to hear it when immersed in it. Rather, his deep sense of being separated from his geographical home in both space and time led him to try to *create* a language that would itself serve as the place of his fiction—which is a somewhat different and more complex artistic impulse. For the creation of this language, Goyen drew sometimes on his mother's speech—he said in an interview that he would call her on the telephone just to hear her talk and would write down some of her expressions. But in a larger and more artistically deliberate way, he seems to have thought of language not only as a means of communication but as the realm in which that communication took place; language was for him part of the very substance of being of the narrator of a story, and often of the characters in that story. As Goyen says in the interview in *TriQuarterly* magazine, the people around him whom he heard when he was a child "got the speech" but he "got the voice." By this he meant that he grew up *in* a way of speaking and that this speaking was his native realm, but that while for those around him this was only their unselfconscious ordinary way of speaking, he was given a kind of artistic consciousness of it, like a singer's perhaps. In his work he was able to transform this way of speaking, to "sing" very deliberately composed notes based on the unselfconscious, folkloristic, improvised notes he heard in his childhood. Goyen's use of the word *voice* suggests his sense of himself as the representative of a community of persons speaking the same language.

"Style," on the other hand, is the *result* in the written composition of the literary artist's transformation of his materials (including language). Goyen's style is closely related to his sense of the importance of "voice." He conceives of his fiction as a "house of breath," that is, an inhabited place made out of the spoken language. Goyen's preoccupation with style (about which he also speaks in the same interview) may partly account for the attention his work has received from translators and readers in France, Germany, and elsewhere in Europe. His translators have included, in German, Ernst Robert Curtius, the great scholar whose learned studies of European literature can be found side by side with his translations of twentieth-century American writers, and, in French, Maurice Coindreau, who also translated Faulkner and Flannery O'Connor. The critics who have commented on Goyen's work have included Gaston Bachelard and Anaïs Nin—uncommon attention for an American author—and some of the best criticism of his work is in French and German. It was often the case during Goyen's later years, and remains so now, that more of his work was in print abroad than in the United States. Goyen felt indebted artistically more to European writers than to American ones, and in fact the idea of "style" is itself somewhat European in the sense that modern European fiction, beginning with Flaubert, has elevated very conscious awareness of style into a position of great prominence in the writer's deliberations. One sees this awareness as part of the Europeanization of Henry James, for example (see Goyen's comments on European writers in the *Paris Review* interview in part 2).

At various times, Goyen spoke of his admiration for a variety of earlier writers. Yet it is their courageous stylistic individualism rather than the relative merits of this or that one's particular style that Goyen seems to have admired. One studies Goyen's fiction in vain for genuine stylistic echoes of his preferred authors, from Samuel Beckett at one extreme to Proust at another. What was perhaps most important for Goyen was the very existence of artistic precedent that spoke to him as a reader. The disparity between his vague youthful artistic ambition and the drab and, as far as he could see, unimaginative life of parents and acquaintances in Houston was painful to him. In his reading, as he remarks when speaking of the great discoveries he made while a college student, he found models of artistic extravagance and flamboyance, dedication and singleness of purpose, success and renown. Temperamentally he felt akin to several writers, but probably for different reasons—to Proust, for example, because of Proust's luxurious exploration of feeling, while to Beckett, because of Beckett's survival and even welcoming of the artist's sense of isolation and apartness from the rest of human society, his having no place to call home.

Readers whose sense of prose fiction responds to Goyen's own (with its gestures of acknowledgment toward such diverse figures as Gustave Flaubert, Samuel Beckett, Henry James, Walt Whitman, and Marcel Proust) can see more readily the correspondences between Goyen's concepts of style and narrative technique, on the one hand, and his sense of story or tale, even of fable, on the other. After Hawthorne (with whom Goyen also felt an affinity), American fiction strikes rather seldom, with the exception of Goyen, into the realm of the fabulous until the influence of Latin American fiction writers, especially Jorge Luis Borges and Gabriel García Márquez (otherwise extremely different writers), is felt decisively in the 1970s. Also during Goyen's writing life, American fiction has steered rather cautiously away from Goyen's notion of intimate, singing *voice*, preferring to conceive of style as (a) an unobtrusive means of communicating narrative events (or the absence of events), (b) a descent into speech (sometimes into dialect—but Goyen was not writing dialect), or (c) a highly artificial construct meant to call attention to itself in that sort of fiction in which the act of writing becomes itself the first subject of the fiction.

Goyen's method, as self-conscious in literary terms as any other, is both more impassioned and more ventriloquistic than that of authors who prefer either a self-advertising authorial presence or a cautious authorial invisibility. Both of those stances involve a double consciousness of the kind that produces irony, and this ironic stance, so much favored in American fiction by the 1960s, cannot often serve as a vehicle for the pressure of feeling that Goyen's stories tap and transmit to the reader. Except for a gentle undercurrent of authorial teasing in a few stories, such as "The Letter in the Cedarchest" or "The Texas Principessa," Goyen is one of the most unironic writers American fiction has produced. His intent as a writer seems to acknowledge something that many readers are not accustomed to looking for, much less finding, in contemporary fiction: the conviction that an intense hidden life (perhaps akin to what Frank O'Connor called "the lonely voice" of short fiction) lies everywhere, waiting to be recognized, and that once heard, it will dominate the imagination, far overpowering the outward and mundane appearances of human action. For all the subjectivity and dreamlike imagery of Goyen's narrators, his fiction is not solipsistic or narcissistic, even in its most rapturous moments of interiority; rather, it directs its vital energy outward toward another person, a listener. What is hidden in the world *outside* the narrator is discovered *within* the narrator and is communicated to another. The sheer exuberance of Goyen's narrators (early signaled and wonderfully accomplished in "Ghost and Flesh, Water and Dirt") impresses the reader with this unmistakable sense of hiddenness in the stories. Such narrative talk, however perfected an artifice it may be, is also passionate and believable, revealing depths where it seems to conceal or merely ramble and offering the reader a transformation of spirit. Goyen's sense of the revelation of the hidden can be illustrated with a passage from "Old Wildwood," a story that holds many keys to his formation: "There was so much more to it all, to the life of men and women, than he had known before he came to Galveston just to fish with his grandfather, so much in just a man barefooted on a rock and drinking whiskey in the sun, silent and dangerous and kin to him. And then the man had *spoken* [emphasis added] and made a bond between them and brought a kind of nobility of forest, something like a shelter of grandness of trees over it all (*CS*, 147)."

In fact, in nearly all of Goyen's work, one can sense a notable faith that the story as a form can carry meanings and emotional power larger than what more genteel or conventional writers and readers may be used to expecting. Sometimes the force of Goyen's fiction seems at the point of breaking the conventions by which we distance ourselves from the fictional characters whom we allow to come to life in our minds as we read. Goyen wants his characters to career into us, into readers, the way someone we used to know who has not been around for a while—strange to us now, and yet familiar—might suddenly show up in our midst. His stories are not like the snapshots of contemporary characters to which literary fashion has accustomed us, to a large extent, but rather like intense, sometimes very self-conscious episodes in the long, untold stories of their lives. Perhaps it was because of the uprootedness and passion of his own life that Goyen was so interested in characters who enact the journey outward from home and family and then return again, only to leave and return many times over. When somebody's aunt ups and runs off with another man, leaving behind husband and child, it is not, for Goyen, an occasion for musing on how feckless and impulsive she seems; nor is it the moment for weary and disillusioned reflections on liquor and mistakes, or a knowing sense that everyone is like that, or close to being like that; nor is it a moment for artistically self-reflexive comment on the impossibility of literarily representing such an event anyway. Instead it is an instance, meditated upon and told over, of the mostly incomprehensible and overpowering feelings that can seem almost to throw someone into another identity. There is in Goyen a kind of rapture of the tragic. And human understanding of such action involves, for Goyen, a receptivity to this rapture and to the fabulous side of the lives he presents ("dancer, singer, fantastico"), as well as to the everyday difficulties that follow, in the wake of the decisive action, for the woman, for her husband and child, for the man she runs off with, and for the one (the nephew, say), who later simply *must* tell what happened. This is not to say that Goyen's work is not aimed at understanding; it is indeed, but not with the expectation that either literary devices or psychological insight will be sufficient to *record* a human action. Goyen is more interested in creating a way of speaking that will, for a moment, house or harbor or shelter the intense feeling that arises from a human action.

Orphanhood (as in "Pore Perrie" or "Old Wildwood"), love and sex (as in "Ghost and Flesh" or "Had I a Hundred Mouths" or "Arthur Bond"), mysteries and fears of childhood (as in "The Grasshopper's Burden" or "The Faces of Blood Kindred"), the powerful effects of chance or accident (as in "Ghost and Flesh" or "Rhody's Path"), the element of the unforeseen and the fabulous and the extreme (like the flagpole sitter in "Figure over the Town" or the sudden visitation of the brothers in "Precious Door"), the unending journey out away from home and family and back again (as in "Rhody's Path" or "Pore Perrie" or "Bridge of Music, River of Sand")—these are a few of the recurring situations and preoccupations of Goyen's stories that I will look at more closely in the chapters that follow. These elements of his fiction are grounded in his experience, even though no experience identified by humanist or scientist has yet explained how what happens to one person, the artist, is transformed by that person into something—art—that then happens, in a concentrated and potent way, to someone else, the reader, in the realm of imagination.

The Teller-Listener Situation

William Goyen's short stories make up an extraordinarily rich and complex body of work. In order for one to read individual stories with the greatest pleasure and understanding and with the greatest profit as one seeks to understand Goyen's artistic vision, it is well to consider some general characteristics that span much of his work, from his earliest fiction to his last.

In the previous chapter I pointed out that certain aspects of Goyen's artistic temperament and some of his fictional themes are present almost from the beginning of his writing career. Other critics have also noted that Goyen's characteristic manner, his artistic signature, was stamped on even his earliest published work. Robert Phillips comments that "some writers achieve their mature 'style' (which is often more a matter of content than of imagery or sentence structure) through a long evolution. . . . Not so with William Goyen. Goyen's manner and content were fully developed from the first page of his first book onward."[6] One might want, in fact, to show a series of noticeable shifts and changes in Goyen's work from beginning to end, but it remains true that the seeds of his fictional strategies, his ideas about language and style, and most of his themes are present from the beginning; while they grow more complex and more potent as his work evolves, and while his attitudes toward them subtly alter, they remain at the center of his work. Goyen's late works are blooms on a single "wonderful plant" (to use one of his titles) that he cultivated throughout his writing career. That he contemplated a final collection of stories that would include both his last finished works and some of his earliest but uncollected pieces stands as evidence of this consistency.

If, then, in the pages that follow, I have chosen stories from throughout Goyen's writing career to illustrate a number of points about his fiction, I do not mean to imply that he lived and worked in some sort of timeless way or that he was immune to the changes in his own life and in the world around him; indeed, there is a particularly notable energy and fresh vision in his last works that will surprise and impress the reader who follows the chronology of Goyen's fiction. But for the purposes of introducing Goyen's short fiction in this volume, I cannot fully answer the question of his overall artistic development, because doing so would require detailed attention to his novels and his nonfiction, as well as to his stories. Further, many readers believe that Goyen's stories, together with his first novel and his last (both of which are akin in different ways to the short story, the first because it consists of meditative chapters that resemble some of Goyen's stories and the last because it is more novella than novel), are his greatest work; despite how little known Goyen is in comparison with some of his contemporaries, these works form one of the great monuments of American short fiction, the genre for which American literature is perhaps best known and, especially abroad, most admired.

Goyen's Short Stories

Goyen's first published collection of short fiction, *Ghost and Flesh* (1952), contained eight short stories, some of which he had written while working on his first novel, *The House of Breath* (1950). Goyen's second short story collection, *The Faces of Blood Kindred* (1960), contained eleven; in the meantime he had also published another novel, *In a Farther Country* (1955). *The Collected Stories of William Goyen* (1975) included all the stories from the first two collections and added seven uncollected stories. Goyen had meanwhile published a short novel, *The Fair Sister* (1963) (which grew out of a short story from *The Faces of Blood Kindred*, "Savata, My Fair Sister"), and another novel, *Come, the Restorer* (1974).

At the time of his death, Goyen had completed a new short novel, *Arcadio*, which was about to be published, and from his papers it is clear that he intended to publish a new collection called *Precious Door.* In the form he first gave it, *Precious Door* was to include twelve stories, of which seven were new and five had been composed years earlier but not collected. His next formulation of the collection, however, dropped two of the early, uncollected stories and added two more new stories, "Had I a Hundred Mouths" and "Tongues of Men and of Angels." This later plan might suggest that for lack of more new work he had at first been intending to fill out the collection with the early work; and yet it also suggests that he found his early work, despite the passage of the years, to be sufficiently of a piece with his latest work to make sense alongside it. His last formulation of the collection withdrew those same two new stories, evidently because out of them he was beginning to shape a new novel, called "Leander."

After Goyen's death, the publisher of *Arcadio*, revealing a failure of vision that Goyen would have found ruefully familiar, did not wish to publish a posthumous collection of *new* stories, professing doubts about the commercial appeal of such a volume, but preferred to issue a volume of *selected* stories. This larger volume contains, in addition to earlier works, some (but not all) of the stories in the *Precious Door* manuscript, including the two that were to have been the germ of the uncompleted "Leander" (for which Goyen had written only a few more fragments and which he had not yet begun to shape as a whole). The collection *Precious Door* as Goyen planned it thus remains unpublished as a cohesive group of stories.

From this publishing history it will be apparent not only that Goyen's short stories were a lifelong endeavor but also that the composition of his novels was closely related to the writing of stories. In addition, considering that all three of Goyen's larger novels are composed of sections resembling the kind of meditative short story that is characteristic of Goyen's most original work, it is no surprise that he could say "Short fiction is my love."[7] In an early letter to Margaret Hartley, the editor of the *Southwest Review*, in which a number of Goyen's stories were published, Goyen wrote "My work, whatever it is I do, is a shaping of patterns . . . and beyond that I do not know whether this work is and has been 'stories' or 'novels' or whatever. . . . I should like the whole to be like the patterns upon water because there has been a deep disturbance below" (quoted by Phillips, 105). Years later, in an interview, Goyen said about his novels, "I generally make the parts the way you make those individual medallions that go into quilts. All separate and perfect as I can make them, but knowing that my quilt becomes a whole when I have finished the parts" (See part 2).

One of the most characteristic elements in Goyen's work is a fictional situation in which one person is telling another a story, or a story in which the narrator speaks as if telling the story to a listening person close to him (or her), not an anonymous reader. Goyen called this essentially dramatic confrontation of two persons the "teller-listener situation." In surveying Goyen's career as a short story writer, I will focus on this situation as the heart of his artistic uniqueness.

Dramatically or thematically, Goyen sometimes incorporates the situation itself as an element in his fiction. I will analyze one such instance, from "Pore Perrie," later in this discussion. For now, let a simpler example illustrate this strategy. In "Old Wildwood," shortly after the passage quoted earlier, we read of the grandson, when he was with his grandfather on their fishing trip years ago, that

> [i]n this loneliness he knew, at some border where land turned into endless water, he felt himself to be the only one alive in this moment—where were all the rest?—in a land called Mississippi, called Texas, where? He was alone to do what he could do with it all and oh what to do would be some daring thing, told or performed on some shore where two ancient elements met, land and water, touched each other and caused some violence in kinship between two orphans, and with heartbreak in it. What to do would have the quiet, promising dangerousness of his grandfather on the rock in it, it would have the grave and epic tone of his grandfather's ultimate telling on the side of the cot under one light globe in a mist of shoreflies in a sandy transient roof of revelation while the tide washed at the very feet of the teller and listener. And what to do would have the feeling of myth and mystery that he felt as he had listened, as though when he listened he were a rock and the story he heard was water swelling and washing over generations and falling again, like the waters over the rock when the tide came in. (*CS*, 147–48)

The secondary oppositions in this plangent passage—land and water, lonely individual and generations, doing and telling, quiet and violence, tide and rock—echo the fundamental opposition of teller and listener, and that pairing of persons is echoed further in such phrases as "two ancient elements" and "two orphans." I will return to a number of the motifs presented in this passage in my discussion of themes in the next chapter, but at this point I am simply calling attention to the intensity with which the teller-listener situation is reinforced by these images, which signal its centrality to Goyen's aesthetic.

Goyen's first two books, the novel *The House of Breath* and the story collection *Ghost and Flesh*, are closely akin artistically. While there is no questioning the completeness and complex structure of *The House of Breath* as a whole, some of its individual chapters nonetheless establish the contours of what in Goyen's short stories is a characteristically meditative, often but not always first-person composition that draws together several events or images in which a powerful feeling was formed and is now remembered (as in "The Faces of Blood Kindred") or in which that remembered feeling leads to further discovery (as in "Old Wildwood" or "The Horse and the Day Moth"). This is not, of course, the only sort of story Goyen wrote; his work is quite varied. But even in a number of other stories not purely of this form, there is a similar development in a subsidiary way, as when a character senses and prizes something Goyen identifies with a "secret" feeling or truth.

It may be important, therefore, for readers of Goyen's short stories to read *The House of Breath*, for in it are found both Goyen's invention of this meditative form and his use of intense, sustained first-person *speech* as a medium of fiction. To put it more precisely, Goyen often employs two kinds of first-person speech: that of a narrator who may use a language of strong feeling, dramatic, exclamatory, and filled with poetic devices; and that of a second character whose story the narrator is, as it were, listening to and retelling to the reader. The narrator is a kind of thoughtful, inquiring medium between the story and the person who hears it told.

Each of the chapters of *The House of Breath* that presents the story of a character (even the chapter about the river) begins with a brief introductory narrator's passage and then proceeds to give to the reader the voice, the distinctive speech, of a particular character, as if that character were speaking to the narrator, and only through him to the reader, who overhears. This way of framing the speech of a central character is critical, because it encloses that character inside an intimate space where there are two people together—one speaking, one listening. One reads this sort of fictionally framed narration—or gathers impressions from it—rather differently from the way one reads first-person narrative in which the speaking character speaks directly to the reader: in Goyen's fiction what one "hears" has already been once transformed, inevitably, by the person who heard it previously and who now "tells" it. The transformation is a compressing and intensifying, yet without loss of the qualities of spoken language.

Furthermore, the teller-listener situation is not only dramatic but also social: not only stories and feelings but also values are transmitted, and, depending on the receptivity of the listener, they take hold or fail to take hold, in another person. In *The House of Breath* the listener who tells again, who re-creates the entire house with his breath, is a young boy remembering in later years. Quite clearly, certain human qualities given to him by members of his extended family are more important to him than others; generally, in that book, he begins to prize freedom of feeling and of action, rather than conventionality of behavior. This transmission of values is partly characterized by the immediacy of the experience of telling and listening; it could not be so memorable an experience were it the experience of reading—for who among one's kin *writes down* such matters or employs writing in the attempt to influence one?

There is thus a certain quality of *orality* in much of Goyen's fiction, in terms of both its aesthetic nature as literature (it is written as if it were spoken aloud) and its themes (people are always *talking*). And the experience of hearing something spoken is quite different from that of reading it, even when the former is in effect a sleight of hand created within and by a written text. The writtenness of the text is shifted at least slightly toward a spokenness.

Oswyn Murray has provided a convenient summary of the difference in question here:

> The spoken text has to be performed in order to be communicated; and the mode of performance in a social or ritual context determines the meaning of the text in ways which are absent from the activity of private reading. That is not to deny that there are analogies between the expectations engendered in oral performance and those which control solitary reading. The ritual of performance in fact lies at the basis of the creation of literary genres: the shared expectations which culturally determine our "reading" of any text begin in social ritual and end in the theory of rhetoric. Yet the experience, and therefore the mental world engaged by oral culture are surely different.[8]

Goyen sometimes called his stories "arias" or "anthems," as if signaling this shift toward spokenness in the genre in which he was working. Recall his experience in theater, first as an aspiring student actor and later as a playwright, and the direction pointed is clear: the quality of orality, an *as if* orality because we are indeed reading a printed text, is a distinguishing mark of Goyen's work. And there is not only a spoken quality but also a *ritual* one (of the sort Murray means) in the most incantatory of Goyen's performances in this mode, such as the stories "Ghost and Flesh, Water and Dirt" and "Arthur Bond." That is, they seem written not only to be told but also to be retold.

One sometimes has the sense that a writer's objective—as it has been shaped by artistic convention and tradition—is to lead the reader decisively through intended stages of reaction to the text, even to force the reader to go this way and that. Such writers entertain, instruct, control, patronize, or even contemn the reader in a way that, once understood in a complete reading, loses rhetorical power because the trick has been divulged. On the contrary, Goyen's characteristic fictional mode—meditative, intimately voiced, passionate—seems, despite its emotional force, appealingly considerate, even tentative, about suggesting his intentions. That is, we are invited into a social, dramatic situation that requires not our obedience but our sympathy, our emotional responsiveness. The story seems to partake of the rhetoric of orality rather more than that of writing.

This rhetoric of orality may be defined succinctly as a revitalization of qualities of language that are organized in *time* by sequence, as when one speaks and listens, rather than in space, as when one reads a written or especially a printed text for meanings organized more spatially and visually. The rhetoric of orality, although it is pure only in cultures where writing is not even known, survives partially in many ways in print culture.[9] For example, it survives in us as individuals, to varying degrees, from the period of our infancy and childhood before we could read and write; and it survives artistically in the fictional illusion of a speaking narrator. Beyond Goyen's attention to these qualities, which include matters of syntax and style, diction and even themes, two more things set Goyen's fiction apart from other first-person narratives. First, all of his work, whether composed in the first person or the third, conveys qualities of spokenness: this is a difference of degree from the work of other writers. Second, his first-person narrators are always situated in an occasion when there is both someone speaking and someone listening; this is a difference in quality from other fictional works. Even when the listener in the teller-listener situation can only be inferred, the inference is powerful and convincingly "realistic." Whereas most first-person fictional narratives lose all situational plausibility as soon as the reader asks, "Who is the narrator speaking to, and when, and why?", Goyen's stories always provide an implied answer to this question: the occasion can be understood to be dramatic and plausible. The narrator of "In the Ice-Bound Hothouse," for example, is giving testimony to the police (and he is writing it down, but as if he were speaking). The narrator of "Ghost and Flesh, Water and Dirt" is talking to a stranger in a bar. The narrator of "Arthur Bond" seems to be confessing, with an attitude of wonderment and in a soft voice, a long-pent-up obsessive recollection of the eponymous protagonist. And most sustained as a performance, Arcadio's story includes an invitation to the listener to join him in the shade under the railroad bridge, to listen to his tale.

In performance, Goyen's stories could quite naturally elicit an unusual response. One anecdote may suffice. At a reading in a large auditorium in New York, Goyen was paired with a then very popular young writer whose work had the reputation of being somewhat hardboiled and hip. After his colleague of the evening had finished and exited the stage, Goyen came tentatively out. Dozens of young people in the audience were already standing up and on their way out, not intending to listen to Goyen, of whom most of them had probably never heard. They had come only for the writer who described a world they already knew and associated themselves with. Goyen reached the podium without being introduced, shuffled his papers, adjusted his glasses, and without any introductory comment began to read into the microphone the story "Arthur Bond," the first sentence of which is, "Remember man named Arthur Bond had a worm in his thigh." He had not read more than three sentences when most of the exiting crowd had stopped to listen, and remained where they stood; a few more sentences and many were now respectfully returning to their seats, embarrassed at moving while he was reading; amazement on their faces, they were asking one another who Goyen was. The very rhythms and cadences of this story drew them back. When Goyen finished the brief story and looked up, unaware of his effect on his audience, there was boisterous applause, and he went on to another story, with the full audience listening raptly.

The fictional situation of teller and listener is, of course, not an actual truth but an artistic device, a deft illusion. Written texts are silent, inert objects, and no one is physically present but the reader, for whom the word *listener* is in fact a kind of metaphor, not in reality an accurate term. What sets Goyen's characteristic use of the situation of a teller and a listener apart from the narrative strategy of other writers is the illusion that the speaker is accompanied by a listener; and given the presence of that second person, the listener (whether as a character in the story itself, as in "Pore Perrie," or in a more subtle way), the quality of the told story becomes that of a ritualized act answering both the listener's eager desire to know and the teller's expressive need to tell (as is the case with the telling uncle in "Had I a Hundred Mouths").

Through this ritualization Goyen conveys the sense that each story is not only a *telling* that breaks free from the printed page but already a *re*telling. Thus Goyen's stories create the impression of having been shaped, smoothed, and intensified by *repeated* tellings; the most *oral* among the stories, such as "Ghost and Flesh, Water and Dirt" or "Arthur Bond," seem of a different order of fiction entirely, in a language as fully charged with meaning and feeling as song or prayer. The orality of Goyen's stories is both *residual* (in that it comes to Goyen from his own experience of listening and may even be a part of the narrative plot itself, as in "Had I a Hundred Mouths" or "Pore Perrie") and *created* (in that Goyen infuses the story with many linguistic signs that implicate the reader as the listener).

In those passages in *The House of Breath* which can properly be attributed to the central narrator, he is himself a creating presence, re-creating the past and other voices with his own breath, his own speech. He is filling their lives with his own breath; he is breathing with their voices. He is in a state of remembering and creating, but he is also in an active state of telling and retelling what he has heard. At the same time that the reader recognizes the great artifice underlying the extraordinary compression and interweaving of themes in that novel, paradoxically the reader is also convinced by the illusion of orality, so much so that those various characters of the novel seem overheard, as if they were speaking again, out of the past, to the narrator. Even in the short stories that pursue a more traditional way of presenting themselves—like the anonymous third-person narratives "The White Rooster" or "Tapioca Surprise," which convey a mild familiarity of tone, as if someone (we do not know who) were telling us the story, or the first-person narratives in which we stand very near the speaking voice, such as "Savata, My Fair Sister," "Rhody's Path," or "Ghost and Flesh, Water and Dirt" (three stories otherwise very different from one another)—there is often this heightened sense of the spoken language, an awareness of its compression and drama.

Goyen's belief was that the presentation of a fictional language resembling speech is like the presentation of a kind of song. By calling some of these pieces "arias" Goyen meant that an intensity of voice could pull the novel away from fictional genres toward a musical one, the opera.

The reader "hears" this singing speech in the short story "Pore Perrie," for example, in which two distinct voices sing their parts—the voice clamoring for the story of Pore Perrie to be told, and the voice telling that story, albeit reluctantly. Thus there is a kind of musical duet of voices in "Pore Perrie," each with solos.

The story—first published in *Ghost and Flesh* and one of Goyen's most haunting tales—is complicated and may contain unresolved mysteries. The structure is a nesting of one telling within another, within yet another. Section 1 opens with a quotation, before the reader knows who is speaking—as if to underline Goyen's belief that the speaking of this question, the live saying of it, is more important than the identity and the fictional situation of who is asking it: "Tell me the story of pore Perrie. Tell how she lived all her life till she died." Immediately another voice replies: "Hush asking me 'cause I don't want to tell it. 'Twas buried with pore Perrie in her grave" (*CS*, 37).

The story continues as a conversation until the asking voice prevails and the answering voice begins to speak of Perrie. The asking voice wants to hear it all the way through, to "get it straight," but the answering voice does not want to speak of Perrie at all.

Section 2 of the story is speech by the answering voice, yielding to the request and adding, "I want you to hush ever asking me about it again" (*CS*, 38). Section 3 drops the quotation marks and begins the story of Perrie, but as if in the questioner's voice, suggesting that this questioner does indeed already know the whole story. In section 3 we are immersed in a storytelling within the storytelling: Son writes to his Aunt Linsie and asks her to tell him of Perrie, his adopted mother; Aunt Linsie, like the voice in sections 1 and 2, does not want to speak of her sister Perrie.

In section 4 the quotation marks return, and a voice—it *must* be Aunt Linsie—is speaking. The reader's understanding deepens by stages: there were two somewhat religious sisters in their small-town home in Texas, the one who is speaking, Linsie, having devoted herself to Perrie, who had a slight deformity of foot.

In section 5 the quotation marks continue, seeming to indicate that our first storyteller is repeating to that first, unnamed questioner the words of Aunt Linsie as she told Son the story of his mother's life. We learn that Perrie married late, to Ace, a man who was himself an orphan, and that they adopted Son from an orphanage. The crux of Son's story seems to be that he was a somewhat odd child—secretive, "very very nervous [sic]" (*CS*, 41). As a teenager, he becomes more strange to his adoptive mother, who has never told him he is not her natural son. Perrie and Ace quarrel, and Ace stays away in his traveling work as a salesman; Son suddenly goes off to find him and stays away. The section ends with a puzzling interruption—someone, most likely the first questioner whom we heard in section 1, wants to hear about "the letters." There might have been double quotation marks around everything that preceded this question, but Goyen's nesting of one storytelling inside another is too complex for the relatively crude device of quotation marks to add much clarity.

In section 6 we learn that Son began to write letters back to Perrie, first of all criticizing her for never telling him he was adopted. He wants to know the identity of his "third" mother, Perrie and Linsie being the first two, but Perrie writes to him that she does not know. He—like Ace and other men in Goyen's stories—is working in a lumber mill in another town. He mentions to Perrie that on the Fourth of July he learned he was adopted; he does not answer Perrie's last letter.

Section 7 departs from what one might call the narrative-of-finding-out, the questioning and answering, the seeking of explanations and answers to one's kinship and that part of one's self-knowledge which must come from others; this section returns to the narrative of the lives of Perrie, Linsie, Ace, and Son together and recounts what happened on that Fourth of July. Our first narrator tells us that Son came home from the cataclysmic fireworks display wounded in some way but will not speak to Perrie or Linsey until the next day, when he reveals he has hurt his sexual organs the night before in an accident. A doctor examines him, but Son is forever changed. In this section there is again an interruption from the original questioner, who calls this narrator Aunt Linsie. This has been Aunt Linsie, almost with an odd detachment, telling of herself all along. She has been telling, in fact, not only of what happened to Perrie, Son, Ace, herself but also of her having been asked and having told, once before, this very story to Son himself. That is, she is reenacting the telling of the story for a new questioner and now feels this is the last time she can tell the sad tale.

The questioner importunes her to finish the tale, and, in section 8, she reluctantly does so. Of course, the questioner has known all along who is speaking and about what; it is as if he already knows the whole story but needs her to tell it all the way through, needs to *hear* it more than know it. Knowing it only restates the mystery of Son and Perrie; hearing it ties him to Aunt Linsie and through her to all the others, in kinship and in common concern, even if not in attitude toward the act of telling. The clever nesting of narratives-of-finding-out serves to focus the story on the relationship between the one who tells the story and the one who listens, rather than on the details of the narrative of events. In this section Linsie recounts the last visit of Son, who is like an apparition in the yard at night and who neither announces beforehand nor then reveals to Perrie that he is coming or has come back. But Perrie, in a final scene during a thunderstorm, seems to know he is out there and shows herself to him at her window, naked as the mother she would have been to him had she given birth to him herself; then she dies. Linsie ends her story as if she were talking to Son again, but he has been replaced by the questioner who began this story and who interrupts no more.

It is he who has the last word, in section 9, when he turns to us, his readers, who have overheard, as if from around the corner of the front porch, the entire exchange between him and Linsie. To us he tells of the mythologizing of the figure of Son, the many versions of Son spotted by people afterward, so they think. Like Son himself, he does not stay in the hometown: "And now I'm moving on (oh hear my song)," he says (*CS*, 49). The social situation of passing the story on from one member of the family to another of a younger generation, has been both a *subject* and the *dramatic* situation of this story (i.e., Linsie gave Son the story of Perrie when he asked for it, and she gave the questioner, later, Perrie's story and the story of giving it to Son). This last section is set entirely within parentheses, which suggest that it is outside the storytelling situation of the rest of the piece.

In fact, what this supremely characteristic Goyen story is about at the deepest level is not Perrie's life and death or Son's mysterious life but a situation in which someone in that family line, someone who already feels a kinship with these lives, wishes to place himself in a relationship with them more definitively, wishes to establish himself in their line, to take their travails to his own heart. He does so by immersing himself in a situation in which, even though he already knows their story, he asks and is told it again and now carries it in himself not as an outline of events but as *speech* about them; this speech *he* now possesses and is shaped by. His own desires and hopes and the trajectory of his own life are now fitted in some way to what went before in their lives, because he has the shape of speech with which to recall them to another person. He may still "look for tongue to tell it with," as he says in section 9, the last part of the story; but he does have the speech within himself already, in the way he has heard it. He has been a part of the "teller-listener situation." The musical duet of voices in the story—Linsie's voice and that of the questioner-narrator—implies a third presence, that of the listener who will hear the next (i.e., *this*) telling of the story of Pore Perrie—Goyen's short story.

Meditative Structure

When what is most vital in a story is not only the information or narrative conveyed but also the way someone is speaking, is making sense of his or her life by telling it *to another person*, there may, naturally, be no strong narrative sequence of events but, rather, a certain consistency of tone and an interweaving and echo of reference that convince us that the speaker's life and experience, of which we hear only a little, are indeed of a piece, are authentic. As in "Pore Perrie," the sequence of events may be told out of chronological order, as a speaking person will do, because the story told out loud is following an emotional thread, not a logical one. The rhetoric of orality, which I have contrasted with other strategies of writing, does not partake of the analytical or logical rigor that depends on the study of printed texts; instead, it suggests the vitality, bright color, and emotional rather than logical consistency of storytelling.

Some of Goyen's stories take a meandering route from event to event or image to image (such as "Children of Old Somebody," "Nests in a Stone Image," and "A Shape of Light"—the three that conclude the volume *Ghost and Flesh*). Goyen has shown elsewhere, as in "The White Rooster" and "The Thief Coyote," that he is quite capable of creating a more familiar kind of narrative structure, and so its absence in the meditative stories is not an oversight but rather the deliberate rejection of storytelling organized around plot. Goyen's preference is for another sort of organization, around (a) a progress from feeling to feeling, from revelation to revelation, from memory to memory, from image to image, and (b) a dramatic situation—someone is speaking and someone is listening. As I have already noted, the orality of Goyen's stories does not resemble that of most first-person narratives, which may often make us wonder in what possible circumstance any such narrator could plausibly be *speaking* the story we are reading; that is, the literary convention of the first-person narrator as used by most writers does not attempt to create a believable teller-listener situation. Goyen's stories take care to imply with great force the active presence of that usually silent listener, there next to the teller, providing a human and dramatic occasion for the telling of the story and calling the story out of the teller. Goyen's preference, either in intense or in diluted form, for the meditative structure over the straightforwardly episodic one is the result of this deliberate artistic choice, as a way of handling events, images, memories, and moments in time in a new way, in order to get at a sense of life through not story itself but story as the human voice breathes life and immediacy into it when speaking to another person. It would not be too much to say that just as Goyen's narrator in *The House of Breath* is most preoccupied to answer Aunt Malley Ganchion's question, "What kin are we all to each other, anyway?"—the first of two epigraphs to the novel—so Goyen establishes with his fictional method a way of making the reader the next in the line of kin, by putting the reader in the position of being on that porch, on that evening, to receive the story.

Thus Goyen's short stories are not so much *narrated*—which would imply a concern with a sequence of events—as *spoken*, created and held in speech: that is, mentioned, referred to, encompassed, recalled, touched upon, and so on. The poet Thomas McGrath, whose work is far different from Goyen's, nonetheless had a striking metaphor for the way spoken language can create a powerful illusion of human presence; he called it bringing characters "into the light of speech." This is Goyen's artistic accomplishment, too, even though he repeatedly discovers that speech, the human breath breathing the story out right now in the moment of telling, remains inadequate, as of course it must be, to restore what is lost and past and gone.

Though Goyen wrote only a little about writing, almost every time he spoke of it he went back to what he called the "teller-listener situation." He mentions this situation even within some of his stories, as we have seen already in "Old Wildwood." The questioner in "Pore Perrie" who has asked for Perrie's story says, at the end:

> (. . . And now I'm moving on (oh hear my song); this is the story as it was told to me; and as I go on, on the road, with a message to deliver, *I* want to get it all straight. There is this Son's pain to understand and *tell about* and I look for tongue to *tell* it with.
>   Pore Perrie.) (*CS*, 49; my italics)

More directly, Goyen says in the preface to his *Collected Stories;* "I've been mainly interested in the teller-listener situation. Somebody is telling something to somebody: an event! Who's listening to this telling? Where is the listener? . . . I've cared about the buried song in somebody, and sought it passionately; or the music in what happened."

By "the music in what happened" we may understand, among other things, a musical sort of organization of Goyen's meditative stories—that is, as already noted, the repetition and echo of themes and motifs, rather than an evolution of one narrative line from beginning to end. Goyen continues: "And so I have thought of my stories as folk song, as ballad, or rhapsody. This led me to be concerned with speech, lyric speech—my heritage."

This situation of the teller and listener arises consistently in Goyen's work not because he formed it as an artistic goal that he then pursued—the way some contemporary painters, for example, paint repeatedly what is essentially the same work, or work based on the same single discovery—but, rather, as Goyen says, living speech was a given; it was his lucky heritage. His use of the teller-listener situation as a characteristic device in his fiction thus derives at least partly from his experience. The important element in this aspect of his formation as an artist is not just that, as a youth, he heard and overheard this story and that, but he heard people habitually using language in a particular and natural way to seek some understanding of their lives. That way is intimately related to elements of rural society, with economic hard times or dead seasons when sitting and waiting (something Goyen often mentions in his stories) are filled with attempts to sort things out by mentioning them, recalling them, laying out this little part or that of some larger story of someone's life—and always in a language rich with expressive resources. In Goyen's childhood, this language contained many varieties of colorful vernacular speech and was still mostly untouched and uninfluenced by the "standard" diction and intonation that infiltrated rural areas first by radio and then, in later generations, by television. Such "standard" language draws all listeners and viewers of these commercial media toward the homogenization of language that follows urbanization and is of use to the commercial economic structure, which sponsors the electronic media *because* they standardize consumer interest. The standard language is inevitably associated, especially among the young, with the luxuries and other commodities it advertises. Indeed, the standard language becomes itself a kind of marketable commodity. But Goyen's language stands in opposition to such language of commerce, just as in his work there are many statements against pollution of the natural environment by commerce (as, for example, by the oil-drilling industry and the sawmills).

In addition, Goyen's early experience of speech "rich with phrases and expressions out of the King James Bible, from the Negro imagination and the Mexican fantasy, from Deep South Evangelism, from cottonfield and cotton gin, oil field, railroad and sawmill" was also the experience of an intimate scale of human relationship. Goyen's time in New York must have helped him—as exile often helps the literary artist in this way—to prize his native speech. Such speech came not in the midst of city noise (which some of his characters experience as a kind of torment) or over airwaves from anonymous faraway studios but on the front porch, in rural quiet, when troubles, sorrows, or loneliness provoked someone to tell (or tell again) of Rhody or Perrie or Grandpa or Boney Benson—to name just a few of Goyen's characters introduced in stories containing a teller and a listener, named and present or merely implied. As Goyen says in one interview, "I always hear somebody telling me the story that I'm writing" (Igo, 275). And so the teller-listener situation can be both method and theme in Goyen's work. That is, he can use the dramatic situation of a teller and a listener both as the occasion of a story (as when the questioner says, "Tell me the story of Pore Perrie") and as a theme, as when Margey in "Ghost and Flesh, Water and Dirt" explains to her listener, "Now I believe in *tellin*, while we're live and goin roun; when the tellin time comes I say spew it out, we just got to tell things, things in our lives, things that've happened, things we've fancied and things we dream about or are haunted by" (*CS*, 58).

Elaborating further on this device as it affects the act of composition itself, Goyen said, "I am responsible as the listener—the responsibility lies with the listener, the re-teller, not the teller, and my responsibility is to know when I'm hearing madness or to know how to give *on* what *I've* heard, because what I'm talking about is the continuity of listening, telling, listening. The listener needs a listener, then, when he now begins to tell the tale *on*. This is what everything I've ever written seems to be about."

Both his last novel, *Arcadio*, and the late story "Had I a Hundred Mouths" embody this insight or method, for in them we first "hear" someone who has already heard the story from another and who then gives us the narrative of events so that, as we read the story, it is being told to us a *second* time. Goyen continues, "So I'm telling *again.*

'Twice-told tales,' Hawthorne called them. . . . Someone wrote . . . about my work [that] the liberating, therefore spiritual, significance of story-telling was in the very telling itself, a kind of a prayer or meditation or apotheosis of feeling, a dynamic spiritual action. So: the need to tell, on the part of a lot of characters I have written about." That last comment alerts us to the presence of the teller-listener situation as a *theme* of Goyen's work. He continues:

> But in some writers what one gets is diction more than voice. That is, it's *thick speech*, rather than voice. There's a great difference between speech and voice. . . . There is a quality of voice that is, I guess, indefinable. I feel I know what that is, and I have to wait for it, and that determines my work: voice. I can't fake it, and I can't find it if it's not there. I have to hear it. This I know for myself. Sometimes the voice, the same voice, tells me a bunch of stories.
>
> People in my life told me stories, and I sang. They had the speech, and I got the voice.

The profound seriousness of this self-description should demonstrate, if any reader required demonstration, that Goyen's use of the colloquialism and folksiness of speech was not in the least condescending or meant to be understood as documentary, but rather was a vital necessity of his artistic project. Even the folksiness of such stories as "Rhody's Path" or "Arthur Bond," while it may be gently humorous, represents a oneness of writer and material, not an ironic distance between them.

Furthermore, Goyen's comments about speech not only echo his youthful personal ambition to sing (or dance, or play an instrument on stage) but also suggest how an artistic device evolved out of both his experience and his talent as a writer: *his structural strategy—meditative and musical—is integrally related to the problems of language that Goyen's stories work out.* What is the most convincing, the most affecting way to frame the language of a teller? What is the most accurate way of presenting, in language, the experience of fleeting, mingling, evolving feelings and memories?

Of course, not all of Goyen's stories are *told* in this way. But it is notable that the structural effects of this aesthetic are visible in Goyen's interesting use of the third-person narrative voice. Perhaps "The Horse and the Day Moth" is the best illustration. In this very short story (dedicated to the memory of Margo Jones, the theatrical director and producer who was an early friend of Goyen) the central character is described at a moment of emotional crisis and of a crisis of *language*, right from the story's first words: "The waked dreamer was sitting on the side of his bed, head in his hands and staring at the floor, remembering his daydream and trying to order it, thinking how we see so much, know so much and yet are able to shape and *tell* so little of it all and that so slowly and with such pain. It was a hot summer afternoon in the great city" (*CS*, 208; my italics).

The story, although in the third person grammatically, remains almost entirely inside this unnamed character. His state of uncertainty is broken by the sounds of a runaway carriage horse outside the window, and he rushes to his window to watch. Then he returns to sit on his bed. Something about this scene makes him think of a "day moth," but this particular memory is left unexplored for the moment. Instead, what he has just seen evokes the memory of a dead carriage horse in an earlier winter. Within that memory there is yet another one, of a summer visit to his mother in a garden. She is naming the flowers, and when he goes to look at one in particular—again associated with a memory, this time of the aunt who brought the plant from Louisiana years before—he sees a shaggy little moth. This image in turn elicits memories of his childhood, and he catches the moth, as he had done often when he was a boy; when he releases it he finds on his fingertips "the faery gilt of the day moth's tiny wings" (*CS*, 210). All afternoon he keeps that gilt on his fingers, until at last he takes his elderly mother's hand and leads her back into the house. The story now broaches its central issue: "How in the world did the horse and the day moth find each other in him, and what had brought them together? He had wondered then [when he saw the dead horse, in a past winter] and wondered now again, sitting on his bed [after seeing the runaway carriage horse out his window]" (*CS*, 211). The only answer he can summon to this question is, "But what is there to do . . . but to let the mind relate them to each other for its own secret reasons, to carry horse and butterfly within oneself, through many seasons, until they find each other and reveal a meaning to their carrier?" (*CS*, 211).

Again he is in the present moment, sitting on his bed, and feels that "there is a link . . . between the happenings of the daily world and the dreaming mind that holds its hidden images. It was as though life were unfolding on either side of a partition, a wall" (*CS*, 211–12). The bed on which he has been sitting is now brought into the story fully, as if it has been waiting for its realization as a potent image: "Now he held

the dream as close as another body in his bed; and there was a joining,
as in love." We have not yet been told anything of this dream, from
which he had awakened in the very first sentences of the story, even
though it was this painful dream that led his mind, by its secret path-
ways, to the memories we have seen unfolding in him. And we are not
told the dream yet, either, because first we must come to the resting
point of the thinking that the story has presented to us, in a passage of
uncommon delicacy and profundity, for which we have been prepared
in a carefully oblique way:

> We cannot believe, he thought, how all things work together toward
> some ultimate clear meaning, we cannot believe. Human life is at
> once in a conspiracy to prove us of small or no end, and a conspiracy
> of incidents and images to lead us to a beginning again. There is the
> constant, gentle and steadfast urging of the small, loyal friendliness,
> the pure benevolence of some little Beginningness that lies waiting
> in us all to be taken up like a rescued lover and lead us to a human
> courage and a human meaning. The rest is death: murder (self or
> other), betrayal, violence and cruelty, vengeance and crimes of fear.
> But the little Beginningness is in all of us, waiting. (*CS*, 212)

The day moth and the dead horse have brought this meaning out of
their apparently chance juxtaposition. And the final words of the story
now restore to us at last the dream with which the unnamed character
began, thus closing the circle on this story; that is, *he* has known the
dream all along, but now *we* are *told* it:

> In his dream he had seen his mother standing half in the doorway
> of the house, in darkling light, in the attitude of an early photograph
> he knew of her, her hair bobbed and graying, for she was so ill, even
> then, calling out to him and his sister in the yard where they had
> drawn a hopscotch in the dirt: "Come on in now, it's darkening."
> And when they had gone in, he and his sister, they had found the
> house filled with the darkening and no answer to the call but the
> low, gentle, echoing cry, "Come on in now, it's darkening."
>   Now all in his room there was the hovering presence of the day
> moth. (*CS*, 212)

Thus one memory has yielded to the next, one past moment to another, and all memories and past moments have intertwined with a new
understanding of the present moment and of life itself. In addition to

the element of musicality in the quality of language, there is in some
stories, like this one, a musicality of structure, a musical repetition and
interweaving of themes and images, something like this:

a dream (its content not revealed), in the present

the horse in the present

the day moth

a horse in the past

mother

the day moth

the horse in the past

after the dream, in the present

the content of the dream of mother

the day moth

Goyen wrote in the preface to his *Collected Stories:* "I have felt the
short-story form as some vitality, some force that begins (and not necessarily at the *beginning*), grows in force, reaches a point beyond which
it cannot go without losing force, loses force and declines; stops. For
me, story telling is a rhythm, a charged movement, a chain of pulses
or beats. To write out of life is to catch, in pace, this pulse that beats
in the material of life."

While it does not mention music, this passage is very like the way
one might also say that music proceeds; that is, the passage describes
the story as a way of organizing time (as well as a way of describing
characters, situations, places, and so on) in the manner of musical im-
provisation or composition. Often, one has the sense that just as Goyen
does not know in advance, he says, what shape a larger work will have
but must trust what connections arise between the "medallions" of it
as he works (this is a spatial, pictorial metaphor), so he wants to create
for the reader a sense of revelation out of diverse materials, out of the
musical path of thought and feeling (this is a temporal metaphor). And
in a way that accomplishment is one of his most notable ones. The
musical path is, of course, more characteristic of speech than of writing,
is more characteristic of the way the mind links things, discovers mean-

ings that it remains for a while unaware of, than of the way the mind constructs a plot or argument. (Unlike Molière's character who is elated to discover that he may think more highly of himself because he has been told he speaks prose—that is, of course he does not speak poetry—Goyen's characters speak *speech;* for them to speak "prose" would be a deadening of the spontaneity and life of speech, a loss of the vital rhythms both of words and of feelings and associations.)

The peculiar quality of a story like "The Horse and the Day Moth" depends both on the way in which it is structurally (musically) organized and on the way it is told (the musicality of the language itself). If one had to identify this narrating voice one would have to say that it is something like what one would imagine the central character's voice to be. We have the odd sensation of the central character's telling us of himself in the third person. That is, he is telling now what he earlier discovered and, in those last two paragraphs, had already told himself. In a way, then, he has listened to his own mind, as if it were speaking to him as an other, and then he has spoken once more to us what he has heard. This double perspective recalls the second of Goyen's two epigraphs to *The House of Breath:* the French poet Rimbaud's famous line "JE est un autre," meaning there is something *other* even about "I." And we might also recall Wallace Stevens's aphorism, from his "Adagia": "When the mind is like a hall in which thought is like a voice speaking, the voice is always that of someone else."[10]

Naturally, since music is not only a temporal but an aural phenomenon, Goyen understands his responsibility as a writer as partly to *listen* to that voice speaking in the hall of the mind, to listen carefully enough to discern the value of what he is already hearing in the voices that arise in him from memory and imagination. In a notebook left at his death was this little reminder to himself of his method and credo:

1. Writing is waiting (for):
2. {Finding the Voice
    {Hearing the Voice   Story is told to
    me, I tell it to you.
        Otherwise I don't write—or
    can't write.

Narrative Voice

Given that the fictional strategies associated with the nature of narration itself and the identity of the narrative voice are especially noticeable in Goyen's short fiction, it is useful to look at his stories in terms of how they can be sorted into several different categories according to their similarities of narrative voice. In this regard, much of what is true of Goyen's stories is also true of his longer fiction.

One can arrange the stories along a scale, moving from the traditional sort of remote third-person narrative, in which the narrative voice is itself not understood to be intimately involved in what happens, to a first-person narrative in which we are listening to one of the principal characters of the story speak and in which he—or she—and we as readers are the intimately related teller and listener. Note that it does not follow from this arrangement that the language at the more impersonal end of the scale must be "standard English"; a third-person narrative can also use the artifice of a folksy tone of voice. And besides, in every story of Goyen's one can see his stylistic touch. But at the other end of the scale the language will indeed tend to be more flavored with the idiosyncrasies of a speaking voice, will sound more intimate, and may make more use of regionalisms. It is in the very nature of third-person narrative not to call much attention to itself, lest the voice that is speaking it develop into a character in his or her own right. "Third person" narrative is therefore the label not so much for a grammatical device as for a certain tone of voice, a certain distance from the action. It should be noted that almost nowhere in the entire range of Goyen's work can one find the tone of voice commonly called "omniscient third person."

These categories cannot be entirely neat, because Goyen did not write according to a scheme. But making allowances for variation from a norm, one could divide up Goyen's stories in this way:

1. One end of the scale holds *third-person* narratives, such as his first published story, "The White Rooster," and, from his second book of stories, "The Faces of Blood Kindred," or the early story that was not collected until later, "The Thief Coyote," in which the revealed self-awareness of the teller or author in these stories is minimal. The somewhat less remote "The Letter in the Cedarchest," "Zamour," and "Tapioca Surprise" also belong in this category. To be sure, there is more intimacy and self-consciousness in the voice that narrates "The Letter in the Cedarchest," as if someone telling this story were at least a little aware of himself. One hears, right from the first word, "Now," a more immediate tone of voice than that of "The White Rooster," and one sees many small signals that the narrator of this tale is very close to the story himself: for instance, it is said of Lucille's husband that he "had evil lips"—this sort of judgment would be made by a character close to the realm of the story, not an all-seeing author above his characters. Similar hints appear in the colloquialisms of the narrator's language—individual words such as "acoming" or phrasings such as the sentence that begins, "Helped her so much that she begun to have giggling and crying spells." Taken together, these linguistic signs do suggest a certain intimacy in the narrative tone. But generally these stories represent a narrator who, while he seems to know all about the characters but is not one of them, is nonetheless another of Goyen's *tellers*. The touch of narrative intimacy—the folksy tone—creates a gentle distancing, a subtle and bemused tolerance.

2. The next category includes those stories in which the grammatical strategy is a *third-person* narrative but whose tone of voice intimately resides near one or more characters—as in "The Grasshopper's Burden," in which the reader is kept closely inside Quella's thoughts (and, for one brief moment, enters George Kurunus's). Other powerful examples include "Old Wildwood" and "The Horse and the Day Moth." This group also includes several stories that make use of the same grammatical strategy, not to take us close to the central character who is *other*, and whom we might identify as being far from the author, but rather to remove us only a little bit from the author himself, as in "The Moss Rose," "A People of Grass," "The Geranium," and "There Are Ravens to Feed Us."

3. The next category includes *first-person* narratives in which the speaker is identified as a participant in the story or someone who was close to the participants. Examples are the sections from Goyen's early unpublished novel, *Half a Look of Cain*, published separately as the short stories "The Enchanted Nurse," "The Rescue," and "Figure over the Town"; and also "Children of Old Somebody," "Bridge of Music, River of Sand," "Had I a Hundred Mouths," "Precious Door," and "Pore Perrie."

4. The last category, the full-fledged "arias" at the opposite end from the more or less impersonal third-person stories of our first category, includes *first-person* stories in which the self-conscious teller is himself or herself present, the principal actor and teller in one, so that the story is notably a *performance* and resembles a dramatic monologue for stage presentation. These stories typically make greater use of the idiosyncrasies of colloquialism, as in "Ghost and Flesh, Water and Dirt," "Savata, My Fair Sister," "The Texas Principessa," "Where's Esther?" and "Arthur Bond."

These four categories represent points on a continuum, not completely separate groups; any careful reader will find that Goyen's stories are not easy to categorize neatly. The purpose of this grouping along a scale is to emphasize that all of Goyen's work in one way or another calls the reader's attention to the narrator's voice and thus opens up questions about not what a "story" is but what the telling of a story is. Although even in the most stylistically aural of his stories, such as "Arthur Bond," there is no denying Goyen's vivid visual description, Goyen's is a literary art more for the mind's ear than for the mind's eye. In addition, Goyen has put his unmistakable artistic signature on the stories of all four categories. The Goyenesque style grows more intense as we move from the first category through the others.

It cannot be an accident that the stories in the first category, in which the language and artistic strategies are more traditionally third person, are also the stories with the more traditional principle of fictional structure—a plot. Yet, even those stories which are most meandering in terms of plot, like "The Horse and the Day Moth" (the second category) or "Pore Perrie" (the third), turn out to contain an important *sequence,* whether of events or of feelings and memories. This quality points not to the absence of plot in some of Goyen's most memorable stories but to a peculiar and interesting use of "plot." Despite the common acceptance of the term *plot* to mean a sequence of actions, the word is actually a spatial metaphor, drawn from measurement of land, diagrams, and so on. While Goyen does use a spatial metaphor, the quilt, to describe some of his longer works, he uses a musical metaphor, "song," to describe his stories. Music organizes recognizable elements that are repeated, sounded in alternation or in other rhythmic patterns. And this is the way Goyen's stories often organize their elements as well.

Thus, the "plot" of Goyen's stories is often indeed an important ordering in time, not of events, which take place in space as much as in time, but rather of memories and feelings, which are interior, which are not bounded by space, which take place in imagination. Goyen's use of "plot" is entirely subservient to language and voice. After all, Goyen did not write a single story in which *all* trace of a teller is absent, even including those stories in the first category. And at the end of his career, especially (as in *Arcadio*), he achieved a kind of fusion of the *theme* of the teller-listener with the fictional *technique* of using the teller-listener situation. The artistic possibilities of the early "Pore Perrie" are again developed in "Had I a Hundred Mouths."

"Had I a Hundred Mouths" first introduces a teller-listener situation; it shows us the uncle telling two young nephews the very story we are about to read. One of the nephews is deeply affected by the tale (the story is lodged and preserved in his consciousness), and the other apparently not so. Then the story shifts into the voice of the uncle, and the narrative is told, through all its bizarre and shocking episodes in which the uncle is implicated morally more than he seems to know. At the end, the frame closes when the nephew who was most affected by that telling is revealed as having ever since been under the burden, as it were, of the uncle's story, so that as the carrier of the tale he himself, as an adult, must tell it once more. Lifelong he has been preoccupied with what he heard from his uncle that day; it seared his imagination with its stark horror, and he has been searching in his own life ever since for "Leander"—that is, for that wrecked, ruined, suffering soul who was created out of others' lust and "betrayal, violence and cruelty, vengeance and crimes of fear" (a phrase from "The Horse and the Day Moth," *CS*, 212).

One might profitably consider how often it is an uncle or an aunt or a person with similar kinship to the listener who tells Goyen's stories; there is an anthropological consistency in the way Goyen's stories are told *of* mothers and sons, for instance, *by* uncles or aunts. The consistency of this constellation implies that the ritual of telling is a way not of enforcing close bonds within the family but of strengthening bonds among those who are not so intimately related, who in fact achieve another kind of intimate relation, perhaps as strong as close blood, when they participate together in telling and listening; they are not inhibited so strictly in telling as the members of the nuclear family would be with one another. (For more examples, see *The House of Breath*, which has a complicated family tree.)

As is often and characteristically the case in Goyen's work, there is an erotic undertone to the intimacy of the teller-listener situation. "Had I a Hundred Mouths" begins this way:

> On Good Friday, in the warm afternoon, the two cousins lay huddled against their uncle's bony body, each nestled in the crook of an arm. Often the cousins would be left in their uncle's care, and their habit was to take off their clothes because of the Gulf humidity and lie cool on the bed together and listen to his stories, which were generally about the joys and despairs of desire. . . . [The older nephew, who was eleven years old] was beckoned by some new feeling and

he felt powerless before it; and, most of all, he didn't care. He felt
that he would go all the way with some feeling, when it would soon
come, and not hinder it because it was wrong, and not be afraid of
it, not care what happened, overwhelmed. His storyteller uncle had
something to do with this feeling, he was not sure what; but surely
it was a feeling that had first come to him from his uncle; it seemed
to be in the command of the man, it seemed called up in him by
the man's very nurturing presence, something like what motherli-
ness had been for him not so long ago but now pushed away forever;
and by the seduction of the storyteller, the surrender of listener to
teller, almost in a kind of love-making, of sensual possession, yet
within innocence and purity.[11]

Now, the rhetoric of orality referred to earlier, or rather the rhetoric
of communication itself, both oral and written, is linked to erotic desire
in several ways, which have been explored by such critics as Roland
Barthes. Language can certainly be turned to seductive purposes, but
more than that, language itself can be a seduction away from the world
outside language to the world of associations and linguistic phenomena
inside language (critics differ on whether this seduction is an achieve-
ment of the human imagination or an unfortunate problem in human
culture).

Further, the relation between reader and text includes elements of
both seductiveness and linguistic reference that together produce what
some have likened to a metaphorically erotic experience. This idea is
not new and is probably experienced and understood by sophisticated
readers in a variety of circumstances and historical eras. In literature,
the rhetoric of orality is not only a linguistic phenomenon but also a
historical one—the way in which this rhetoric lures, seduces, or con-
vinces the reader so as to carry him or her to a relationship to meaning
has evolved historically and is different from the relationship in which
we now usually stand, as late twentieth-century readers, to written
texts. One can see that in the history of the development of literacy,
for example, the social relationship of teller and listener is different
from that of writer and reader. In ancient Greece, for instance, when
oral and written culture existed for a time simultaneously in a stage of
transition, very different attitudes were held toward each, and literary
creation was instrumental in effecting these changes. According to Oswyn Murray, the scholar Jesper Svenbro relates "the transition to an
autonomous form of literacy"

to the development of silent reading among at least a literate elite
in the late fifth century [B.C.], . . . and to the impact of the theatre,
which, in its full impersonation of the individual character by the
actor, broke the spoken bond between writer and active reader [i.e.,
broke the illusion that the writer of a text always spoke honestly *as
himself*]. Henceforth the image of the reader is pederastic: he is (in
the Platonic metaphor) the beloved conquered and penetrated by
the lover-writer, and despised for his perhaps too complaisant submission. . . . [This was in a society] which believed that pederasty
was a necessary stage in the process of education, and hence of
learning to read. But it also represents the move from written text
as autonomous oral act to written text as violation of the solitary
reader. (Murray, 656)

In other words, society moved from (a) conceiving of communication
as an event during which the speaker was who he seemed to be and
early written texts were a kind of impersonation of speaking persons to
(b) conceiving of communication as a kind of seduction, that is, containing the possibility of untrustworthy meanings, hidden authors, and
even a forcing of a vulnerable reader. Goyen's storytelling, for all its
late twentieth-century sophistication and historical situation, its ventriloquism, and the analogy it establishes between sexual seduction
and the seduction of compelling storytelling, nonetheless creates to
some extent the illusion of an earlier pre-textual attitude, in which the
relationship between writer and reader, between teller and listener, is
"loving," analogous to tender desire, and not manipulative or calculat-
ing. Like the teller and listener nestled against each other, it is rife
with a kind of erotic tenderness, not conquest. Don Juan may have
been the model of the writer working within the rhetoric of writing,
which was, after all, dominated by male writers. But the writer within
the rhetoric of orality does not contemn a conquered reader and depart;
rather, this writer remains and allows himself (or herself) also to feel
the power of the bonds of intimacy. Goyen writes, in the passage just
quoted, of "the surrender of listener to teller, almost in a kind of love-
making, of sensual possession, yet within innocence and purity." One
may recognize in the ancient evolution of literacy toward a relationship
in which reader must distrust writer an analogy to the highly self-conscious and even archly manipulative American fiction of the sixties and
later, the "postmodern" school. Although Goyen is a literary experi-
menter of the first rank, that was not his experiment. He went in the
opposite direction, linking speaking and telling to desire and dreaming.

Insofar as his artistic method has genuine points of contact with pre-textual culture or residual orality, it is for the purpose of creating a social situation of reading that unites teller and listener in moments of shared feeling rather than in mutually skeptical attitudes with regard to communicative reliability.

Goyen's work reminds us of a basic distinction of language: the difference between spoken utterance, whether spontaneous, rehearsed, or ritualized, and written text. Goyen adapts some elements of spoken utterance to the written text, and in doing so he both comments on the nature of the spoken and alters the nature of the written. It is not that he "realistically" reproduces or records the diction and phrasing of speech; his motive is not documentary but expressive. Rather, he refers to, or represents, spoken language as one part of his overall artistic strategy to create a peculiar bond between teller and listener. It only trivializes Goyen's accomplishment to regard his colloquial speech as dialect; it is far more than that, as he suggests when he distinguishes "speech" from "voice." A story in dialect may in itself be very effective storytelling; but it does not necessarily represent an intensification of the signifying powers of language, especially the poetic powers of association, connotation, echoes and interweavings of themes, and so on, to all of which Goyen's especially distilled language gives special power. Nor does a story in dialect necessarily make the situation of the teller and the listener itself an element on which the art is trained, or achieve any sophistication of thinking about what narrative is, how it works, and what it accomplishes.

Those stories of Goyen's which fall into the third category, of which "Had I a Hundred Mouths" is one of the most astonishing, are precisely the stories in which the transition from oral to written—that double existence of language—is most finely balanced and in which the poetic and rhetorical resources of language are most potently deployed. (The performance pieces of the fourth category of Goyen's stories are, as noted, more like theater. Just as theater creates the illusion of an actor becoming a character—an illusion that spectators simultaneously see through yet do not always question—the performance also breaks "the spoken bond" between writer and reader; that is, it destroys the illusion that the writer is speaking, in his writing, as himself.) At the beginning of "Had I a Hundred Mouths," after the older nephew's soul-searching meditation has led him only into insoluble quandaries, abruptly the narrative continues: "It was in the dark afternoon on a November day of sleet, told the uncle" (*HIHM*, 6). The voice of the story descends into the uncle's intonations, which are very different from the nephew's. While the nephew is troubled deeply, at his tender age, by the imponderable mysteries of adult life, the uncle speaks casually of the most shocking and barbaric violence, merely to lead up to his story of what happened to Louetta (which is no less shocking). To the two little boys listening, the uncle—incongruously, almost abusively, one might say—recounts Louetta's double rape, by the black stranger and by himself. The story takes no note of the shock the two boys must have felt, for it has moved away from the older nephew's point of view entirely and lies only within the uncle's. From time to time the uncle reminds us, by implication, of the presence of the two silent, presumably spellbound, and even frightened boys: "And now I'm going to tell you something" (*HIHM*, 11). But the story remains within his voice, giving him time to sing. I will not here go over the events of the narrative itself—suffice it to say that the uncle tells of tragic violence and striking pathos. What most matters at this point in my analysis is to note the delicate touch with which Goyen keeps the story within the uncle's voice and yet at the same time reminds us that the story is all this time a remembering by the uncle, a telling to the two boys, and a subsequent retelling by one of the boys. Another example of the balance of these simultaneous perspectives:

> That night Kansas Tate in her misery fell of a stroke and died, and I run far into the woods and drank my whisky in the dark of the deep woods and laid like a log in the leaves. And then I crawled and hid in the dark of the cave.
>
> The uncle took a long swallow of whisky. And then he said, very low, I've never told a soul this story until now. Had I a hundred mouths I could not have told this story; it was too much of a story to tell. I've kept the tale of Leander and Louetta a secret all these years and have drank a ton of whisky on it. And now I've told it to you boys, my brother's son and my sister's son, one just becoming a man and the other still adozing in his little boyhood. And the uncle reached again under the bed and brought up the bottle to his mouth. (*HIHM*, 13–14)

These are deft modulations: that last sentence interrupts the uncle's voice with stage directions. But the next sentences afterward interrupt the stage directions with a retrospective consciousness, before dipping down again into the uncle's voice:

The golden fumes of whisky spread over the nephews, and the carnality of that moment, the despairs of the flesh and the sorrows of the story of Leander brought life down upon the older nephew so heavily that it seemed unbearable; and he wondered how he would ever hear his feelings that his heart and his body were just beginning to give to him. He understood then his uncle's feelings and the ton of whisky used to deaden them, but he vowed he would never deaden life, that he would feel his feelings full and that he would not fall under their burden as his uncle had, in hiding and numbness. He would feel and he would tell, even as his uncle had, finally, this afternoon.

But the uncle had more to tell. His voice went on, graver than the nephew had ever heard it. That day as I laid in the cave and wanting to die, I heard a sound. (*HIHM*, 14)

When the uncle finishes his narrative, the older nephew asks what became of Leander, and the uncle says he does not know. The story presents once more the scene of the man and two boys lying together, the man sleeping now, the boys awake. Then a surprising turn makes us hark to a different voice. The story leaps ahead to the uncle's funeral. The older nephew is shocked by the sudden appearance of several hooded members of the Ku Klux Klan—those who had destroyed Leander. One of them lifts his mask and reveals himself as the younger nephew, and the older nephew feels "terror and rage." The voice of the story clearly remains with the older nephew, and we are by now able to *hear* this episode in the same way that we hear those intimate but third-person narratives of our second category.

The voicing of the story reveals to us how the social and psychological situation the story recounts both transmits and fails to transmit moral values. The older nephew feels something of himself being formed in the experience of listening to and being with the uncle. The younger nephew, who will grow up to join the Klan, responds differently: "The younger nephew lay like a blank-eyed doll nested in the uncle's embrace; he might even have been dozing; he seemed to be in some peace under his uncle's arm, in some kind of haven, unthreatened. . . . But did the younger nephew need anybody? Who knew? He did not seem to hear. Or did he hear and just not care? Who knew?" (*HIHM*, 4–5).

As yet unalive in his feelings, the younger nephew, if this glimpse we are given of his adult life is meant as an indication, appears to have absorbed from his uncle only the superficial prejudices embedded in the tale. But the older nephew is filled with the complexities and imponderables of the uncle's story and feels allied to all suffering life. He wonders why one person *hears* a story and another does not—that is, why one person is engaged with the life of feeling and another is not. He has no answer. The situation in which he begins to sense tragic elements in life was the same one that may have aroused in the younger nephew only an admiration for the brutality of the Klan. The story does not portray the transmission of values, whether correct or corrupt, but rather the confusion of the transmission itself. Thus Goyen implies an equal artistic interest in both the substance of the values transmitted and the way in which they are transmitted—almost unknowingly by the uncle, but not quite; there is an element of prurience in his habit of undressing with the boys and telling them of rape and castration. *Both* children suffer wounding consequences, as the ending of the story implies.

As an adult, the older nephew has repeated all too much of the uncle's life—the drunkenness, the lust, and the loneliness. But he has not absorbed the racial hatred or the coldness toward life that infected the younger nephew. And late at night on a city street, in a mood of despair, the older nephew comes on a bizarre, fantastic figure, a black man dressed in scales of glass and in feathers; white man confronting the African-American life unknown to him except by signs of suffering, the nephew calls to him, "Leander!" But the figure moves on, not acknowledging him except with a forbidding glance. The older nephew's reaction is to be plunged into a sense of the flesh, the physical body—the site of both lust and mortality. His awareness of mortality creates not fear but a kind of tragic calm, in which he is able—and feels compelled—to write down and tell the buried story of the uncle: "And all that night the nephew put this down and told again the story that his uncle told him, a story that he could not have told before had he had a hundred mouths to tell it with. In the morning, in the silver light of dawn over the old city of his miracles, miraculously refreshed he saw in the mirror his naked body, its skin, its haunch, its breast: the ancient sower's flesh, the reaper's" (*HIHM*, 19).

In other words, in this third-person story the narrating voice quite explicitly reveals itself as artificially couched in the third person by the very nephew who is at the center of the story. What we have been reading he has written about himself, we now discover, in the third person. Note that it is not the author, Goyen, who has done this but a character in the story. Thus perspectives nest inside each other, as they did in "Pore Perrie."

This story more than any other joins the teller-listener situation to the erotic life and does so in several ways. First, there is the homoerotic intimacy of the uncle and the boys; second, the prepubescent feelings and thoughts of the older nephew, who begins to grasp that erotic passion will consume him and wishes to yield to it; third, the lust and violence that destroy Louetta's life, as told by the uncle, who himself raped her; fourth, the use of the seductiveness of language itself—Goyen's deft and perfectly timed modulations, the richness of his narrative skill, and so on—to create the complex illusion of the story as a whole; and last, the significance of the ending of the story.

"Haunch" and "breast" are ambiguous terms and suggest both male and female bodies—suggest, more than anything, an erotic life, "the ancient sower's flesh." And this erotic rejuvenation has arisen out of the nightlong work or *writing* and *telling* the old story. This willing donning of the mantle of the storyteller, *because of having been awakened to life earlier as a listener,* is the conclusive and concluding gesture of the story and exemplifies the driving force behind all of Goyen's work. Sexual experience is both a sowing and a reaping, a greening of life and a reminder of mortality; when it is violent (as also at the end of *Arcadio*) it is a destruction of life.

As with the two brothers who appear in the story "Precious Door," the figure of Leander remains a potent emblem for the older nephew in "Had I a Hundred Mouths," and although the story recounts mostly an event from his boyhood, it gives to that event the perspective of adult, and tragic, experience, by means of the last short sections. Thus it, like many other stories by Goyen, functions as a recovery of the past, a memory piece, as well as a meditation on lust and tragedy and the life to be regained, or to be initated once more, by the telling of story. And throughout this story, as in so many others, the power of the work lies not only in the events or feelings brought to the reader but also in the uses of the language with which they are conveyed, from the ventriloquism of the uncle's colloquial speech, which ranges through the nearly affectless early passages and the later confessions of trouble and sadness, to the magnificent narrative rhythms that call up the chilling apparition "Leander" in the city night, years later. Complex layers of perspective and seductive interrelationships among them are created by the author's powers of fictional illusion. As Goyen said in an interview, "the language is always a principal character in the story for me." In his work, perhaps the most striking feature of this centrality of language is the way in which he creates out of the teller-listener situation a rhetoric of the erotic, as complex and profoundly contradictory as the erotic can be in life. As I have already suggested, Goyen woos his reader with this fictional strategy, but he does not seduce in the sense of an unemotional exercise of power over another. Rather, he creates in the teller-listener situation between text and reader an echo of that situation between characters.

And while from his earliest student days Goyen engaged in a struggle over values with his father and the life around him, he did not later idealize either his own art or the rural life from which he drew it and simply set it against crassness, conformity, small-mindedness, or modern city life. On the contrary, that first house, that emblem of stability and peace and the restoration of soul, as we see it in "Rhody's Path," is also a place of oppressive attitudes, which is why Rhody leaves it in the first place. The ending of "In the Icebound Hothouse," acknowledges the darkness in that house. Goyen offers no evidence that the teller-listener situation is inherently opposed to the horrors he describes in "Had I a Hundred Mouths"; rather, he opposes it to lifelessness in the way that life—all of it, including the horrific elements—is opposed to death. He says, "I'm not talking about the horror of life. But the horrible and terrible element in life. Why would I endure life if I thought *life* were horrible? What good would I gain by enduring? Enduring is a hopeful action."

Some Thematic Elements
in Goyen's Short Fiction

I have mentioned that there is a striking consistency in Goyen's fiction, from his earliest work to his last—a combination of characteristic style, subjects, situations, and narrative strategies that readily conveys to us that a short story is unmistakably Goyen's. This consistency arises also from the presence throughout Goyen's work of certain predominant themes.

In addition to the thematic, as well as technical, significance of the teller-listener situation and the emphasis this theme places in turn on the theme of the power of language as a place in which the past can be sung out, understood, and partly recovered, there are at least five other prominent themes in Goyen's writings: (a) the effect of the past; (b) the experience of leaving home and returning repeatedly; (c) erotic life; (d) persons who are orphaned, deformed, outcast in some way; and (e) the harsh inhumanity of industrial and urban society, which destroys the natural environment and estranges people from one another. In many of Goyen's stories (as well as in his novels), several or all of these themes may be sounded, and therefore it is somewhat arbitrary to consider a story in terms of only one theme. Further, not all the themes are present in equal measure in each stage of Goyen's career, much less in every story. But for the sake of the analyses that follow, I survey some of the stories in terms of their central focus on one of these themes, after indicating generally the boundaries of these thematic categories.

Theme 1

The effect of the presence or absence of the past in the lives of the living: this is most notable in Goyen's first novel, *The House of Breath*, but it is also an important element in such stories as "Pore Perrie," "The Faces of Blood Kindred," "Old Wildwood," and "Had I a Hundred Mouths." This theme, embodied in the phrase "ghost and flesh," is central to the entire volume of that name, Goyen's first book of stories.

Goyen shows that we are both attracted to the past and trapped by it; we wish both to free ourselves of it and also to recover it. These paradoxes are part of our formation as individuals, and when not only our family but also our cultural background have put their stamp on us—for example, in the way we speak, in our attitudes, in our habits of speech, dress, and eating—then we may be caught in a back-and-forth movement between the past that has shaped us and the future we are trying to shape for ourselves. We are looking, as Nietzsche put it, for a past from which we may spring, rather than that past from which we seem to have derived. Goyen's treatment of an individual's origins may be more background than foreground in most of his stories, but the subject remains an important one in all his work.

Discovering the family past from which he may spring, the central character of "Old Wildwood" gains his first clear sense of what he wants his own life to be like. The names of ancestors given to him by his grandfather in Texas sound in his mind years later in Rome, when he himself has come as far from the time of his grandfather as his grandfather had come from the time of John Bell and others. Hearing of heroic forebears, the boy formed his desires on a heroic scale; hearing of his grandfather's death, the young man is reminded of the standards he wants to hold himself to—standards of scale rather than type. That is, he wants not the outward accomplishment of his forebears (road building or woodcutting) but accomplishments of feeling on a scale with those material feats.

In "Bridge of Music, River of Sand," the lost past of the landscape itself haunts the present as a promise that might have been delivered, had men and women of the modern time only cared for it. The unknown man who jumps from the bridge would jump into what is no longer there—a river that has dried up. He cannot get back to the past (the river), yet he does disappear in sand quite as effectively as he would have in water. Thus the story seems to say that one might mistakenly, desperately, leap out of the present into an illusion. And the end of generations that is portrayed in "The Armadillo Basket" signifies that the end of the lives of the old women is the end of a way of life, and this latter end will haunt their descendants, to whom a basket made from an armadillo shell will undoubtedly seem as foreign as an artifact from another civilization.

Whether it is a personal past or a cultural one—echoing either the consequences of an individual's deeds and experience or the cumulative effect of many persons' decisions on a town or the environment—Goyen's stories describe, many times over, those moments when the past reaches forward to shape a present moment, when it cannot be escaped. Goyen also describes some paradoxes: (a) the past cannot be fully grasped, anyway, as when the narrator of "Had I a Hundred Mouths" wants to confront Leander and cannot find him, and (b) the veil of attractiveness over the past hides horror, not solace (as in the ambivalence of the design etched in glass on the childhood front door in "In the Icebound Hothouse").

Theme 2

Failing a home that can remain unchanged through time, the experience of leaving and returning many times, as one strives to find a place to rest: this theme is especially notable in such stories as "Pore Perrie," "Rhody's Path," and "Bridge of Music, River of Sand." A preoccupation with leaving and returning is mentioned in many other stories and is related to a feeling of withering or burning out and then coming back, revived, to life, as in "Nests in a Stone Image," "The Horse and the Day Moth," and "The Geranium." It is also related to the portrayal of persons who are wanderers and without a home, as in "Children of Old Somebody" and the novel *Arcadio;* and such persons are of course akin to the orphans and foundlings mentioned in many of Goyen's stories, most dramatically in a figure like the flagpole sitter. This theme is really a dramatization of a felt exile and estrangement from others. In an interview Goyen says:

> I had a sense of myself—which has lessened a bit, but is still an underlying sense of myself—as a *passager,* as someone passing through. So many of my stories were almost ballads—saying that I'm on my way, I'm just passing through, I've sung out of my feeling that I couldn't live in Texas, that I couldn't live among my own, that something alienated me, that I was drawn apart. And that was a heartbreak for me. I accepted it as a kind of destiny and often as a curse. . . . An artist moves, goes out, comes back and then leaves again. . . . When I went back, it was almost—just a death, one of my deaths. I couldn't get over waking and hearing Texans. . . . I talk like that, that's my speech, and those are all my people, but why is it I can't be a part of them? Why am I here in this room alone, isolated and exiled from them, just outside my door?

Naturally, one supposes that Goyen's own experience is at the heart of his preoccupation with this theme. His journeys away from home were repeated—first from his childhood home in Trinity, Texas, to which he never returned, and then from his family into the world of larger possibilities that he discovered when he attended college. When he went to Iowa for graduate school he returned in three months. After his wartime tour of duty in the navy, he never lived in Texas again for any significant period of time, although he sojourned there and visited frequently. Again, his leaving of New York for Los Angeles in the mid-1970s was another such loss, inasmuch as his apartment in New York had for more than fifteen years given him a sense of home and had been a place of composition for him as well.

But beyond these geographical removals also lies the repeatedly experienced emotional removal from past security into present uncertainty. Goyen felt this emotional loss not only about his own early childhood but also about some of the stages of his life, as when his years of success, beginning with the publication of *The House of Breath* when he was thirty-five, led to years of disappointment and as when his period of artistic plenitude led to years when he did not write. He also had occasion to wonder, as one who sometimes felt left behind, about those who left and did or did not return, as Rhody does in her story. The romance of leaving, of setting out on a journey, of "having a plan," as the older brother says in "Precious Door," appears in a number of stories. There are those who do not get to leave, like the young boy Jim in "The Thief Coyote," and those who are sorry to have had to leave, like Princis Lester in "Zamour." Goyen's uprootedness finally made him feel an affinity with Beckett, who said that the artist lives nowhere.

Theme 3

Erotic life: this theme is present from the beginning of Goyen's work and ranges from the excitement and exaltation of love in "Ghost and Flesh" and the awe and curiosity expressed in "Old Wildwood" through the disillusioned wonderment at sexual desire in "Arthur Bond" to the dark and even demonic, ungovernable lust of "Had I a Hundred Mouths." In Goyen's earlier stories and in *The House of Breath*, sexual freedom is often hinted at as the hidden desire that sends people running away from their small-town homes to life in a larger world. In "Ghost and Flesh, Water and Dirt" there is a lovely and frank portrayal of sexual desire and excitement, without any hint of the darkness of sexual obsession that will appear in *Arcadio*, years later. But even in "Ghost and Flesh, Water and Dirt," while the narrator's life shows us the sweetness of her passionate love for Nick Natowski, the story also robs her of this sweetness and brings her back to her small town to tell and retell the tragedies of her love and grief.

In Goyen's work, where both heterosexual and homosexual lovers have a place (Goyen's work is discreet in its presentation of the sexual experience itself, until we reach his last work, *Arcadio*), erotic experience is often tied to spiritual suffering as well as ecstasy—that is, Goyen is interested in sexual experience beyond the distinctions of heterosexual and homosexual. Rather than treating sexual experience as a matter of sexual preference, Goyen presents a kind of cosmic eroticism. In *The House of Breath* this eroticism is part of the spiritual experience of the vast dimensions of the human soul and its capacity for feeling; in the stories, where the scope is more limited, the portrayal of sexual experience also seems more limited and yet is still akin to the cosmic eroticism of *The House of Breath*, and is identified with exaltation as much as with guilt and a remorse. Moreover, in the stories the subject of sex may be displaced or disguised in other images or figures, as it is in the evangelist, snake, and flagpole sitter—all of them with relation to Rhody—in "Rhody's Path." The conjunction of flagpole and sex reappears in "Figure over the Town."

Much spiritual suffering seems tied specifically to the experience of sex. The accidental wound suffered by Son in "Pore Perrie" is a mutilation of his genitals; a similar but worse wound is deliberately inflicted by the Ku Klux Klan on Leander in "Had I a Hundred Mouths" and accidentally befalls Boney Benson in "A Shape of Light." Such woundings are not, in Goyen's fiction, statements about sex so much as ways of using sexual life to represent a larger condition of profound psychic wounds of deep disappointment or betrayal; thus Goyen also shows how erotic intoxication separates those who feel it from all others. Yet it would be a great mistake to associate the erotic only with disillusionment and emotional pain; as in *The House of Breath*, Goyen's stories also richly suggest the power of the erotic to give the individual an ecstatic sense of his or her place not only among men and women but in nature itself, as we noted earlier.

This leads me to mention briefly how Goyen writes of sexual identity in his fiction. His treatment of this aspect of human nature goes beyond his ability to write so convincingly, as he often does, from the female point of view (as, for instance, in "The Grasshopper's Burden," "Ghost and Flesh, Water and Dirt," "The Texas Principessa," "Where's Esther?" and other stories). Readers of Goyen's fiction will also have already noticed an interesting and complex portrayal of gender identity and sexual attraction. There are many examples of conflicted sexual identity, beginning with Christy and Folner, and Boy himself, in *The House of Breath*. And the castrating wounds suffered by characters in a number of stories serve to make ambiguous their sexual identity. There is also the homoerotic quality of the physical therapy performed by the male nurse on his patient in "The Enchanted Nurse" and "The Rescue," of the relationship between the two brothers in "Precious Door" and between the nephews and uncle in "Had I a Hundred Mouths."

"Precious Door" hints that there is a sexual element in compassion, through such details as the description of the young wounded stranger: "[W]e saw in that moment when his face and his look came clear to us what would have been called a beautiful young girl if it had been a girl; but it was a man" (*HIHM*, 41). And brotherly love is similarly qualified by the passionate embrace into which the surviving, murderous brother gathers the body of his dead brother near the end of the story. Readers of Goyen's longer works will have been struck also by the exploration of sexual identity and experience that forms the heart of *Arcadio*. Arcadio is a hermaphrodite and, having been raised and abused in a whorehouse, has much to tell of sexual experience. While sexual experience itself is a matter often implied or mentioned in the stories and novels, although rarely brought into view directly, in *Arcadio* Goyen discusses it explicitly. He describes an obsessive and destructive lust, seen in both Arcadio's father and his father's lover, Johna; absent from this work is a tender passion that could be felt as a positive and even visionary possibility of life, despite its being also overwhelmingly puzzling and mysterious.

In many of the later stories, as if in preparation for *Arcadio*, sex becomes a more central subject. In "Had I a Hundred Mouths" and "Tongues of Men and of Angels," Louetta is sexually victimized not only by the man who first rapes her, and then later, and horribly, by her own son, but also by her cousin—the uncle who is telling the story to the two boys lying in his arms (as noted earlier, a sexually charged situation). "Arthur Bond" is an astonishing treatment of sexual desire, which appears metaphorically as the "worm" in Arthur Bond's thigh.

A last note: there are two ways in which the erotic is present in Goyen's fiction. First it appears as subject, as in these stories and others; second, it can be present as the emotional undercurrent of the teller-listener situation itself, which Goyen even describes in erotic terms in "Had I a Hundred Mouths." Thus the erotic operates both thematically and rhetorically in terms of an erotics of reading.

Theme 4

The presence of those who are deformed or outcast, whose *difference* from others is marked in their bodies and whose special burden of consciousness is not only thus marked but honored as well: this sort of figure is akin to the wanderers mentioned in regard to theme 2. This is the realm of Goyen's orphans and foundlings and other isolated persons. Goyen associates physical deformity or injury with intensity of feeling, a special capacity for feeling, or a special suffering that awakens or charges spiritual life. One thinks of the small boy sick with overpowering feeling in "A People of Grass." In the same interview quoted earlier, Goyen says he is really interested more in "a spiritual deformity. Of course, dwarves, and humpbacks, and harelips, and so forth. That's only the beginning for me. I can't linger on that very long but it delivers me from the boring reality of realistic reporting. . . . I'm aware that there is no everyday trivia in itself; that beneath it, or going on within it, there's always some slight deformity of thought or action. It's the hidden life I'm talking about."

That Goyen felt himself marked by difference is incontrovertible. As a boy he suffered from occasional seizures, and his emotional sensitivity and dreams of artistry early set him apart from many others. Near the end of his life, Goyen had prepared for his publisher a proposal for a new novel to be based on the Greek myth of Philoctetes. This figure was the archer who was abandoned by the Achaians on their way to war against Troy because he had been bitten by a snake and the bite had turned into a noisome wound that others could not bear. But prophecy later revealed that Troy could not be defeated without Philoctetes' bow and that it would not be enough for another to steal the bow and use it; Philoctetes himself must be brought back, wound and all, to the battle. Philoctetes is thus a figure with both a gift and a defect, a figure who despite his gift is abandoned by others because of the defect—an exile, an estranged person. His wound is a deformity that not only torments him but also makes others uncomfortable and isolates him from their love; yet his talent—his bow—is unmatched by anyone else's and is something others need. It is easy to see why

Goyen wanted to write this story over again, for he saw in it that the gift not only is the opposite of the wound but is in a way available only because of the wound—that is, in the modern psychological reading of the myth, the wound not only necessarily accompanies the gift but also is the origin of a gift that evolves in compensation. This story had already been used by a number of modern writers, and it was taken by the critic Edmund Wilson, years before, as the title metaphor of *The Wound and the Bow*, a study of the modern literary artist.

What many of Goyen's characters have in common is having been *marked* in some way—as Philoctetes is by his wound—as different from others. In Goyen's work such marking may be first a sign simply of suffering—of the bodily suffering inflicted by one person on another, as in the case of Leander's scars and castration in "Had I a Hundred Mouths," and, in an outward way, of the suffering psyche, as in the case of the sadly monstrous figure of George Kurunus in "The Grasshopper's Burden." Deformity is also a sign not of grotesque contrast to others for the sake of dramatic effect (Goyen did not really like the hunchbacks and other figures of deformity of so-called southern Gothic writers) but of individual identity. With deformity Goyen gives a character sufficient identity for beauty as well as ordinariness or ugliness to be seen and acknowledged, for the beauty that ugliness makes apparent by contrast to be perceived *in the same person* (as in the figure of Arcadio), and for beauty itself to be redefined in a more profound way. Another example may be taken from the interview:

> I saw a great photograph yesterday in a book store, a huge life-size photograph of a very beautiful woman with a wonderful breast, and on the other side was a tattoo of roses across no breast at all. She had had one removed, and yet the photographer was saying, "This is all right. This is beautiful. Don't be horrified. She *has* one breast! But it was a *creature:* it seemed almost like Leander. . . . That's why that picture of that woman with one breast, and one scar, was such an *affirmation:* She said, "I am beautiful."

We see a similar mark transformed from deformation to honored difference in "Old Wildwood," when the grandson's attitude toward his grandfather's twisted foot changes. First he sees it as a kind of repellent creature, bare on the rock where grandfather and grandson sit fishing by day. But then the boy comes to see the foot differently:

Something began between the two, between the grandfather and the woman, and the grandson feigned sleep. But he watched through the lashes of his half-closed eyes as through an ambush of grass the odd grace of his grandfather struggling with the woman with whom he seemed to be swimming through water, and he heard his grandfather's low growl like a fierce dog on the cot, and he saw his grandfather's devil's foot treading and gently kicking, bare in the air, so close to him that he could have reached out to touch it. And then he knew that the foot had a very special beauty and grace of moment, a lovely secret performance hidden in it that had seemed a shame on his person and a flaw upon the rock. It had something, even, of a bird's movements in it. It was the crooked foot that was the source and the meaning of the strange and lovely and somehow delicate disaster on the bed. (*CS*, 148)

Of course, what such difference finally serves to show is that there is *no* difference except of appearance, that all persons are imperfect and weak, and that the humanity of all is beautiful. Any physical difference—deformity or weakness—thus serves as an especially evident sign of the mortality we all share. Recall the intimations of mortality— "the ancient sower's flesh, the reaper's"—connected to the apparition of the wounded Leander at the end of "Had I a Hundred Mouths." And in "A People of Grass, " the young boy who has been embarrassed and filled with remorse at his sister's physical weakness, revealed when she fell and tore her paper costume at the town's maypole dance, hides behind the family piano and weeps: "And he felt again as he had so many times before, already, in his very beginning life, that gentle blue visitation of a sense of tragic unfulfillment, a doom of incompleteness in his heritage, never quite brought to perfect bloom, as though its lighted way had been crossed by a shadow of error; and mis-touched, stumbling, bearing its flaw upon its brow and shying for the touch of a magical wand, it could not rise, but struggling to rise it tore its flesh and limped into its dance" (*CS*, 179–80).

Insofar as all the "touched," damaged, or deformed show us, as they discover it for themselves, the bow that compensates for or balances their wound, they are also in a way marvels. For Goyen, the bow is often simply and splendidly a capacity for feeling, and so there is an exciting *intensity of being* around some of his characters, like the flagpole sitters in "Rhody's Path" and "Figure over the Town," or Arcadio, or the doomed and frightening brothers in "Precious Door." In fact, there is marvel in the very first such characters in Goyen's published work, the white rooster, "in rags of feathers, like a beggar-saint," and Grandpa Samuels, its murderous defender, as well as in the bizarre persons in "The Letter in the Cedarchest," in Savata, in the bearded sisters in "Zamour," and so on.

Thus Goyen's use of deformity or the grotesque is not at all the same as, for example, Flannery O'Connor's. O'Connor wished to portray men and women as "fallen" in a "fallen world," as conceived within Catholicism. Goyen portrays not the result of any fall, but, rather, a shared human vulnerability to failure and weakness. Goyen's sense of Christianity gives prominence to compassion and forgiveness rather than reckoning and judgment. In fact, after the publication of his non-fiction work, *A Book of Jesus* (1973), one sees more of an interpretable Christian symbolism in Goyen's work generally and even scenes of careful, allegorical, symbolism, as in "Precious Door." There we find the figure of the dying brother who, like Abel, has been slain by his own brother and whose silent suffering also echoes Christ's.

A case could also be made that the violence represented in Goyen's stories intensifies in the last period of his creativity, from the mid-1970s to his death in 1983. As the dramatically different creature Arcadio describes the debased life he has led, mostly as the victim of others and of his cruel and lust-crazed father, he also expresses his desire for reconciliation and forgiveness; he recalls his white Bible. That Goyen's depiction of violence reaches its apex in his last two works—*Arcadio* and the two stories that were to be the germ of a new novel ("Had I a Hundred Mouths" and "Tongues of Men and of Angels")—coincides with his most complex and most convincing creation of stories as "arias." That is, the rhetoric of orality also reaches its peak in these works.

According to Walter J. Ong, it is a characteristic of oral culture that figures of myth and story show exaggerated characteristics and traits, as of strength and weakness, of size or temper, and so on. While not wanting to press the comparison too much, I would suggest that the physical violence in Goyen's stories derives more from the nature of his language and his aesthetic conception of fiction than from the presumed similarities of cultural background that he is said by some to share with such southern writers as Flannery O'Connor, Carson McCullers, or others to whom he has sometimes been likened. Violence is not precisely a theme in Goyen's stories, yet if one surveys them with an eye toward categories of human action, one notes in some of them a striking drama of physical attack and repercussion, including the murder in "The White Rooster" (two murders, counting the death of the white rooster at the hand of Mrs. Marcy Samuels), the violent deaths of Margy Emmons's daughter and both of her husbands in "Ghost and Flesh, Water and Dirt," the accidental shooting of Jim in "The Thief Coyote," the wild ravages in "Had I a Hundred Mouths" followed up in "Tongues of Men and of Angels," the killing of one brother by another in "Precious Door," the deaths in "In the Icebound Hothouse," and other, smaller such events. In his remarkable, original voice Arcadio recounts many violent events of almost fantastical character, and a tendency to recount events with melodramatic exaggeration also marks certain earlier moments in such narratives as Aunt Linsie's ("Pore Perrie") when she tells of Son standing outside the house in a storm with lightning, or "Rhody's Path" when the snake hunt is on, and so on. Qualities of the rhetoric of orality can push story toward this pole, just as qualities of the rhetoric of what is thoroughly *written* push story toward a pole of ever more refined subtleties and qualifications, such as we encounter in Henry James or Proust. And it is a sidelight on Goyen's use of deformity or marked difference that his violence is another fictional element that marks some persons as set apart from others.

Another sense in which persons are marked as different is in terms of their race. In "Pore Perrie," Son is remembered not only as "very very nervous" but also as "real dark complected" (*CS*, 49). Different from others, he is viewed with suspicion outside his adopted family: "Some came to Perrie and said Son probably had some foreign blood in him, did he have nigra blood in him?" (*CS*, 42). Son is the anguished center of the story, more than Perrie herself or Linsie, because he must live out unresolved problems and suffer unhealed wounds. As marginal characters, Goyen depicts not only black but also Mexican-American and native American figures in his fiction. Because these figures appear almost entirely in the stories set in Texas and because in those stories Goyen makes use of a fictional narrative voice not his own, the attitudes toward race in his fiction are other than what they at first appear—often crude and racist, at best uncomprehending and indifferent.

This is not to excuse the racism of many of Goyen's characters (including two who belong to the Ku Klux Klan—one in *The House of Breath* and one in "Had I a Hundred Mouths," who is himself later tortured by the Klan because he reveals their secrets). Rather, for us to disentangle the attitudes and opinions of fictional characters from Goyen's own views, we must look at the ways in which Goyen situates each character and voice. For the most part, Goyen presents without comment the inherited racism of the generation he most often writes about (those born about 1870 to about 1915), using their language—as when the grandfather in "Old Wildwood" speaks of "Nigras" (*CS*, 143).

To show that Goyen's own attitudes were not these, it may be enough, in this brief context, to point out that his Arcadio, a creature of halves—half-white, half-Mexican, half-man, half-woman—is invested with tenderness and pathos. It is also worth listening to Goyen speak of the Klan. In an interview he says the secrets that the younger nephew in "Had I a Hundred Mouths" was tortured for revealing were

> [t]hat they [the Klan] had had children by black women, and that they had hanged black men for fucking white women. They had scapegoats. Those are horrors, horrors! A medieval world of terror. You know it *was* like that to me; as a child I really felt that. I lived around all of that. There was a man preaching the salvation of my soul in a tent across the road from my house, but up on the hill beyond there the Ku Klux were burning their crosses and I saw them run tarred and feathered Negroes through the street. I saw them running like that, twice. Aflame. We stood and watched that.

If the attitudes toward race represented in Goyen's work are more or less the conventional attitudes of the white people he portrays (although in his fiction there is also imaginative identification with people of color, most notably in "Savata, My Fair Sister," which Goyen expanded into a short novel, and *Arcadio*), in Goyen's last works the attitudes of his white narrators and central characters toward race seem changed, deepened, both harrowed and hallowed by a fresh sensitivity to suffering. For example, while in "Figure over the Town" (first published in 1953) the narrator mentions the Ku Klux Klan without any special awareness of conscience but as simply one more fixture of the generally intolerant town that has become enraged at Flagpole Moody, in "Had I a Hundred Mouths" (first published in 1982) the Klan's attacking Leander genuinely horrifies the narrating uncle, even if the actions of Leander's "red nigger" father and of Leander himself also horrify him. The uncle's own complicity and guilt in Louetta's fate, the willful misinterpretation of her sexual suffering that leads him to assault her, complicate his ability to judge Leander or any other person around him. Thus his tender solicitude for Leander when he saves him and heals him in secret in the woods is, for all its value against the terror of the rural society in which they live, contradicted by his keeping Leander a captive, albeit not a very carefully held one. The uncle is still trapped in his own conception of Leander as in some ways little better than a caged creature, not a fully human being. But the older, compassionate nephew finds in Leander the image—given back to the reader at the conclusion of the story—of all victims of the destructive and ungovernable powers of lust and flesh. In *Arcadio*, Goyen, while portraying sex as a nearly demonic force, finds a way to reconcile persons of white, brown, and black skin in a common human torment of loneliness and abandonment.

Theme 5

The harsh inhumanity of industrial and urban society, which destroys the natural environment and estranges people from one another: beginning with Goyen's earliest work, *The House of Breath*, his fiction resounds with an unusual sensitivity to the natural world. In an early letter Goyen wrote: "There is so much beauty in the world, so much beauty that must be told about powerfully that one must save his power for it. The natural world has such a secret power for me, it is such a source of strength and affirmation, that in Taos I lived many days on end like a sleep-walker and Oh I miss it so!" Goyen's feeling for the natural world was not, however, that of a naturalist who prefers nature to human society. The letter continues

> But then there are human beings, too, and they, too, are beautiful and treacherous and full of such mystery. God knows we need someone to tell us the human is beautiful these days, and we need to hear ever and ever again that even in our ugliness we must be loved into something more than ourselves and more than ugliness. My side is on the side of the human being, and the human being moving in nature, which is spirit; and nothing else seems important to me, and if I thought I could not spend my life laboring to perceive and to understand and to clarify what happens to us in the world then I would want to die.[12]

Earlier I quoted "Zamour" on the inability of one of Goyen's characters to adjust to city life. Regarding this large theme, I would also point to the ecological awareness in "Bridge of Music, River of Sand," to similar attitudes in *Arcadio* and even in *The House of Breath*, and, in many of Goyen's stories set in small-town Texas, to a reverence and even an awe before the natural world—for instance, from the thunderstorms of "Pore Perrie" to the hurricane of "Precious Door." Recall also Goyen's characterization of his place of origin as "the soft woods-and-meadows area of East Texas" (in his introduction to his *Selected Writings*) and his saying that the "landscape of my stories, generally East Texas, is pastoral, river-haunted, tree-shaded, mysterious and bewitched" (preface to his *Collected Stories*).

Goyen's portrayal of the natural world is a smaller theme than the first four I have listed, yet it forms a persistent background to them. It is often against the beauty and variety of nature and also the scale of force that nature's cataclysms define that Goyen represents human beauty and ugliness and human destructiveness. One sees this element both in the way in which *The House of Breath* is situated in rural Texas and again at the end of Goyen's writing life, in Arcadio's lament over the destruction of the natural world. The settings or details of such stories as "A Shape of Light" and "Zamour" also represent the natural world as a background against which human action is played out, in both senses of the word *against*—as a mere setting and as if it were a foe to be conquered by human exploitation. Goyen often represents nature as wholly good, as when the forests cleared by the grandfather in "Old Wildwood" symbolically suggest a realm of unconstricted feeling and freedom that the grandson must recover in an interior way. That story and "Zamour" also contrast city with country, giving nature a privileged place. In the context of more densely crowded human life, Goyen uses animals or plants to represent possibilities of human life that have been denied or constrained—this is the resonance of, for example, the forest in which the hunters pursue the coyote in "The Thief Coyote"; the humid density of cultivated, protected plants and blossoms in the icebound hothouse that is violated and wrecked by human beings; the renegade, hobo rooster in Goyen's first story or the little cock killed by accident in "The Faces of Blood Kindred"; or such stimuli to feeling as "The Moss Rose" and "The Geranium."

Goyen equates something like a simple life force with the untroubled unconsciousness of the natural world; but he also seems to associate with that world the self-aware vitality of human erotic energy, especially in his earlier work. And by the time of the writing of his late work, such as "In the Icebound Hothouse," *Arcadio*, and the linked stories "Had I a Hundred Mouths" and "Tongues of Men and Angels," the images of nature have grown more complicated and provide not a clear contrast to human life but rather a parallel despoliation. Whereas, for example, in an earlier story like "A Shape of Light" the woods seem a place of fertility and nurture, in "Had I a Hundred Mouths" Leander is conceived in the woods only because it is there that Louetta is twice raped; moreover, Leander ends up a captive there, as if he were a wild animal, tied with a rope.

There is, in other words, a progression in the way Goyen presents images of nature. This progression does not quite leave behind early positive associations with nature, especially as Goyen continues to depict "the soft woods-and-meadows area of East Texas," but these associations become more complicated as Goyen comes to dwell not only on the destruction of the natural environment by industry but also on aspects of the natural environment that already suggest an ambivalent reading of "nature." For example, the uncle in "Had I a Hundred Mouths" mentions the Cushata Indians, but the story does not permit us to idealize them and identify them with a natural environment in which human violence plays no part; while they are as much exploited and tormented by white people as the forest itself is, they are not animals or plants but human beings, and so their struggle against whites implicates them in a complex cycle of violence: the uncle says, "Course the Cushatas was thieves and come in and stole at the Commissary and from people's houses, couldn't trust one of em, black niggers hated red Indians, red Indians despised the black niggers, the white man didn't trust either one of em, black *or* red, so—the best thing to do was drink a little whisky and stay away from all of em" (*HIHM*, 7). Detailed study of the representation of nature in Goyen's short fiction would show the stages of a progress from images of the Edenic nature of childhood to the ambivalent images of an exploited and polluted area of human struggle, but such a study would have to include analysis of Goyen's novels, especially *The House of Breath* and *Come, the Restorer.*

Thematic Analysis of Stories

Ghost and Flesh. The stories in *Ghost and Flesh* must be considered not only individually but also as the parts of the book they form. As Patrice Repusseau writes, this is "a collection of stories which all treat the same subject, but which are progressively more profound"

(Repusseau, 460; my translation). Recall our scale of narrative voices: the volume begins with the somewhat remote third-person narrator of "The White Rooster"; the next three stories ("The Letter in the Cedarchest," "Pore Perrie," "Ghost and Flesh, Water and Dirt") are narrated by character-voices; then come two stories whose third-person narrative stays very close to the central characters ("The Grasshopper's Burden" and "Children of Old Somebody"); "Nests in a Stone Image" attains the unusually close third-person narrative voice also evident in "The Horse and the Day-Moth"; and the final story, "A Shape of Light," goes beyond all these in two ways—its language is truly a kind of "aria," and its structure is as unplotted as it could be. Thus the sequence of stories advances through possibilities of narrative voice from the least intimate to the most.

Throughout the sequence of stories, the words *ghost* and *flesh* appear repeatedly. These key words signal a preoccupation with a partial and therefore painful but nonetheless desired recovery of the past. (This is the first of the five themes outlined earlier.) Those who have read *The House of Breath* will not be surprised that this loss of the past and the attempt to recover it in a realm of language if not in reality are at the heart of Goyen's first story collection as well. Even the more antic "Letter in the Cedarchest" concludes with the notion that everyone has a "ghost story or a flesh story." And when the first voice to speak in "Pore Perrie" asks to hear her story, the second voice says, "The flesh of it is buried, but we have the ghost of it again." In "Pore Perrie" it is clear that the recovery of the sad stories of the past is painful, and some who know them would rather not speak them; yet there are others (that first voice, the intelligence that will "tell the story *on*" again) who must know, who clamor to know, for the sake of standing in that relationship, of being the listener, then the teller to another listener, perhaps a loved person. In this story one of the clamoring questioners is none other than Perrie's adopted Son himself, who long ago wrote to Linsie and asked her to tell him of Perrie's life and death; but behind him or through him clamors that other voice, that first voice we hear, and its echo as a kind of implicit narrator for most of the story and then, in the last section, more clearly out in the open. There is a distinction to be drawn between these two questioners in terms of their desire to know the past: Son labors under a burden of guilt because of his history with Perrie; the new listener, who then relates the story to us, bears not guilt but a grief for the sadness borne by his kin through their lives. To him, Perrie, Son, and Ace are all ghosts.

"The Grasshopper's Burden," which seems at first glance somewhat removed from this concern with the past, nevertheless not only voices the other themes discussed earlier in this chapter but also brings in the key word *ghost* and links it to George Kurunus, the deformed boy who fascinates and repels the main character, the girl Quella:

> On the blackboard were written the lines in beautiful penmanship:
>
> > "Come into the garden, Maud,
> > For the black bat, night, has flown. . ."
>
> and under the lines was—what? Was it a joke or what? There was a curious disheveled chaos of giant and dwarf runaway shapes, tumbled and humped and crazy . . . like the Devil's writing or like a ghost's. She ran. (*CS*, 73)

This "devil's writing" is the work of George.

"Children of Old Somebody" raises the theme of the past explicitly: "there is this loss to recapture, to salvage up from the fathoms, hovering over the depths to rescue the shape when it rises" (*CS*, 77). But this story broadens the idea of "ghost" to include the child that is "the ghost" of the passion of its parents, and it invests in the figure of "Old Somebody," the evanescent shape of change and mystery and death, the power to return the past to the present: "If we build the bridge of flesh we must cross over, over it, into the land of dust, and burn the bridge of burning flesh behind us: *cross over flesh to reach ghost*. The dust yearns for dust, but dust will have its flesh and, having it, deliver it over with its own hands, into dust" (*CS*, 85). The passion of life that is *flesh* is given urgency by the knowledge of death that is *ghost*. In "Children of Old Somebody" these ghosts from the past are part of what must be recovered, and every strange figure, beggar at the back door, or face at the window is a reminder, even an embodiment, of the lost past, which can frighten like death as well as restore like a remembrance of love.

The central character in "Nests in a Stone Image" says out loud to himself: "What vanishes returns, again and again in any room at any hour; there is no room in the wide world will shelter you from it, no place to go into out of it, no refuge, no asylum. Stand and face it and endure it, the vision; but tell of it, in its multifarious ways and changes and appearances, its hundred faces and cries and sounds, its infinitely elaborate wardrobe of masks and costumes; everything contributes to the whole image, there is the total contribution, there is the listening and the speaking" (*CS*, 95).

He too, to recover his past and make sense of it, "brought all the *ghosts* of these rooms, boxes of light and darkness that had captured him for a time and from which he had escaped, to this room where he lay, *flesh*, upon this bed" (*CS*, 92; italics added). Those two words sound and resound through the stories like musical themes that link each story to the next, establishing and echoing from time to time an elegiac tone akin to the tone of *The House of Breath*.

"Ghost and Flesh, Water and Dirt" announces the presence of the past in its very title. In it, Margy Emmons tells of her own tragedy—but again, not simply to tell the story but as if to live in it again through the words, the language, with which she shapes it. And she passes on to her listener that wisdom which she has gained, even if slowly, from her friend Fursta Evans and which she has made her own:

> Now I believe in *tellin*, while we're live and going roun; when the tellin time comes I say spew it out, we just got to tell things, things in our lives, things that've happened, things we've fancied and things we dream about or are haunted by. Cause you know honey the time to shut you mouth and set moultin and mildewed in yo room, grieved by a ghost and fastened to a chair, comes back roun again, don't worry honey, it comes roun again. There's a time ta tell and a time ta set still ta let a ghost grieve ya. So listen to me while I tell, cause I'm in my time atellin, and you better run fast if you don wanna hear what I tell, cause I'm goin ta tell. (*CS*, 58)

Unlike Aunt Linsie of "Pore Perrie," she believes that one should tell the stories of sadness; she understands that those stories cannot be escaped, that they always return, and that they must be told again and again, while the telling mood is on one, if one is not to deny one's own life, one's own history, and also a fundamental aspect of one's own connectedness to life and the lives of other people. While Margy Emmons may remember the past in solitude, the teller-listener situation she seeks in the barroom will restore the past in a different way because she is bound in a human relationship when she tells it. It becomes not only memory but also ritual.

"Ghost and Flesh, Water and Dirt" is one of Goyen's masterpieces. Its structure is simple: it opens with an unidentified voice—we may take it for a bartender or someone else sitting at the bar when Margy comes in—saying, "Was somebody here while ago acallin for you" (*CS*, 50). Then the story plunges into Margy's voice, where it will stay. The story adjusts us to the urgency of her speech by presenting the first paragraph—Margy's immediate reaction, her talking to *herself*—in italics. Then she settles down, having found someone to talk to next to her at the bar, and she tells her tale from beginning to end.

She is troubled by the ghost of her first husband, who after their only child was killed in a riding accident killed himself out of grief. When Margy goes back into her own mind, her speech is again represented by italics. But mostly she tells of the accident; of her great grieving; of her decision, at her friend Fursta's urging, to start life over again; of moving to California—the time is World War II—and working in shipbuilding and meeting a sailor with whom she falls in love; of her grief at his death at sea during the war; of her return to Texas; and of her alternating rounds, now, of quiet grief, when she lives with the ghost of her first husband and is lost in images of the past, and her "time a tellin," when she bursts out of this grief and is active again, out and among other people and telling her story.

Little in the plot itself is remarkable; all that is remarkable is the language with which Goyen creates Margy Emmons out of her own mouth—her convincing intimacy, her good humor, the depth of her wisdom about the natural course of great feeling, and her need to find, from time to time, someone living, someone next to her, to whom to tell her story. She is fully immersed in a rapture of the tragic, and although she says things that are funny, and can laugh about them, she never breaks out of that rapture, which is what drives her language forward through her narration.

This is a quintessential Goyen story—not as complex as stories in which the narrative voice moves around (as in "Pore Perrie" or some of the subtle third-person pieces that are very close to their central characters)—but wonderfully energetic, psychologically profound, flawlessly paced, and containing the greatest authenticity of voice. It is worth pointing out that in addition to raising the themes of sexuality and telling, the story also touches on the urge to leave and return—one among Goyen's five main themes. Margy says that when she was in California, after she learned that Nick Natowski had died, "[s]omethin drew me back [to Texas] like I'd been pastured on a rope in California" (*CS*, 57). The story ends with the line with which Margy had originally settled into her telling: "Saw pore Raymon Emmons all last night, all last night seen im plain as day." This circularity suggests the unending cycle of Margy's feelings and the ritual nature of her telling, and it marks the story as the center of *Ghost and Flesh*.

The Faces of Blood Kindred. In "Old Wildwood," a story central to Goyen's next volume, *The Faces of Blood Kindred*, there is a similarly satisfying proportion and closure in the way the story is set in a present moment, with the central, unnamed character, "the grandson," receiving while in Rome a letter that awakens profound memories. The letter says that his grandfather has died. Returning to his most vivid memories of his grandfather, he also discovers the memory of a moment of self-understanding, of that threshold of knowledge in his childhood when he began to understand what adult feeling would be like and when he first understood what his hopes for himself might be. The story concludes by restoring us to the scene in Rome; while we have been listening, as it were, to these memories, the grandson has been sitting on the Spanish steps, "supporting himself upon the opened palm of his hand" (*CS*, 141). Now, "engraved in the palm of the hand he had leaned on, was the very mark and grain of the stone, as though his hand were stone" (*CS*, 151).

His reverie and memories of his grandfather have led him into discoveries that give him, by sharp contrast with his present existence in the ancient city of Rome, a far clearer sense of himself than he had had: "He would not have a hand of stone! He would carry a hand that could labor wood and build a house, trouble dirt and lay a highway, and blaze a trail through leaf and bramble; and a hand that could rot like wood and fall into dust" (*CS*, 151). The grandson's journey of self-discovery has been his chance to recover some of his past, the past of his family, and to acknowledge how he has been defined by it, shaped by it.

It is also worth pointing out that this story, one of the richest in Goyen's work and one that repays many readings, establishes the grandfather's identity with an important and characteristic theme, that of physical deformity—the grandfather's twisted foot—and it introduces the theme of erotic life, not only the awakening erotic life of the boy-child the grandson remembers himself to have been but also the still-vigorous erotic life of the grandfather. The passing portrait of sexuality acknowledges both its animal quality and its strange, ungainly, but transcendent beauty. The story is a key to Goyen's work because of its presentation of characteristic themes and fictional technique, such as its juxtaposition of the old man's death with both his own earlier, vigorous life and the grandson's two awakenings (one remembered, into the life of adult feeling, and the other in the present moment, to the direction in which his past has pointed him); its lack of traditional plot and its dependence on meditative structure; its language of reverie and hope in the grandson's mind and its language of story and wonder from the grandfather's mouth; its portrayal of how the past comes into and reshapes the present moment; and more.

Another especially important work is "Rhody's Path," also from *The Faces of Blood Kindred*. It begins with a linguistic signal that we are in the rhetoric of orality—the intimate "you" and "us," the colloquial "twould" and the confiding tone and syntax of the second sentence, and the shared belief and convictions of the unidentified teller and the implied listener ("a pattern of the Lord above"): "Sometimes several sudden events will happen together so as to make you believe they have a single meaning if twould only come clear. Surely happenings are lowered down upon us after a pattern of the Lord above" (*CS*, 165).

The tone of voice is folksy but, as I noted earlier, does not at all suggest an ironic distancing between Goyen and his narrator. There is a large cast, including a revivalist, a plague of grasshoppers and a rattlesnake, a flagpole sitter, and the family which Rhody periodically leaves and to which she returns unannounced. And there are characteristic touches: the extravagant figures of the revivalist, the flagpole sitter, and Rhody all mark varieties of human difference from the stay-at-home family, some member of which is telling this tale. There are the themes of erotic life and of leaving and returning; and there is intimacy of tone: "Just even to mention the pestilence of hoppers makes you want to scratch all over" (*CS*, 165).

In this summer of the grasshoppers, Rhody returns and a revivalist sets up his tent. Rhody is a young woman who, like Sue Emma in *The House of Breath*, is forever in search of an elusive excitement, partly erotic no doubt, that will free her from the claustrophobic imaginative and moral confines of small-town and family life. The revivalist is in some ways a familiar figure in Goyen's work, not because Goyen often writes of preachers but because he often portrays characters whose spiritual ambitions are thwarted or perhaps, more interestingly, fed by their pleasure in the senses: they are torn between spirit and body, and not infrequently they combine excesses of both (as in Arcadio). These several fictional vectors converge on the night when the revivalist's rattlesnake escapes its cage. During a search across the fields lighted by a bonfire, the snake is found only when it bites Rhody (and, another

Goyen touch, it bites her on her bad leg). The snake—emblem of outlaw feeling, perhaps, of ungovernable natural instinct—is shot and killed by the flagpole sitter, who has come down to participate in the hunt. And while Rhody lies attended to by family, the revivalist and all his people decamp without a farewell.

Of course it is Rhody whom the snake bites, because in her way she is already "bitten"—she is subject to follow her unbidden instincts, which seem as contrary to custom and as frightening to the homebodies as snakebite, and she is already marked as different by her bad leg. Yet it is not the revivalist's remedies or prayers that cure her (he himself is of that other world, and he runs back to it; he and his people can only react by destroying temporarily—and thus suppressing—that part of themselves [the snake] which is so dangerous, yet it will always be replenished); the seductive but dangerous world outside the small town cannot heal its own wounds. Rhody is cured of the venom of the snake (of her own stay in that world) by home remedies, by the dose of (apparent) stability and comforting sameness. It is for this very re-assurance of home that Rhody periodically returns; yet she cannot stay. When she has recovered from the snakebite (that is, when she has been sufficiently reassured and comforted by her visit home), she is once again restless. Rhody's path is right across the field, back toward the outside world, and she packs her things and takes it once more. "We all kissed her good-bye and Aunt Idalou cried and asked the plain air what had branded her youngest child with some sign of restless wandering and when would she settle down to make a household as woman should; and we watched Rhody go on off, on the path across the pasture with her grip in her hand, going off to what, we all wondered. . . . Rhody went out and took the world's risks and chances, but simple remedies of home and homefolks rescued and cured her, time and time again" (*CS*, 173).

The permanence of home life is only apparent, however, as the homebodies know: " 'The sad thing is,' Idalou said, rocking on the front porch looking at the empty pasture and the sad-looking path that Rhody took, 'that years pass and all grow old and pass away, and this house will be slowly emptied of its tenants.' Had Rhody ever considered this? And what would she do when all had gone and none to come home to?" (*CS*, 173).

This dilemma of life has no solution; and the narrator indicates that this conflict within Rhody, and all like her, cannot be resolved but cannot be avoided, either: "But surely all of us who were listening to Idalou were thinking together that the path would remain, grown over

72

and hidden by time, but drawn on the earth, the pasture was engraved with it like an indelible line; and Rhody's feet would be on it, time immemorial, coming and going, coming and going, child of the path in the pasture between home and homelessness, redemption and error. That was the way she had to go" (*CS*, 173).

It is tempting to regard this story as also an allegory of the writing life, as Goyen conceived of it and lived it. The writer must leave to accomplish his or her work, but the exciting journey away from home is also a depleting exile, and the writer must return periodically to be restored to the materials of art. In Goyen's case, the writer leaves, as it were, a culture more oral than written and pursues his writing, but he must return to refresh his ear for the spoken language on which he bases his work.

For its stylistic and atmospheric effects alone, this story is memorable; but as the most concise telling of this dilemma of leaving and returning and leaving again, "Rhody's Path" lies at the center of Goyen's work. What Goyen does here with fictional technique is not so far from garden-variety narrative, perhaps—this happens and then that and then that. But even when constructing something of an ordinary plot, Goyen's signature is in his style and in the system of figures, emblems, and themes he made characteristically his own.

The Collected Stories.   The intimacy of first-person narrative draws us immediately into the perplexity of the narrator of "Bridge of Music, River of Sand," a story from the 1970s that compresses into only a few pages a haunting evocation of the lost world of East Texas that is Goyen's characteristic mise-en-scène. It begins,

> Do you remember the bridge that we crossed over the river to get to Riverside? And if you looked over yonder you saw the railroad trestle? High and narrow? Well that's what he jumped off of. Into a nothing river. "River"! I could laugh. I can spit more than runs in that dry bed. In some places is just a little damp, but that's it. That's your grand and rolling river: a damp spot. That's your remains of the grand old Trinity. Where can so much water go? I at least wish they'd do something about it. But what can they do? What can anybody do? You can't replace a *river*. (*CS*, 280)

There are several important echoes here. Readers of *The House of Breath* will recall the reluctance of Malley Ganchion to ride across the bridge in the car—she would insist on getting out and walking, so frightened was she of the bridge (*HB*, 84). In this story the narrator says the same of his mother; but the significance of the echo lies not so much in the biographical origin of this Goyenesque motif as in what Goyen makes of it in *The House of Breath* and here. That bridge lies over the fertile, ungovernable, larger-than-human river, which in *The House of Breath* is identified with erotic life. Here is that bridge again (as it will appear, a final time, in *Arcadio*, who sits *under* it to tell his story), but now the river has run dry. Malley Ganchion, abandoned in the old house, her husband and children gone, was once afraid of the life that now she misses. Arcadio sits beside the river to tell of his wandering life, both debauched and saintly (body and spirit, once more); and here our narrator has come upon the bridge only just in time to see a man leap off it, to kill himself. If that man had wished to drown himself in the river (given everything the river might stand for), he has only thrown himself into a dry riverbed instead. Yet after diving headfirst into the sand, he is slowly swallowed by it and vanishes without trace, and so the narrator is unable to convince anyone that the suicide even happened. His telling is in effect his effort to convince his last listener, the reader. If the reader believes him, then reader and narrator (listener and teller) reenact the ritual passing of values from one person to another that the teller-listener situation embodies. If the reader remains unconvinced, then the narrator—the teller—must seek another listener. The illusion of speaking and hearing is thus powerfully conveyed, especially since a portion of the teller's authority comes from his own self-doubt, his convincing practicality when he ponders what he has seen. What the teller effectively does convey, whether or not the listener believes that a man leapt from the bridge, is the force and authenticity of his voice, his being, in a changed, somewhat unrecognizable world.

Not only is the river dry, but the town beside it is filled with the "stinging fumes of the mill." The fouling of the natural world, which Arcadio will also lament, is connected to an end of feeling, an end to the rushing current that spoke of raw sopping life to the narrator of *The House of Breath*, both intoxicating and frightening him with it. The narrator wonders if he could be "suffering a kind of bridge madness, or the vision that sometimes comes from going home again, of going back to places haunted by deep feeling" (*CS*, 283). Then he recalls his memory of the bridge as he had seen it in his childhood, so delicate and lovely it seemed made of music. The river was once the very stream of life; and the bridge, once beautiful even if never very practical, was once as much the other half of the landscape as spirit is the companion to body in the landscape of human life. But now the river is dry and the bridge condemned. The narrator has driven onto it illegally, only to see a man throw himself off.

The elusive, complicated, symbolic resonances of the river and bridge fill the story; not only is the past lost in time, but it too has run dry, is decrepit, is befouled by manufacturing. Was the man who threw himself off the bridge fleeing the ruined present? Was he trying to throw himself into the past? That the narrator cannot know is less important than that he desperately wants to know, because these are his choices as well. Must he kill himself in order to escape the pain of the despoiled present? Or might he be able to recover something of value even in the dried up past were he to plunge fully into it? This is a place that is, for him, "haunted by deep feeling" (Goyen uses the word *ghost* again in this story, in the same way he used it as a frequently sounded motif in *Ghost and Flesh*). The narrator does not answer his own questions; he thinks he has been "brought to some odd truth which I could not yet clear for myself" (*CS*, 284). And he drives off the bridge and away from it, toward the pitiable little town he once knew; like Rhody, he can only pursue the path in front of him, unable to reconcile the clanging opposites of his desires, his hopes, and his feelings.

The flagpole sitter of "Rhody's Path" reappears in "Figure over the Town." Although this story was originally a part of Goyen's unpublished early novel, *Half a Look of Cain*, he placed it at the end of the volume as a valedictory comment when he reprinted it in his *Collected Stories*. Of a meditative sort, the story recounts in a first-person voice the appearance during the narrator's childhood of a flagpole sitter. The narrator remembers having been disturbed by this figure over the town: he dreamed of the man's falling; he worried about his being rained on. Because Flagpole Moody stays atop his pole so long, he eventually ceases to be the center of the town's excited attention, but the narrator recalls that he formed a secret attachment, a sense of kinship—which will not be surprising at this point in our analysis—with this strange figure whose apartness from the town is quite literally his being *over* the town. This story is set during an unnamed war, which signals us, early and subtly, that Goyen is putting an element of fable to work: "Everywhere there was the talk of the war, but where it was or what it was I did not know. It seemed only some huge appetite that craved all our sugar and begged from the town its goods, so that people seemed paled and impoverished by it, and it made life gloomy—that was the word" (*CS*, 287).

Moreover, such crimes as the town suffers—robberies, a disappearance, a racial murder—are laid to the war. Since nowhere do we read of soldiers being conscripted or of anything overtly military, it is permissible to interpret this war as the raging confusion and danger of life in the larger world. As the narrator implies at one point, that larger world is simply beyond his imagining and is filled with "the general lawlessness and demoralizing effect of the war" (*CS*, 287). Because the town suffers deprivation and crime, however, excitement and then indifference are supplanted by suspicion: some people begin to blame the flagpole sitter, who comes "to be regarded as a defacement of the landscape, an unsightly object, a tramp" and is threatened by the Ku Klux Klan—who, in Goyen's stories, as in life, are the violent agents of crude general intolerance as well as of racial hatred.

The continuing presence of the flagpole sitter excites violent hostility, yet also evokes fervent devotion. He is a catalytic and intrusive creature, come unbidden, who changes the town around him. The story takes on the proportions of the absurd and the fabulous. Flagpole Moody attracts a fanatic evangelist but does not reply to his messages or to anyone else's. He is utterly independent and alone, and with a terrific power of endurance atop his pole. He becomes the psychic center of the entire town, the repository of fears, hopes, desires, and greedy schemes: "Dogs howled and bayed at night and sometimes in the afternoons; hens crowed; the sudden death of children was laid to the evil power of Flagpole Moody over the town" (*CS*, 291). A tale of the way in which anyone who persists in his *difference* is usually cast out of the human community and blamed for its ills, "Figure over the Town" reprises Goyen's preoccupation with all sorts of outsiders (orphans, foundlings, deformed or wounded persons, failures, anyone who acts in an unexpected way or persists in an uncommon course, and so on).

The narrator's identification with the flagpole sitter is at first qualified but then grows clear. It is qualified by his wanting to distinguish himself from the town's "sensitive and intellectual people, poets and artists," not only when he was a child but also now, in retrospect (*CS*, 292). One might have expected the narrator to put Flagpole Moody *among* such outsiders as poets and artists, but he implies that *their* difference is fake or inauthentic, whereas Flagpole Moody's is genuine. The narrator's identification with Flagpole Moody is clear in his increasing admiration when Flagpole Moody becomes active, performing "acrobatic stunts" atop the pole (*CS*, 293). He also recounts how a carnival set up its Ferris wheel "so close to Flagpole that when its passengers reached the top they could almost, for a magical instant, reach over and touch his body. Going round and round, it was as if one were soaring up to him only to fall away, down, from him; to have him and to lose him" (*CS*, 293).

But then the perspective is abruptly reversed, and the narrator's real point of connection to Flagpole becomes evident: "This must have tantalized Flagpole, and perhaps it seemed to him that all the beautiful and desirable people in the world rose and fell around him, offering themselves to him only to withdraw untaken and ungiven, a flashing wheel of faces, eyes, lips and sometimes tongues stuck out at him and sometimes a thigh shown, offering sex, and then burning away. His sky at night was filled with voluptuous images, and often he must have imagined the faces of those he had once loved and possessed, turning round and round his head to torment him" (*CS*, 293–94). Well, did he? The reader has no access to Flagpole Moody's thoughts, but must assume that it is the narrator who has experienced these feelings, and having had them, has turned back to the memory of the flagpole sitter and found in him an emblem for his own complicated emotional experience. For as he knows, or perhaps knows to imagine, "there were men on the wheel who made profane signs to him, and women who thumbed their noses. . . . [And] [s]oon Flagpole raised his tent again and hid himself from his tormentors. . . . But he had not turned away from me. I, the silent observer, watching from my window or from any high place I could secretly climb to, witnessed all this conflict and the tumult of the town" (*CS*, 294).

He dreams Flagpole Moody secretly comes down to him; he dreams the town sends him up the flagpole to tell Flagpole to come down. Thus the narrator's link to the strange figure of the outsider is reinforced. But his dream reveals to him that Flagpole is gone, having left only garbage inside his tent. The idealization is shattered. After he calls down to the people on the ground that Flagpole is gone, however, he stays inside the tent, "to make Flagpole Moody's place my own" (*CS*, 296). The garbage suggests that Flagpole Moody's charismatic hold on the town and on the admiring narrator is founded on illusion and idealization. Flagpole Moody's isolation and aloofness are not aspects of a purity of purpose but are themselves problems. He depends on the town for sustenance and attention, and when he departs like a ghost he leaves behind the trash of physical fleshly life, which shows that he is as much like the townspeople as he is different from them. The narrator takes Flagpole Moody's place no longer believing in the ideal. Apartness is not a purer life, only a different one.

The story of Flagpole Moody does not resolve the *plot*—that is, it does not bring the town's pitch of emotion to a climax—but simply brings Flagpole down after his forty days and forty nights, without further comment or reaction. Thus the story's structure is meant not to create tensions of plot and then resolve them but to create instead a window into the early formation of possibilities of feeling in the narrator. As he says at the very end, "I did not tell my dream, for I had no power of telling then, but I knew that I had a story to one day shape around the marvel and mystery that ended in a dream and began in the world that was to be mine" (*CS*, 296). The "story" of Flagpole Moody offers no dazzling conclusion—all the dazzle was in *not* knowing what he was doing up there; all the mystery and marvel were not in what he did but in not knowing why he did it: in the sheer, simple fact of his doing it at all, and without explanation. And to that "story," the ending can only be simple: he came down; and his coming down ends his story. But the narrator's story has only now just begun; his feelings and fantasies have been awakened by Flagpole Moody, and now he has found an entrance to "the world that was to be mine" through his secret attention to and kinship with the flagpole sitter. What is that world? It is no more pure or "clean" than ordinary life, but it is still preferred by the narrator because it gives a central place to imagination and to acknowledgment of difference. At certain moments in the story, the fervor and intimacy of tone of voice reveal where the narrator's feelings are most heightened—in being a secret witness (watching and seeing without being seen), in imagining the procession of human relationships that will fill his adult life (the Ferris wheel), in discovering sympathy with those who are outside routine life, in accepting disappointment and disillusionment, and in not allowing them to bring down hope. As Goyen saw them, these are ingredients of the artistic life.

Goyen's Last Stories

"Had I a Hundred Mouths" is one of the fourteen stories Goyen wrote or revised from early work between the composition of "Precious Door" in 1976 and his death in 1983.[13] As a group and looked at along with his last novel, *Arcadio*, these stories represent an interesting and important development in Goyen's work. I noted earlier that something in Goyen's fiction—a matter of both style and subject—was recognizably his own, was Goyenesque, from the beginning of his career. I also noted that the continuity of Goyen's fictional signature does not necessarily suggest that he failed to change or develop as an artist, only that his signature effects—especially the voicing of his stories, as well as his characteristic themes—remain more or less consistent. In these last stories, however, the signature effects and reaches of imagination and potency are taken to impressive new heights. In addition, some of Goyen's attitudes appear to change.

My discussion of "Had I a Hundred Mouths" showed how this story is a thorough display, with an extraordinary intensity of effect, of a number of Goyen's fictional techniques and themes. Its companion piece is "Tongues of Men and of Angels," which begins with the words,

> I started out to tell about what became of two cousins and their uncle who loved them, according to what the older cousin told me. But some of their kinfolks' lives would have to be told if you're going to talk at all about the cousins and their uncle. So what I have to tell about first is all one family, what I heard told to me and what I watched happen. I have been here in this family's town longer than any of the family, and have in my long time noted—and wonder if you have, ever—the turning around of some people's lives, as if some force moved in them against their will: runaways suddenly arrived back, to the place they fled; berserk possessed people come serene; apparently Godblessed people overnight fall under malediction. (*HIHM*, 61)

In this passage one sees—or rather hears—elements that by now are familiar, especially the concern with *telling* (reinforced by that sudden interjection to a listener, "—and wonder if you have, ever—") and the theme of leaving and returning. Proceeding in a fashion somewhat fantastic yet, because of its intimate colloquial style, convincing, the story picks up the threads of some of the characters introduced in "Had I a Hundred Mouths" and, almost without dialogue, in a narrative storytelling way carries each to its end. The sections are smaller medallions than a story would be; and in fact from Goyen's papers it is clear that he had begun rethinking the two stories as parts of a longer work he intended to call "Leander," perhaps something of the length of *Arcadio*. He might have expanded each of the sections of "Tongues of Men and Angels," but he did not live to finish the project.

The new stories are perhaps the most powerful and wide-ranging group Goyen wrote, even more impressive than the stories brought together in *Ghost and Flesh*. The first new theme introduced is that of reconciliation, in "Precious Door"; and in fact on the manuscript copy of what he had intended to be a collection of stories by that title, he put this epigraphic excerpt from that story:

> "The love of God works through reconciliation."
> "Father," I asked. "What is reconciliation?"
> "It means coming back together in peace," my father answered. "Although there was torment between the two brothers, they have been brought back together in peace."[14]

The quest for reconciliation is a vital portion of Arcadio's purpose in his odyssey. Arcadio dwells long on his struggle with demons—his father, especially, but also his own lustful nature—and the demons are also present in the stories of this period of Goyen's life. There is a heightened sense of this struggle, not only in the two stories already mentioned but also in the supremely compressed and intense performance "Arthur Bond" and in the dark fable "In the Icebound Hothouse." "The Texas Principessa" is, by contrast, light and airy and filled with the narrator's humorous appreciation and tolerance of human weakness; and "Where's Esther?" while it touches on the darkness of alcoholism, does so in a plaintive, melancholy way, with deft touches of humor. And in his posthumously published essay, "Recovering," Goyen was writing of his reconciliation with his own illness.

"Precious Door" was the first short fiction Goyen wrote after the long fallow period during which he had worked on only one novel, *Come, the Restorer*, and the nonfiction *A Book of Jesus*. The conflict and tension of erotic life and the sadness of the loss of the past are kept offstage (though not entirely absent) in this story. Goyen had rediscovered in himself the centrality of his concern with spirituality, which can indeed be seen, subtly indicated, in many earlier works. (Goyen's sense of the "spiritual" should be studied in the *TriQuarterly* interview: his beliefs were, on the one hand, not at all conventional but, on the other, based on his interpretations of the accepted Christian figures of Jesus and St. Francis.) The focus on reconciliation in "Precious Door" partakes of Goyen's understanding of spirituality, and he regarded this story as a regeneration of his gifts as a writer of fiction.

"Precious Door" is set in a rural household during a hurricane. Father and son are confronted by two strangers whose violent relationship seems to have the force of the storm itself. In an early draft, more members of the family were present and active. The father and mother talked about the coming hurricane, the father then sent the mother and other small children off to a safe refuge from the storm, and the father and older boy remained in the house alone. But Goyen dispensed with the full scene in which this decision is made, only sketching it rapidly in the final version:

> Storms scared my father where little else did. He felt afraid in our old house and always took us to the high school basement. "Mary, you and the children go on to the high school and hurry up," my father called. At this I rushed into the house.
>
> "I'll stay with my father and the hurt man," I announced. There was going to be a discussion of this, but little time was left for it; and I could see that my father was glad to have me stay. (*HIHM*, 41)

The importance of this revision is that it calls our attention to the arrangement of characters. One might guess that Goyen's experience writing for the theater brought him to the dramatic scheme of this story, for in removing the mother and small children entirely from the scene, he is able to present us with only four figures and to focus our attention on all of them in more concentrated fashion. Indeed, except for its visionary conclusion, the story has the shape of a one-act play set in one room.[15]

"Precious Door" is told from the point of view of a man remembering an incident when he was twelve years old; as the story progresses, his memory of what happened on that day leads him to understand

how this disturbance and troubling of the household was also the beginning of his awakening into a more adult consciousness, a wonder
and sadness about the larger world (a moment of insight that we may
recall Goyen treating earlier in such stories as "Old Wildwood" and
"Had I a Hundred Mouths"). This familiar distortion or fictional manipulation of time creates the illusion of looking forward into time, but
in truth it is a looking backward. While presenting the child's hopes
for his future, Goyen is actually presenting the narrator's memory of
the emotional experience of holding those hopes; this technique resembles others by which Goyen brings the past into the present moment, where it has the effect of turning the course of the narrator's
central character's life in a new direction. That is, an adult looking
back at his own childhood or youth finds there the *confirmation* of his
present intuition (often about the crucial importance of feeling in his
life and of continuing to pursue his early hopes), and this confirmation
gives him the strength to choose a course of feeling that would otherwise be more difficult to choose. It is all a masterful trick of perspective, an illusion—a specimen either of the seductiveness of language
that recasts reality as it is not or of the rhetorical power with which
Goyen can pursue a truth of the life of memory and reverie. One's
appreciation of it depends on one's critical point of view. But the last
thing Goyen ever claimed to be was "realistic"—he specifically disavowed that fictional approach espoused by Zola and Dreiser.

The narrator's tone of voice is intimate and reflective. And he is
good at telling the story. The opening lines irresistibly raise the curtain:
"'Somebody's laying out in the field,' my little brother came to tell us.
It was eight o'clock in the morning and already so hot that the weeds
were steaming and the locusts calling. For a few days there had been
word of a hurricane coming" (*HIHM*, 40). Here are two important matters on which the story will turn—matters that will together awaken
the child's adult consciousness: first, the introduction of a foreign element into the stability of the family (the mysterious and ominous
stranger), and second, the highly theatrical immensity of the surrounding natural world. The story also explores the possibilities of language
for narration and for reflection. At the beginning of the story the narrator's colloquial expressions convey the comfortable familiarity of the
world of childhood and of his father's authority but also show us that
this familiarity is broken by the presence of the wounded stranger.
There is a tone of pathos in the narrator's voice as he recalls his father's
fruitless questioning of the unconscious boy. There will be no answer

to this mystery; it is evidence of a tragic, unknowable dimension of life of which the narrator—as a child—had had no experience until now. The subtle implication *in the present moment of telling* is that the adult narrator again faces, or has recently faced, some event of similar tragic dimension and, in recalling and telling this story of his childhood, is able to gather the emotional strength to take from present tragedy not the impulse to shrink from life but the will to embrace it despite emotional pain.

In Goyen's work, an intensity of being emanates from the person at the center of tragedy. Here, before tragedy is even evident, the narrator gives us a first hint of the extraordinary quality of the stranger's presence—not only that he was unknown to them and wounded but something more than that: "Something shining came through the damaged face and we knew we had brought a special person into our house out of the weeds of the field" (*HIHM*, 41).

At first thought to be only a sleeping drunk, the stranger turns out to be terribly wounded, and he brings fear and foreboding into the house—and also dramatic intensity, as the storm gathers force in the distance. Mother and small children are sent off to safety elsewhere, after the boy that the narrator was claims a right to stay with his father. The storm rises. Father and son carry the dying stranger into the heart of the house, the parlor (etymologically, a room where one *talks*). The stranger, although he says only two words before he dies, is nevertheless as if centrally lighted on stage, mostly because of the way he is treated by the father, whose generous tenderness and alarm convert stranger to friend as soon as he sees the knife wound in the unconscious boy's chest:

> "He may be dying," my father said, "can't rouse him. Call the doctor, son, then get me some warm water. Hey," my father called loudly at first and then lowered his voice to a soft summons, "Hey, friend, hello; hello . . ."
> The battered friend did not budge. . . .
> "Pardner, you might not make it," I heard my father say. . . .
> "Help me put our friend on the pallet," father asked.
> When we lifted our friend . . . (*HIHM*, 41–43)

More than any other story by Goyen, "Precious Door" portrays kindness and tenderness and does so while suggesting a biblical, allegorical meaning in this scene of fatherly love and the later scene of the reconciliation of the two warring brothers (too late to save the younger, more vulnerable one).

Goyen skillfully paces the story as he alternates the narrator's anxiousness at the impending storm and his father's efforts to revive the wounded boy. Because the mother and smaller children are gone, the story can portray the son's unusual closeness with his father as if they both can already sense that whatever will unfold in the next hours will bind them together in a new way. In the narrator's account, we note his pride that his father could depend on him to help in this double emergency: "I covered things on the porch and pushed things back and brought some firewood to the parlor. 'I thought we could build a fire in the fireplace,' I announced. 'That'd be fine,' my father said. 'You know how to do it, like I taught you'" (*HIHM*, 42).

The drama of the wounded stranger and the storm, for all its own inherent power, is employed to advance the drama of the narrator's awakening consciousness of the life of feeling. In such scenes as this in his fiction, Goyen's interest centers not on feeling itself, which of course all people, children and adults, experience, but on a consciousness of the important place of feeling as a determinant of adult life. Goyen employs both the direct expression of inner life and fictional scene setting to convey to his readers the intensity of this awakening—and sometimes both together, as in this juxtaposition of the two in the narrator's consciousness:

> "God bless you, pardner," my father said, and I patted the man's head. My breath was caught in my throat, that he was with us.
> The storm was here, upon us. (*HIHM*, 42)

Seeing trees felled onto the road by the storm, the boy and his father know the doctor will not reach them. They wash the stranger's wounds, they pray over him, and he dies. The shock of his death, right at hand, makes the boy cry, and his father comforts him. And the storm of feelings roused in the boy by this sudden intrusion into their life, this death in their midst, begins to clarify. The narrator thinks: "I hoped then, with a longing that first touched me there on that wild and tender night in our faraway parlor in that hidden little town, that one day I would know the love of another, no matter how bitter the loss of them would be" (*HIHM*, 43).

He feels like a three-year-old as his father rocks him and he cries, but his regression marks the moment when he advances into a knowledge of the bitter loss of love between grown persons. Immediately after this death and comforting, and the revelation of feeling, the story describes the height of the storm, the waters rising around the house to a flood that seems about to carry everything away. (For other instances in Goyen's work of water as the complex emblem of feeling, so intense that it threatens danger, see the river chapter and others in *The House of Breath* and the story "The Rescue.") The change from living being to mere body that has come over the stranger gives the narrator his first boyhood understanding of grief, and the story seems to have resolved its tensions.

But now Goyen introduces a fourth—and most surprising—character. Out of the blowing storm comes the frightening apparition of another stranger whom they must quickly admit into their parlor. Feeling has been very much the substance of the narrative so far—the father's compassion for the dying youth and his fear of the storm, the son's awakening to tragic loss, the shattering consequences of violence, and the possibilities of emotion so intense that it leads to this violence. Now the new character is introduced as another creature of feeling—of the passionate, impulsive rage that killed his younger brother, of bitter remorse, and, finally, of self-condemnation for his crime. He will exact a retribution on himself for what he has done.

Tears flow readily from the young man come out of the storm. Goyen pushes the allegorical hints beyond correspondences with biblical story, for just as the boy's father has been an example to the boy (of compassion and competence, yet also of fear), so the young man shows him another model of human feeling (of passion and ready feeling, yet of a murderous lack of control over feeling). In the parlor, candles and the fire on the hearth are alive and flickering but the body of the younger brother is lifeless and still. The young man and his dead brother take a posture that the father and son unwittingly mimic: "And then I heard him say clearly, 'Put your head on my breast. boy! Here. Now, now boy, now; you're all right, now. Head's on my breast; now, now.' . . . My father and I were sitting on the cold springs of the daybed whose mattress was the dead man's pallet, and I could feel the big, strong wrap of my father's arm around me, pulling my head to his breast" (*HIHM*, 45).

Yet in the narrator, pulling against his comfort in his father's love and strength, is a fascination with the two young men, dead and alive, as examples of a kind of freedom of action he had not known before. It is first a freedom of feeling more passionately demonstrative than what he has known in his life: he hopes that one day he "would have enough courage to be this tender as this man was now at this moment, if ever I was lucky enough to find someone who would take my tenderness." It is also a freedom of action unlike the settled life of his family: he hopes he too will have, as the two young boys did, "together with someone, a plan" (*HIHM*, 46).

The one-act play ends with the living brother picking up the dead brother in his arms and going back into the storm with him, clearly with little chance of surviving. And father explains to son the word *reconciliation*.

But the visionary element in Goyen—which appears even more often in his last works than it did in his earlier ones—leads the story onward past the end of the one-act drama. There is a rapturous coda in which the story of the two brothers is set within a far larger context than the parlor and the life of one young boy. We return to the storm, and to an earth so sodden and flooded it resembles a biblical scene. In that swirling flood of the earth, rumors travel about the two brothers, Goyen's Cain and Abel. No one but the boy and his father know who they are, but others see the strange figures floating on a door that rafts them along the flood tide, out toward the sea.

The visionary, the fantastic, and the intensely dramatic also define two other striking stories in Goyen's last group, "Arthur Bond" and "In the Icebound Hothouse." These stories return us to the demons that drive the darker moments of *Arcadio*, "Had I a Hundred Mouths," and "Tongues of Men and of Angels."

A story of greater wonderment and less anguish than those last two, although fully as wild and certainly more hopeful of some redemption from the agony of human excess, is the very brief "Arthur Bond," which is also focused on the life of ungovernable passion. Like *Arcadio* or the early "Ghost and Flesh, Water and Dirt," "Arthur Bond" conveys an extraordinary authority of voice, embarking from the first sentence on an aria or hymn, as Goyen might have called it. As in those other works, the tone of "Arthur Bond" is again of a rapture of the tragic (tragedy that does not disallow laughter). That unforgettable first sentence, the rhetorical effect of which was so evident in the recital hall where Goyen read it aloud, establishes the governing metaphor of the story, that Arthur Bond's life was lived as if an *other*, an inhuman force or being, shared his body and he could not control it: "Remember man named Arthur Bond had a worm in his thigh."

The worm is a symbolizing of the penis; yet the narrator, who has a conventional southern religious point of view, seems not to be aware of the referent of the symbol. The worm is also a symbolizing of wild drunkenness. (The reader will have noticed that in a number of these last stories alcohol is a recurring subject.) In fact, the worm comes to seem like the emblem of any obsessive, uncontrollable behavior and leads the narrator into the heart of the story, which is a pure wonderment at the inexplicable afflictions that may visit without apparent cause or justice. The teller of this tale, speaking intimately ("One more thing and I'm done talkin about it"—*HIHM*, 31), carries his meditation into a plea to God for explanation. The story rises, thus, into prayer—a prayer, Goyen seems to suggest, likely to have been heard before in many a corner of church and house.

A fine-tuned performance, the narrative stream of the story is highly rhythmical, greatly varied in diction, and exquisitely timed. The language is rich with puzzlement and pondering, folksiness, a hint of confession, and, as we might expect, meditative intensity. The worm is a real affliction, treated by doctors but never killed, so that the story has the ring of a fable, but at the same time the worm never ceases to be interpretable, decodable, as the symbol of the underlying subjects of the story, especially Arthur Bond's obsessive sexuality. We may suspect that although our apparently somewhat pious, even if earthy, narrator can speak openly of drink, he might not feel comfortable speaking so openly of sex; thus Goyen's metaphorizing of sexual desire as the worm in Arthur Bond's thigh is a feat of figuration quite befitting the narrator, whose imagination would naturally reach for some such euphemism for what he was referring to.

The story creates an effect almost like that of peeking behind the curtain of a puppet show and seeing both puppet and puppeteer at once; this aspect leads to an interesting complexity in the narrative voice, which at one moment seems naive and unsophisticated, and at another wise and experienced in profundities of trouble. The interest of the story and its power thus lie not only in the extraordinary events it relates but also in this narrator's relationship (emotional, intellectual, personal) to those events and in his way of describing them and trying to understand them. The narrator creates a tale of the fantastic, yet remains "believable."

A similar kind of self-questioning appears in "In the Icebound Hothouse," also a fable but one far more complex and difficult. This story has the form of a rambling deposition given by another of Goyen's unnamed narrators. Not surprisingly, the narrator's concern is not only to understand what happened but also to find a way to *say* what happened. The story opens, "It is true that I have not been able to utter more than a madman's sound since my eyes beheld the sight. I've lost speech. And so they have asked me to write. Since you are a poet, write, they told me. Little do they know what they might get. Little, even, do I" (*HIHM*, 48).

Unlike other Goyen first-person narratives, this one attains to the appearance, the texture, of a written piece rather than a "time a telling." The first condition of our narrator is that he *cannot* talk. He has lost speech, which is both the sound that distinguishes us as human and the words we speak to communicate with one another. He adds, "So I'm writing this in the Detention House, where they're holding me until I can give word." "Give word," to mean "speak aloud," is especially rich with meaning.

The poet-narrator also refers to himself as a witness, and thus he resembles the many other narrators in Goyen's work who see what others have done and tell of it as much as they tell of themselves. These circumstances make this story an interesting variation on Goyen's characteristic teller-listener situation, for the narrator's document, despite being requested by the police, yet sounds as if it has been written not for them but, rather, for someone else, someone outside the moment.

He is not only a witness. He haunted the hothouse and was several times sent away by the inhospitable Nurseryman; and once inside, he savagely stabbed a shovel into the breast of the already-dead Nurseryman. It soon becomes clear, in fact, that he has been chased by, and has been chasing, his own demon, and this situation was what brought him into (deservedly) suspicious relation with the two dead persons.

The story is constructed out of several units of different size. The first two paragraphs introduce two of the elements that will later be narrated and explained—(a) the narrator's obsession with the hothouse and (b) the dead girl. The next four paragraphs describe in detail, with flights of descriptive rhetoric, the drunken Nurseryman and the hothouse itself. This passage deepens the strength of the narrator's obsession with the hothouse and its keeper. There is obsession with the place and the plants, but there is also a dogged, repetitive return to the puzzle of the Nurseryman's drunkenness: his motives and excuses. (But these will never be discovered.) He is an afflicted person who incongruously attends the flourishing plants. There is also a hint of sexuality in the greenhouse—not only in the figure of the naked dead girl, which the narrator has already mentioned without yet explaining, but in the profusion of plant life itself. (And in the sentence, "What is the canker worm that ate at your roots?" we hear a link to "Arthur Bond.")

The next section of the story relates the narrator's attempts to get inside the greenhouse—at first perhaps only out of having been charmed by its lush appearance in the midst of a frozen northern landscape. He becomes obsessed with gaining entry but is turned away several times by the Nurseryman. The third time he approaches the greenhouse, at daybreak, as he stands before it the naked girl, murdered or suicidal, comes plummeting down from an adjacent roof and shatters the glass she falls through, jarring the locked door open: "I entered, at last, the ripe heat of the Nursery. I was admitted. I was in. The smell of humid mulch and sticky seed was close to the smell of sex, genital and just used. I was for a moment almost overcome with the eroticness of it" (*HIHM*, 53). The narrator finds the girl on the floor, mysterious and dead, scarcely marked by injury, and sees the drunken Nurseryman shuffling around the room, obviously both disturbed and unable to react within the bounds of reason. Some echoes of Goyen's other stories resound at this point. Puzzling over the Nurseryman's reaction to the extraordinary death of the girl, he imagines him thinking that the girl is "a self-delivered foundling" and he sees in the gardener's eyes "the look of Cain." Foundlings figure in many of the more fabulous stories by Goyen, and *Half a Look of Cain* concerned itself with, among other things, unusual and intense human relations among extreme conditions of biblical proportion (including a flood).

The narrator interrupts his tale at this point to reveal that he himself, far from resembling the lavish beauty of the young girl or the plenitude of flowering and leafing in the greenhouse, is a poet gone dry, unable to write anything. Although the story is presented as his written document, there is a quality of performance to it, as we have seen in other stories, so much so that at one point the narrator even seems to call out to "you back there," as if an audience were in attendance. The impulse to write is now tinged with the coloration of speech, of declamation. The rhetoric of this fictional deposition straddles the border between text and speech and signals Goyen's preoccupation with the creation of a way of writing that will convincingly represent speech without sacrificing the artistic deliberateness of writing.

At the moment when the narrator confronts his own artistic deadness and cries out over the thanklessness and frustration, the unrequited-ness, of his artistic career, the text grows more complex. An unex-plained phrase from early in the story now grows more resonant: he hints that his own spiritual condition is extreme, he is "dying," and he has written, "I was walking around with a hole in my breast." Just as an implicit emotional pain lies behind a narrator's responsiveness to remembered tragedy in such stories as "Had I a Hundred Mouths" and "Precious Door," here some spoiled love lies hidden in the narrator's extremity of emotion, some lost or ruined possibility of feeling that is haunting him. The vision of the green glowing hothouse in the frozen winter world had been incomparably enchanting and promising to him; but that vision was spoiled, first because he was not allowed to enter and then because, entering at the moment of calamity, he was robbed of his hoped-for enchantment and made witness instead to the bizarre death of the young woman and the repugnant act of the Nurseryman.

He recounts, without divulging his motive, that almost casually he stabbed the Nurseryman with "a little spade," aiming it at the dead man's heart. This act he leaves an enigma—perhaps it is no legal crime but it is a moral one. The rest of the story is all aftermath, but, sur-prisingly, not *events* of aftermath but rather meditation. The narrator writes that he sat down beside the bizarre figures, the dead girl locked in the Nurseryman's dying clutches; he felt ill; and when police arrived they took him away. The recollection of all this leads in an interesting direction: first to a hope that his extremity of despair will awaken his "old wild poetry" again and then to a sudden memory, which seems to arise out of nowhere, disconnected from the hothouse and what hap-pened there, and with this memory the story concludes.

Passion, an excess of lust, a quest for the mesmerizing vision of plen-itude amidst a landscape of frozen life and feeling—these have been the backdrop of the fable—for that is what it seems—of a young girl falling to her death, a drunken gardener who assaults her dead body and dies, and a pained, obsessive artist who witnesses all, attacks the dead gardener as if in revenge or punishment and then cannot speak, and is arrested. Now, human feeling, maturing emotions, the human "sentimental education" are in a way outgrowths of memory; that is, we learn the range and reach of human feeling as we live and grow from childhood to adulthood and then into our years of adult life, and we return to memory for our benchmarks of feeling. In the midst of his despair, having relived it as he has written of what happened, the narrator finds himself as if in the presence of a memory larger than he—the house in which he was raised.

This is both the real ancestral house of wood and the house of breath "built once more" in memory: "it blows into shape before me" (*HIHM*, 59). Image of quiet, simplicity, humility, and safety until now, it has a darker look in the aftermath of the bizarre and violent: "Surely it led me to poetry, for it had given me early deep feeling, mornings of unnameable feeling in the silver air, nights of visions after stories told by the lamplight. But oh I see that it held a shadowed life" (*HIHM*, 59).

A flawed hand mirror, a monitory figure etched in the glass of the front door (for the life model of this fictional door, see the *TriQuarterly* interview in part 2)—these suggest a "dark host," a "rearing suspicious horse and suspicious plumed dark rider shying back from the homeless traveler, from the guest half-welcome" (*HIHM*, 60). Having stabbed the dead Nurseryman, the narrator seems to feel that he himself has finally been claimed by the darkness of his origins, half-hidden from him until now, now recognized. The fable becomes confession and cry of despair.

If the complex full significance of this story remains elusive, it is nonetheless a cardinal expression of the struggle between opposites in much of Goyen's fiction. Here it is not between ghost and flesh but as if again between two brothers, one of whom, like the gardener, is drunk with ungovernable rage, is at the bidding of dark feeling, hostility, and violence. And the stricken narrator has found himself undone morally and emotionally by events and actions—even his own—which he cannot fathom but which return him to an ominous early memory of his own origins. In light of what he has done, he now fears his own origins and regards them darkly.

These late stories in a somber vein are somewhat leavened by two others in which there is more humor and lightness of touch, "Where's Esther?" and "The Texas Principessa." It seems no surprise that Goyen's last period of writing, in which he reworked his old themes in a new way that carried them toward the added theme of reconciliation, also includes openly humorous work. In this prolific period the emotional reach of his work widens; now it ranges from the savagery of "Had I a Hundred Mouths" to the comparatively innocent ribaldry of "The Texas Principessa." To be sure, there are even touches of humor in the darker stories, especially in "Arthur Bond."

The sweetness at the end of "Precious Door" and the mixture of wonder and grief in *The House of Breath* may be more profound than the humor in "Where's Esther?" and "The Texas Principessa," but these two late stories recover the lighter elements of earlier stories, like the black humor of "The White Rooster" and the satire of "Tapioca Surprise." Along with the tragic dimensions of a story like "Precious Door," this humor closes and caps Goyen's writing career. Like the pathos of the darker stories, the humor in both these stories conveys forgiveness and reconciliation.

The wonderfully controlled tone of voice in both humorous stories make them two of Goyen's virtuoso performance of fictional ventriloquism. In the monologue "Where's Esther?" the female narrator describes the drunken but socially imperious Esther, whose attention she and others constantly sought. Around Esther, everyone agreed, despite their own hurt feelings when she wounded them, things were very jolly and enviably exclusive. But Esther, now drying out, is altogether different, is dull and ordinary, and the narrator, one of many hangers-on, finds herself bored and at wit's end to create some excitement for herself. While she freely admits that Esther, when drunk, was horrible to others, she is just as quick to defend Esther and to lament her sobriety. There is no plot to the story; there is only the deft portrait of the narrator, who reveals more of herself than she knows and does so to her own disadvantage. But Goyen's portrait is not deeply critical; it seems, on the contrary, tolerant and forgiving, although it does not fail to ridicule the narrator's alcoholic illusions.

"The Texas Principessa" is similar in that it is told in the first person by a woman narrator, only this time there is a more linear plot, and the prevailing feeling-tone of the story is not critical of the narrator herself but, rather, generous toward her, valuing her sincere, unaffected manner. Unlike the narrator of "Where's Esther?" she is not self-deluded. Quite the contrary, she is an acute observer of herself and others around her, and she is struck with awe by the twists and coincidences in her life and confides them with convincing frankness. Repeatedly her telling includes phrases ("that ever happen to you?") that draw the reader into serving as her listener. She has inherited an Italian palazzo from her wealthy old Texas friend Horty Solomon and speaks as if she has just been asked how that came to happen. She meanders through the story, interrupting herself often, seeming as amazed by what she is telling as her listener must be. Even her reaction to Horty Solomon's death is colored more by wonder than by sadness (very like the reaction of the teller of "Arthur Bond"). Where there is wonder (even at calamity) instead of, or at least in equal measure with, rage or grief or despair or fear, there is hope of a restorative energy and love of life. In this connection these two lighter stories seem especially akin to "Precious Door."

The emotional range of Goyen's last work shows, more than any shift away from his lifelong artistic obsessions and themes, a blending of their diversity in more complex creations. There is an unmistakable valedictory note in some of them as well, especially in "Precious Door" and "Tongues of Men and Angels," just as there is in the novel *Arcadio*. In "Recovering" and in comments in his *TriQuarterly* interview, Goyen also speaks as one whose perspective on his work is that of an artist looking back at what he recognizes is his entire accomplishment. When his complete stories are finally available to readers, the full range of his accomplishments—the striking distinctness of his conception of the short story and of his genius for narrative voices, his deeply tolerant and humane sympathy for all those who are marked as different from others, and his sensitive alarm over the fate of the natural world—will be seen as one of the most capacious and original artistic visions in American fiction of this century.

Notes to Part 1

1. For some of these details, as well as much additional information about Goyen's early life, see Patrice Repusseau, *The House of Breath dans l'oeuvre de William Goyen: Thèse de Doctorat es lettres* (Lille, France: Atelier Nationale de Reproduction des Thèses, 1980), 14–87. This is the most important study yet done on Goyen's work. Although short fiction is not its central concern, this book includes many comments on individual stories and invaluable analysis of Goyen's work as a whole.

2. *The Collected Stories of William Goyen* (New York: Doubleday, 1975), 144; hereafter cited in the text as *CS*.

3. "William Goyen: A Poet Telling Stories," in *Talking with Texas Writers: Twelve Interviews*, by Patrick Bennett (College Station: Texas A & M University Press, 1980), 240.

4. See "While You Were Away" (pamphlet) (Houston, Tex.: Houston Public Library, 1978), passim; hereafter cited in the text as *WYWA*.

5. William Goyen, *The House of Breath*, (reprint, 1986), New York: Persea Books, 1–2; hereafter cited in the text as *HOB*.

6. Robert Phillips, *William Goyen* (Boston: Twayne Publishers, 1979), 33. As of 1990, this remains the only full-length treatment of Goyen's work in English. Hereafter cited in the text as Phillips.

7. John Igo, "Learning to See Simply: An Interview with William Goyen," *Southwest Review* 65, no. 3 (Summer 1980): 277.

8. Oswyn Murray, "The Word Is Mightier Than the Pen," *Times Literary Supplement*, 16–22 June 1989, 656.

9. For a full discussion of the nature of oral culture and the rhetoric of orality, see Walter J. Ong, *Orality and Literacy: The Technologizing of the Word* (London: Routledge, 1982; reprint, New York, 1989).

10. Wallace Stevens, *Opus Posthumous* (New York: Knopf, 1957), 168.

11. *Had I a Hundred Mouths: New and Selected Stories 1947–1983* (New York: Clarkson N. Potter, 1985), 3–4; hereafter cited in the text as *HIHM*.

12. Letter of 21 September 1948 (from Portland, Oregon) to Margo Jones, from the Margo Jones Collection of the Dallas Public Library.

13. The revised stories are "The Mockingbird's Song," "The Seadown's Bible," "The Storm Doll," "Simon's Castle," and "A Parable of Perez." The new stories are "Precious Door," "Arthur Bond," "The Texas Principessa," "In the Icebound Hothouse," "Right Here at Christmas," "Black Cotton," "Where's Esther?", "Had I a Hundred Mouths," and "Tongues of Men and of Angels."

14. Goyen's papers, including manuscripts, letters, and photographs, are held in two main collections: at the Harry Ransom Humanities Research Center at the University of Texas, Austin, and in the Fondren Library at Rice University, Houston, Texas.

15. Among the many critical inquiries remaining to be made into Goyen's work, one of special importance will be a consideration of the figure of the mother and the way in which Goyen portrays relationships between mother and son.

Part 2

THE WRITER

Introduction

Unlike many writers, William Goyen made several remarkable and extended statements about his work. When, after a period of literary neglect, his *Selected Writings* and the twenty-fifth-anniversary edition of *The House of Breath* were published in 1974 and 1975, he prefaced the former volume with a frank and open comment about his artistic origins and hopes. Again, to his *Collected Stories* (1975), another retrospective occasion, he added as preface an interesting commentary on his sense of short fiction. And while he gave quite a number of published interviews, three in particular are extraordinary portraits of the artist. (These were conducted by Robert Phillips for the noted series published by the *Paris Review,* by Rolande Ballorain for *Delta,* and by me for *TriQuarterly;* they are the result of many hours of talk and, in the case of the *Paris Review* and *TriQuarterly* interviews, further refinement of meaning in the editing of the transcript.) Given these valuable resources, it is only natural to include Goyen's two prefaces and two of the interviews in this volume.

There is a further richness of comment on himself, on his work, and on art generally in Goyen's correspondence, which will eventually be selected and published. Some letters have been published and may be consulted, along with Rolland Ballorain's interview with Goyen, in the special issue of *Delta,* the notable French magazine on outstanding American writers of fiction, which devoted its ninth issue to Goyen.

Of particular interest in the prefaces and interviews that follow are Goyen's comments in two areas. (1) Goyen had a strong sense of how his personal background prepared him for his particular understanding of fictional style (above all, his talking about storytelling and language). (2) Goyen's deep and unconventional spirituality led him to see the writing of fiction not as a solitary enterprise but always as a kind of compact between people—first, between the writer and the voices that speak to him out of his memories and imaginings, almost as if these were persons to whom he had a certain kind of special loyalty and in whom he held a special kind of faith, and second between the writer and the reader. For Goyen, the writer and the reader are in a relation-

Part 2

ship echoing that between one who tells a story and one who listens, with an important condition: that the teller of the story has himself already been a listener. What happens between the teller and the listener, then, is the establishment of a relationship that is not, as Goyen says in one of the interviews, material (they are giving each other nothing tangible) but spiritual. The telling of the story has, as he says, "a spiritual significance. Someone wrote that about my work—that the liberating, therefore spiritual, significance of story-telling was in the very telling itself, a kind of a prayer or meditation or apotheosis of feeling, a dynamic spiritual action." This is not only an unusual way of looking at fiction; it is also closely related to the special qualities of Goyen's work, including the intimacy of voice and the central elements of the erotic and a kind of radical rejection of industrial and urban life. The careful reader of the following documents will find many striking and profound statements that illuminate not only Goyen's fiction but also much larger aspects of living and making art.

98

Introduction to *Selected Writings* of William Goyen

My birthplace, once a thriving railroad and sawmill town by the Trinity River, is Trinity, located in the soft woods-and-meadows area of East Texas. My father's family brought him as a young man to Trinity from Mississippi. They were sawmill people. My mother's family, native Texans, was made up of carpenters, railroad men (there was a prominent roundhouse in Trinity), but her father was Postmaster of the town for many years. We lived in Trinity until I was seven. The world of that town, its countryside, its folk, its speech and superstitions and fable, was stamped into my senses during those first seven years of my life; and I spent the first twelve years of my writing life reporting it and fabricating it in short fiction. In my seventh year we moved to Shreveport, Louisiana, lived there a year, thence to Houston. I was educated, from the third grade, in that city: grammar school, Junior High School, High School, Rice University. As a child I was quick and scared; serving, secretly unsettled; imaginative and nervous and sensual. When I reached Sam Houston High School, I thought surely I would be a composer, actor, dancer, singer, fantastico. My mother and father were embarrassed by such ambitions. Nevertheless, I found a way to study dancing, music composition, singing, clandestinely. When this was found out by my parents, who were outraged by the extents of my determination, I did not run away from home to a city. I decided to go underground at home, and write. No one could know that I was doing that. It was my own. This was my sixteenth year, and what I wrote was lyrical, melancholy, yearning, romantic and sentimental. Above all, it was homesick—and written at home.

College for me was intolerable. I hated the classes, the courses, the students. I wanted to make up new things, not "study" what had al-

From *Selected Writings of William Goyen* (New York: Random House/Bookworks, 1974), [ix-x]. © 1983 by Doris Roberts and Charles William Goyen Trust. Reprinted by permission.

ready been made. In my Junior year, the thunderstrike came. I discovered Shakespeare, Chaucer, Milton, Yeats, Joyce, the French Symbolists, Flaubert, Turgenev, Balzac, Melville, Hawthorne. I was at literature, insatiable, for the next three years, reading, and writing under the glow and turmoil of what I was reading. Suddenly—it seemed—I had accomplished the Masters Degree in Comparative Literature (1939). I had been writing plays and stories, and in my Junior and Senior years I took all the prizes in both forms.

At the end of the war, I went to New Mexico (El Prado, above Taos) and began to write from myself. It was clear to me now: I saw life as a writing life, a life of giving shape to what happened, of searching for meanings, clarification, Entirety. It was my Way: expression in words. From then on, I managed to write, with little or no money, with growing distinction—which, I have come to see, brings little usable reward—awards, honors, little money. What I wanted was to make splendor. What I saw, felt, knew was real, was more than what I could make of it. That made it a lifetime task, I saw that. All forms of writing excite me and pain me and labor me; but the printed word, the Book—especially the short narrative form—most challenges and most frees me.

Preface to *The Collected Stories of William Goyen*

Of the twenty-six stories in this volume, nineteen were originally published in two volumes under the titles *Ghost and Flesh* and *The Faces of Blood Kindred*, and the remaining seven in American and European magazines. Some of the uncollected stories have enjoyed a long-time popularity in Europe and have only recently been published in America ("Tenant," "Tapioca Surprise," "The Thief Coyote"), years after they were written. The stories cover a span of nearly thirty years: "The White Rooster" was first published in 1947 in *Mademoiselle;* "Bridge of Music, River of Sand" was published in 1975 in *The Atlantic Monthly.*

A number of these stories were written in the fifties, which now turns out to have been a kind of Golden Age of the short story in America. In those days we were all publishing in several magazines, large and small. *Mademoiselle*, with high enthusiasm, published many of us young story writers, including James Purdy, Truman Capote, Jean Stafford, Shirley Jackson and Tennessee Williams. This was because of two women, Cyrilly Abels and Margarita Smith, the editors. Many serious American writers owe a debt to these two women of taste, courage and belief.

But no matter where these stories of mine were published, a small but enduring and distinguished magazine has played the most prominent part in my writing over the years. This is *The Southwest Review.* Through the years, since 1946, the editors, Allen Maxwell and Margaret Hartley, fervently and faithfully published my stories. I cannot imagine my life and its work of writing, from the very beginning, without Allen and Margaret and *The Southwest Review.* Whatever its meaning, the progress of my work is documented in its pages and issues, year after year. It is a calendar, a diary. And Margaret Hartley and Allen Maxwell have been a presence in the life of my writing.

From *The Collected Stories of William Goyen* (New York: Doubleday, 1975), x-xii. © 1983 by Doris Roberts and Charles William Goyen Trust. Reprinted by permission.

For what it is worth to those who want to write stories or simply to know something of one writer's insight in the writing of short fiction, I have felt the short-story form as some vitality, some force that begins (and not necessarily at the *beginning*), grows in force, reaches a point beyond which it cannot go without losing force, loses force and declines; stops. For me, story telling is a rhythm, a charged movement, a chain of pulses or beats. To write out of life is to catch, in pace, this pulse that beats in the material of life. If one misses this rhythm, his story does not seem to "work"; is mysteriously dead; seems to imitate life but has not joined life. The story is therefore uninteresting to the reader (and truly to the writer himself), or not clear. I believe this is a good principle to consider.

But for me, as I have written, I've been mainly interested in the teller-listener situation. Somebody is telling something to somebody: an event! Who's listening to this telling? Where is the listener? I've not been interested in simply reproducing a big section of life off the streets or from the Stock Exchange or Congress. I've cared most about the world in one person's head. Mostly, then, I've cared about the buried song in somebody, and sought it passionately; or the music in what happened. And so I have thought of my stories as folk song, as ballad, or rhapsody. This led me to be concerned with speech, lyric speech—my heritage. Since the people of the region where most of my stories start—or end (they do, I believe, move in and through the great world) are natural talkers and use their speech with gusto and often with the air and bravura of singers; and since the language of their place is rich with phrases and expressions out of the King James Bible, from the Negro imagination and the Mexican fantasy, from Deep South Evangelism, from cottonfield and cotton gin, oil field, railroad and sawmill, I had at my ears a glorious sound. A marvelous instrument of language was *given* to me. I worked with this instrument as though it were a fiddle or a cello, to get its true music out of it; and I was finally able to detach myself from this speech so as to be able to hear it almost as a foreign language; and in several of my stories (most notably "Ghost and Flesh, Water and Dirt") I have wanted to record as closely as possible the speech as *heard*—as though I were notating music.

The landscape of my stories, generally East Texas, is pastoral, river-haunted, tree-shaded, mysterious and bewitched. Spirits and ghosts inhabit it: the generations have not doubted their presence, their doings. Here there exists the local splendor of simple people who "wonder" and "imagine." Some heartbreak is here, too; and something of doom. The landscape of these folk, and mine, is more like Poussin or Claude or Manet than Grant Wood or Norman Rockwell or Rosa Bonheur.

Landscape and language and folk, I seized it all, early, as mine to work with and to make some manner of art out of. It truly was, early, my absolute life's work and my dedication. In Europe, in nearly a dozen states of the United States, this was my work. Living in Rome, it was never more urgent, this faraway haunting landscape, this ringing speech, this tender and yearning, rollicking people, this notion, this vision of "home," this ache of "homesickness." It seems to me that I was always homesick. Standing before great paintings in Venice or Paris, I saw my own people in Rembrandt's, my own countryside in Corot's. Europa was my fat cousin in Trinity, Texas (pop. 900) and the bull that was "raping" her was our own, named Roma. I wrote quite a bit about them.

When I was two-thirds through my first novel, *The House of Breath*, I announced to my editor, Robert Linscott, that I was going to live in Europe for a while. He was astonished that I would make such a radical move and seriously concerned that the book would lose focus and vitality. I went, and the immense experience disturbed my concentration not at all: what I saw in Europe I put right into my novel: it fit very well—ancient frescoes, grand avenues, plazas, noble ruins—into the little town of "Charity" that I was creating out of my own home town of Trinity, Texas. Ernst Robert Curtius, the distinguished German translator of this novel wrote in his Preface:[1] " 'The House of Breath', to be sure, tells us about Charity and East Texas; yet when it does extend itself, it reaches only as far as neighboring Louisiana. And for all that, this book is different from a regional novel. No regionalism is offered here. The language and the landscape of East Texas are only foils to a fabric, in which vital and neighborly human beings talk and move about. In the kitchen of the house near Charity hangs a map of the world. To a boy, whose story is being told, the outlines of countries and continents seem to be the organs of the human body. The organization and formation of the earth has imprinted itself upon the child's consciousness, and in the most perceptual form. In sleepy Charity he had sensed the quality of the whole world and realized that he belonged to it. So it is that this novel of a childhood has become a book of universal scope."

So, I could hope, for these stories that came out of that same child-hood, that same town, that same breath.

Note

1. "Haus aus Hauch," *Verlag Der Arche*. Zurich, 1952. (English translation by Michael Kowal, in *Essays on European Literature*, E.R. Curtius, Princeton University Press, 1973, 456–64.)

Interview, 1975

The interview with William Goyen took place on a sunny Saturday afternoon in June, 1975—the spring of Goyen's sixtieth birthday and also of the publication of the Twenty-fifth Anniversary Edition of his first novel, The House of Breath.

Taped over a three-hour period in the home of a friend in Katonah, New York, Mr. Goyen remained seated on a sofa throughout the interview, sipping a soft drink. He requested that baroque music be played over the stereo, "to break the silences." There were *silences—long, considering pauses between thoughts.*

William Goyen is slender and lanky, and a handsome figure at sixty. His aspect is intense and patrician, his manner gracious and courtly. Goyen's hair is silver; he speaks with a strong Southwestern accent.

PHILLIPS: In the Introduction to your *Selected Writings*, you stated that you began writing at the age of sixteen, at a time when you were also interested in composing and dancing and other art forms. Why writing as a career rather than one of the other arts?

GOYEN: My foremost ambition, as a very young person, was to be a composer, but my father was strongly opposed to my studying music— that was for girls. He was from a sawmill family who made a strict division between a male's work and a female's. (The result was quite a confusion of sex roles in later life: incapable men and oversexed women among his own brothers and sisters.) He was so violently against my studying music that he would not allow me even to play the piano in our house. Only my sister was allowed to put a finger to the keyboard . . . the piano had been bought for her. My sister quickly tired of her instrument, and when my father was away from the house, I merrily played away, improving upon my sister's études—which I had learned by ear—and indulging in grand Mozartian fantasies. In the

"Interview with William Goyen" by Robert Phillips, first published in the *Paris Review*, no. 68 (Winter 1976): *58–100*. Reprinted in *Writers at Work: The Paris Review Interviews*, sixth series, ed. George Plimpton (New York: Viking, 1984), *169–204*.© 1984 by the Viking Press. Reprinted by permission.

novel *The House of Breath*, Boy Ganchion secretly plays a "cardboard piano," a paper keyboard pasted on a piece of cardboard in a hidden corner. I actually did this as a boy. My mother secretly cut it out of the local newspaper and sent off a coupon for beginners' music lessons. I straightaway devised Liszt-like concerti and romantic overtures. And so silent arts were mine: I began writing. No one could hear that, or know that I was doing it, even as with the cardboard piano.

PHILLIPS: You weren't having to write under the sheets with a flash-light, were you?

GOYEN: You know, I *was* playing my music under the quilt at night, quite literally. I had a little record player and I played what music I could under the quilt and later wrote that way. So I did write under the sheets.

PHILLIPS: What was your father's reaction to writing?

GOYEN: Something of the same. He discovered it some years later, when I was an undergraduate at Rice University in Houston. He found me writing plays, and to him the theater, like the piano, was an engine of corruption which bred effeminate men (God knows he was generally right, I came to see), sexual libertines (right again!), and a band of gypsies flaunting their shadowed eyes and tinselled tights at reality. When my first novel was published, my father's fears and accusations were justified—despite the success of the book—and he was outraged to the point of not speaking to me for nearly a year.

This could, of course have been because the book was mostly about his own family—the sawmill family I spoke of earlier. My father, his brothers, his father, everybody else were lumber people, around mills . . . and forests. I went around the sawmills with him, you see, and saw all that. He loved trees so! My God, he would . . . he'd just *touch* trees . . . they were human beings. He would smell wood and trees. He just loved them. He knew wood. He was really meant for that.

Poor beloved man, though, he later came around to my side and became the scourge of local bookstores, making weekly rounds to check their stock of my book. He must have bought a hundred copies for his lumbermen friends. God knows what *they* thought of it. Before he died he had become my ardent admirer, and my *Selected Writings* is dedicated to him.

PHILLIPS: Do you agree with the theory that an unhappy childhood is essential to the formation of exceptional gifts? Were you genuinely unhappy?

GOYEN: How could it have been any other way? My own nature was one that would have made it that way. It was a melancholy childhood. It was a childhood that was searching for—or that *needed*—every kind of compensation it could get. I think that's what makes an artist. So that I looked for compensation to fulfill what was not there.

PHILLIPS: How have the physical conditions of your writing changed over the years? What is the relation between the creative act and privacy for you, today? In your *Note* on the Twenty-fifth Anniversary Edition of *The House of Breath*, you stated that part of the novel was written on an aircraft carrier in the Pacific.

GOYEN: Since my writing began in the air of secrecy, indeed, of alienation—as the work had to be done without anyone's knowing it— forever after my work has had about it the air of someone in solitude having done it, alienated from the press of society and the everyday movements of life.

On the ship, where I continued working, I found that there are many hidden places on an aircraft carrier where one can hide out and do secret work. And this was easily achieved. Also on the night watches and so forth, there was a lot of time. There is a great deal of free time aboard a ship in wartime, ironically. This kind of tradition in my work had been mine all my life, and I have generally lived in hidden places. In New Mexico it was at the beautiful foot of a mountain (the Sangre de Cristo in the primitive village of El Prado), and also in a mysterious mountain (Kiowa Mountain—the D.H. Lawrence Ranch called Kiowa Ranch over San Cristobal, New Mexico, near Taos). And in Europe— Zurich, Rome—I worked in back-street *pensions*.

Yet more and more, as I get more worldly and have the security of having survived, I feel that it is not necessary to be *that* far removed from the workings of daily life and the daily lives of people. Indeed, the older I get and the more I write, the more I feel it important to be part of daily life . . . to know that it surrounds me as I work. I presently live in a large apartment on the West Side of New York City. One of those rooms is mine, and it's an absolute hideaway, yet all around me in the other rooms the life of a family goes on, and I like to know that. I also like to know that twelve flights down I can step onto the street in the midst of a lot of human beings and feel a part of those. Whereas, in the old days, in New Mexico, I was brought up—taught—by Frieda Lawrence to see that simple manual endeavor is part of art. I would work in gardens and dig water ditches and walk in mountains and along rivers when I was not writing, and I felt that it was absolutely essential to my work. That's changing for me now. I'm more city-prone. Maybe the world is changing, too. Maybe solitude is best had in the midst of multitudes.

It's amazing how quickly something gets written. Now, when it comes, it can be on a bus, or in a store. I've stopped in Macy's and written on a dry-goods counter and then suddenly had a whole piece of writing for myself that was accomplished, where earlier in my life I felt I had to spend a week in a house somewhere in the country in order to get that. Conditions change.

PHILLIPS: Some say that poverty is ennobling to the soul. Is economic stability helpful to a writer? On the other hand, do you think wealth can be harmful?

GOYEN: It can be harmful. This depends on the stage in a writer's life, of course. As a young man, for me—I speak now not as a wealthy or an impoverished man, but as a man looking back when he was younger—it was imperative that I live *very* simply and economically. Living in Taos where—who would have believed it then, fifteen or twenty years later a whole migration of young hippies would come to live and meditate in the desert just where I had lived—I was totally solitary. It was imperative for me and my work that I keep everything simple and have practically nothing at all. I lived in just a mud house with a dirt floor on land that Frieda Lawrence gave me out of friendship. I built it with a friend and a couple of Indians. Yet to live in absolute poverty all his life could harm a writer's work. The hardship and worry over money in writers as they get older is a social horror; grants given to writers should be *sufficient*, so that they are able to live with amplitude and, yes, some dignity.

PHILLIPS: The genesis of it all goes back to that aircraft carrier, doesn't it?

GOYEN: I thought I was going to die in the war. I was on a terrible ship. It was the *Casablanca*, the first baby flattop. There were always holes in it, and people dying and it was just the worst place for me to be. I really was desperate. I just wanted to jump off. I thought I was going to die anyway, be killed, and I wanted to die because I couldn't endure what looked like an endless way of life with which I had nothing to do—the war, the ship, and the water . . . I have been terrified of water all my life. I would have fits when I got close to it.

Suddenly—it was out on a deck in the cold—I saw the breath that came from me. And I thought that the simplest thing that I know is what I belong to and where I came from and I just called out to my family as I stood there that night, and it just . . . I saw this breath come from me and I thought—in that breath, in that call, is *their* existence, is their reality . . . and I must shape that and I must write about them—*The House of Breath*.

I saw this whole thing. I saw what was going to be four–five years' work. Isn't that amazing? But I knew it was there. Many of my stories happen that way. It's dangerous to tell my students this because then these young people say, "Gee, all I've got to do, if I really want to write, is wait around for some ship in the cold night, and I'll blow out my breath, and I've got my thing."

PHILLIPS: So this sustained you?

GOYEN: It brought my life back to me. I saw my relationships; it was extraordinary. Lost times come for us in our lives if we're not phony and if we just listen; it hurts, but it's also very joyous and beautiful . . . it's a redemption . . . it's all those things that we try to find and the world seems to be looking for . . . as a matter of fact, that's the *hunger* of the world. So there it was on the ship and it just came to me. I saw so much . . . that I wouldn't have to go home and they wouldn't have to suffocate me; they wouldn't kill me; I'd find other relationships.

PHILLIPS: So after the war you didn't go home.

GOYEN: When the war was over, I just dipped into Texas and got my stuff and left and headed towards San Francisco. I had come to love San Francisco when it was the home port for my ship, the aircraft carrier, and I thought that it would be a good place to live. But I passed through Taos, New Mexico, in winter, in February, and I was enchanted. It really was like an Arthurian situation . . . I couldn't leave. It was beautiful and remote, like a Himalayan village, untouched, with this adobe color that was ruby-colored and yellow, all the magical colors of mud. It's not all one color. It's like Rome. Rome looks like that. And the sunlight and the snow . . . just about everyone on foot . . . a few cars . . . high, seventy-five hundred feet.

PHILLIPS: Did the D.H. Lawrence commune in Taos have anything to do with your staying?

GOYEN: I didn't know anything about the Lawrence legend. Had I, I might not have stayed at all. But I did, and right away I thought that I'd better get a little more money for myself before I settled in to work. So I got a job as a waiter at a very fashionable inn called Sagebrush Inn. I worked as a waiter for a few months until I met Frieda, who came in one night and I waited on her. The whole Lawrence world came to dinner there: Dorothy Brett and Mabel Dodge, Spud Johnson, Tennessee Williams: he was living up at the ranch. They all came to my table. And then the owner of the inn had to come out and say, "This young man is just out of the war and he wants to be a writer." The *worst* thing I wanted said about me; it almost paralyzed me. Well, of course, Tennessee thought, Oh, God, who cares about *another* writer. But Frieda said, "You must come and have tea with me." She said it right away. I went and from that moment . . . we just hit it off. It was almost a love affair. It was the whole world.

So it wasn't Lawrence that brought me to her; circumstances brought me to Frieda and I found her a great pal and a luminous figure in my life on her own terms.

I would go to teas with her. She would have high teas. In Texas we had a coke. But here it was the first time I met someone who baked bread, you know? She made a cake and brought it out . . . it was wonderful. She wore German clothes, like dirndls, and peasant outfits, and an apron. She was a kitchen frau. A few people came . . . Mabel Dodge had given her this great three-hundred-acre ranch in return for the manuscript of *Sons and Lovers*. That was the exchange. Except she never took *Sons and Lovers* away, so that the manuscript and many others, *Women in Love*, all holograph . . . were there in a little cupboard at the ranch. I could read them and look at them in amazement.

PHILLIPS: What sort of things did you talk about?

GOYEN: We talked about the simplest things . . . well, really about love, about men and women and about sex, about *physical* living. Of course, I didn't know that I was hearing what Lawrence had heard. Because it was Frieda who gave Lawrence this whole thing and it overwhelmed me.

The various people would come up in the summer and spend time with us, all kinds of people. Just simple people; Indians . . . she was close to Indians. I got very close to three Indians who were really like my family and helped me build my house.

PHILLIPS: And then people like Tennessee Williams came.

GOYEN: Yes, Tennessee stayed up there with his friend, Frank Merlo. Tennessee told us that he heard Lawrence's voice . . . he was a haunted, poor thing, but he did go a little too far. D.H. Lawrence was whispering things to him. Suddenly Tennessee had a terrible stomachache and it turned out that he had a very bad appendix and had to be brought down to Mabel Dodge. Mabel owned the only hospital; built it and owned it. It was like a European town and we were the only Americans, and I went to this hospital to witness Tennessee's dying . . . he was dying, you know. He was dying in this Catholic hospital screaming four-letter words and all kinds of things with the nuns running around wearing the most enormous habits, most unsanitary for a hospital. Mabel was wringing her hands and saying, "He's a genius, he's a genius." The doctor said, "I don't care; he's going to die, he's got gangrene. His appendix has burst. We have to operate at once." Tennessee said, "Not until I make my will." The doctor said, "How long will the will be?" "Well, everything's going to Frankie," so they sat down, with Frank going through an inventory of all Tennessee's possessions. "What about the house in Rome? You left that out." Tennessee was just writhing in pain. So they made a list of all the things. And then wheeled him off and he indeed had this operation, which to everyone's surprise he managed to recover from. Eventually he got out of there. . . .

PHILLIPS: All this time you were working on *The House of Breath.* How did it get published?

GOYEN: It got published through Stephen Spender, indirectly. He came to that little village where I was living. I had sent a piece of it to *Accent*, a wonderful early magazine; it caused quite a kind of thing. I began to get letters. Random House wrote me a letter and said that they hoped this was "part of a book." (All editors do that, I later learned.) They'll say that even if it's just a "letter to the editor" they've seen. That's what editors have to do, God bless them, and I'm glad they do. About that time, Spender, a man I scarcely knew, whose *poetry* I scarcely knew, arrived in Taos on a reading tour. A wealthy lady named Helene Wurlitzer, of the family who made the organs, lived there and brought people into that strange territory to read, and give chamber concerts and so on. I never went to those things because . . . well, I didn't have any shoes; I really was living on mud floors in an adobe house that I had built, utterly primitive, which I loved. I was isolated and terrified with all those things going on in me . . . but I was writing that book. Well, Spender heard that I was there . . . he heard through Frieda, who went to the reading, and so then he asked me if he could come to see me; he treated me as though I were an important writer. He had just read that piece in *Accent* and he asked if there was more that he could read. I showed him some other pieces and he sent those around. They were published and then somebody at Random House sent me a contract right away of two hundred fifty dollars advance for the book, and then promptly was fired. But Spender was very moved by the way I was living there; he wrote a well-known essay called "The Isolation of the American Writer" about my situation there. Nothing would do until Mr. Spender would have me come to London because he thought I was too isolated, too Texan, too hicky. . . . He really took it upon himself to make that kind of decision for me. It was a wonderful thing that he did. The stipulation was that I would bring a girl who had come into my life with me (this blessed girl has passed on among the leaves of autumn), and she was very much a part of my life there in London, and together we were real vagabonds, embarrassing everybody—people like Stephen, and Cyril Connolly, and Elizabeth Bowen, Rose Macauley, I mean, all of them. . . .

PHILLIPS: You stayed in Spender's house?

GOYEN: I had a room at the top and Dorothy had a room in the basement, with the stairs between us, creaking stairs. It was an elegant house, an eighteenth-century house in St. John's Wood. At four o'clock teatime in the winter it was dark, and they pulled Florentine brocaded curtains and turned on lights; it was a time of austerity still, but people came to tea. Veronica Wedgewood would arrive. Dorothy wouldn't come up from the basement. She really hated this kind of thing. She vanished. She just wouldn't participate. So I was really quite alone with this. I guess I must have kept her under wraps. I must have been very bad to her. I don't know. I have to think about that some time. But here they would come: Natasha, Stephen's wife who was a gifted pianist and wanted to be a concert pianist, and so musicians came, and painters. Cyril Connolly was often there because he and Stephen were working together. Dame Edith Sitwell came. We went to her house and she read one night; she sat behind a screen because she wouldn't read facing anyone or a group . . . behind a marvelous Chinese screen and you would hear this voice coming through the screen . . . all those people . . . that was a world that Spender gave me and was a great influence in my life and on my work.

PHILLIPS: What an extraordinary change.

GOYEN: I was thrown into this elegant surround which was precisely the opposite of what I had been doing. It was right for me because my character, Folner, yearned for elegance. Suddenly my country people were singing out their despair in those great elegant houses. I saw cathedrals for the first time . . . I'd not really seen cathedrals . . . I was able to get to Paris and all around there. All this went into *The House of Breath.* I saw the Sistine Chapel—well, that's the first page of *The House of Breath,* "on the dome of my skull, paradises and infernos and annunciations" and so forth. Europe just put it all right—everything that started in a little town in Texas, you see. It saved the book, I think. Because it made that cry, you know . . . it was an *elegant* cry . . . there's nothing better than an elegant cry of despair. . . .

PHILLIPS: Did people worry what this tremendous change in venue—from Taos to Europe—would do to *The House of Breath?*

GOYEN: Some people worried about it. James Laughlin of New Directions, when I had published a bit, wrote me, "You are ruining your work fast; the influences you are coming into are coming too soon, and you're allowing your personality to overwhelm your talent. Obviously people find your *Texas* personality . . ." (and he could be a snide guy too) ". . . charming and you might be of interest to them for a little while. But you are writing a very serious book and this will be permanently damaging to your work." He really wanted me to get out of there.

PHILLIPS: Were there other Cassandras about *The House of Breath?*

GOYEN: Well, Auden had kind of looked down his nose at me. He said it's the kind of writing where the next page is more beautiful than the one just read. "One is just breathless for fear that you're not going to be able to do it," he said, "and that makes me too nervous. I prefer James."

Christopher Isherwood said, "You know, my dear boy, you'll never make it. That is what one feels when one reads you. You'll never survive with this kind of sensibility unless you change, get some armor on yourself." As a matter of fact, he wrote me and warned me again . . . he put it all down in a letter. And that *did* scare me. I was young and I was scared. But I knew that I had no choice. Then that feeling of doom *really* came to me . . . because I had no choice. I knew that I couldn't write any other way.

PHILLIPS: When you began writing *The House of Breath*, did you expect it to be published? Were you writing for publication?

GOYEN: I was most surely not "writing for publication." But I don't think there is any piece of the novel except one that was not published in magazines before the book itself was published.

PHILLIPS: You said earlier your father was upset by the book when it was published. Had you been concerned about the family and hometown reaction?

GOYEN: Concerned, yes. I fell out of favor with many people in the town, let's put it that way, and just about disinherited by my own family. I had nasty letters, bad letters from home and heartbroken letters from my mother and my father. Generally the attitude was one of hurt and shock. It was not until fifteen years later that I was able to go back to the town! And even then rather snide remarks were made to me by the funeral director and by the head of the bank. We met on the street.

PHILLIPS: So when you apply for a loan, you won't do it in that town?

GOYEN: No, and I won't die there, either.

PHILLIPS: How long did you and the girl stay as Spender's guests in England?

GOYEN: I settled in for the whole year of 1949 . . . and I finished the book in that house at St. John's Wood, in Stephen's house. The girl was there until it got very bad; we had problems, and so she moved to Paris; that made me have to go to Paris to see her there and we had this kind of thing that was going on. When I came back, bringing my manuscript on the *Queen Mary*, she came with me to New York. But then we had one visit with Bob Linscott, my editor, who said to her, "My dear, do you like to eat? Do you like a roof over your head? You'll never have it; he's an artist. I feed him and Random House has kept him alive and probably will have to from now on. Don't marry him, don't even fall in love" . . . and he broke her heart. He really did. Poor Dorothy. He was right; I wasn't about to be saddled down. And so it broke away, and that's okay. Many years later I found a woman exactly like her. Her name was Doris, and so often I say to Doris, "Dorothy," and I'm in trouble.

PHILLIPS: That was quite a step for an editor to take. What do you think their particular function should be?

GOYEN: Well, really caring for authors . . . not meddling with what they did but loving them so much and letting them know that he cares. Generally at that point, when you're starting, you feel that nobody does. Linscott looked after you and if you had no money, he gave you money. Once Truman Capote met me at the Oak Room of the Plaza. "I'm embarrassed to sit with you," he said when I sat down, "your suit is terrible." I hadn't really thought about what I was wearing. He said, "I'm not going to have you wear that suit anymore. But," he said, "I've ordered drinks for us and if you'll just wait, I'm going to call Bob and tell him that he must buy you a suit that costs at least two hundred and fifty dollars." And he did. Bob gave me money and he told me, "Well I guess he's right." He was lovable, Truman. He did sweet lovely things then.

PHILLIPS: Carson McCullers was one of Linscott's authors, wasn't she?

GOYEN: I had first known her in this nest that Linscott had up there for these little birdlings of writers. Carson had great vitality and she was quite beautiful in that already decaying way. She was like a fairy. She had the most delicate kind of tinkling, dazzling little way about her . . . like a little star. Like a Christmas, she was like an ornament of a kind. She had no mind and she could make no philosophical statements about anything; she didn't need to. She said far out, wonderfully mad things that were totally disarming, and for a while people would say, "I'll go wherever you go." She'd knock them straight out the window.

PHILLIPS: What sort of people interested her?

GOYEN: She had a devastating crush on Elizabeth Bowen. She actually got to Bowen's Court: she shambled over there to England and spent a fortnight. I heard from Elizabeth that Carson appeared at dinner the first night in her shorts, tennis shorts; that poor body, you know, in tennis shorts and she came down the stairs; that was her debut. It didn't last long. But that was Carson.

PHILLIPS: What was distinctive about her stories—as, say, compared to the other Southern "magnolia" writers?

GOYEN: She would try to make her stories scary and the word "haunted" was used, of course, by the literary critics, "the haunted domain." I think that was the French title for Truman's first novel . . . *Other Voices, Other Rooms. Les Domaines Hantés.* But Carson was . . . she was a really truly lost, haunted wonder-creature. It's hard to be that and grow old, because of course you either go mad out of what you see, or I guess you try to imitate that kind of purity. She was a bad imitator. So it was just a bore.

PHILLIPS: She was not a person to have as an enemy.

GOYEN: She was . . . not tough but she had a nasty . . . well, she had a way of absolutely devastating you; the kind that hurt, that little kind of peeping "drop dead" sort of thing. She had an eye for human frailty and would go right to that; that's why people fled her. They thought, Who needs this? Why be around her?

Then, of course, she was terribly affected by not being able to write. It was a murderous thing, a death blow, that block. She said she just didn't have anything to write. And really, it was as though she had never written. This happens to writers when there are dead spells. We die sometimes. And it's as though we're in a tomb; it's a death. That's what we all fear, and that's why so many of us become alcoholics or suicides or insane—or just no-good philanderers. It's amazing that we survive, though I think survival in some cases is kind of misgiven and it's a bore. It was written recently about Saul Bellow that one of the best things about him is that he survived, he didn't become an alcoholic, he didn't go mad and so forth. And that the true heroism of him lies simply in his endurance. That's the way we look at artists in America. People said to me when I was sixty, "My God, you're one of the ones, how are you. But you look *wonderful*. We didn't know where you were." They thought I was dead, or in an institution or something.

PHILLIPS: Could her editor, Linscott, help McCullers at all?

GOYEN: Poor Linscott couldn't get any more out of her and then he died before he could help her. I doubt whether he could have; no one could have. She was hopeless. She was just kind of a little expendable thing, you know? She would stay with me days at a time. I put her to bed; she had a little nightgown. I was playing sort of dolly; I was playing house. I sat with her while her Ex-Lax worked. Two or three chocolate Ex-Laxes and three wine glasses, and about three Seconal. And I would sit by her bed and see that it all worked, or at least it all got going in her. And then she was off to sleep.

She had some awful cancer of the nerve ends. This caused the strokes and she had a stroke finally on the other side until she was very badly paralyzed and then she had just a massive killing stroke. She was absolute skin and bones. They took her down there to Georgia, not far from where Flannery O'Connor lived, where they buried her.

PHILLIPS: Could she have written an autobiography?

GOYEN: She did not have "a hold of herself," as a person would say, enough to look back and see herself in situations. She never could have written her autobiography; it would be impossible for her . . . she had disguised herself so much. . . . And what a past, you know? Her mother . . . the Mother of *all* these people . . . thank God mine seems to be quite okay—I'd be raving mad at this point. Carson's mother was an aggressive lady, all over the place, and she came here once and worked at *Mademoiselle*. She had a notorious time as a fiction editor there. She did the oddest things . . . rejecting stories in her own Georgian way, generally in terms of cooking. I think she wrote to a writer once, "The crust of this story holds its contents well . . ." (she was off on a pie) "but my dear, by the time we get to the custard, it runs." The pie image went on and on. "This pie won't do," she said, " . . . came out of the oven too soon." She was a self-educated lady from the South who very early on had read Katherine Mansfield, for instance, and had told Carson about Mansfield, which was the worst thing she could have done. Once I went with her to meet Carson's plane. When she saw her daughter step out of the plane, she turned to me and said, "I seen the little lamp." I thought, "That's some allusion I'm going to have to find out about." When Carson reached us, she said, "Carson, you know what I told Bill when you appeared?" (She was the kind of lady who would repeat a thing she'd said.) "I told him that I seen the little lamp." Carson burst into tears. I said, "Please tell me what this is that hurts you so." She said, "Well, it's that beautiful story called 'The Doll's House' by Katherine Mansfield. It's the last line of the story. A poor little girl peeks in a garden at a doll's house owned by a snobbish family, and she sees this glowing little lamp inside. Later when the little girl's sister asks why there is a curious glow in her eye, she says, 'I seen the little lamp.'"

PHILLIPS: What about your own mother?

GOYEN: As a literary person I truly am the offspring of my mother and women like my mother. There's no woman like a Texas woman in her eighties. It's not Southern. She wouldn't have a clue as to what a "Southern lady" was. Hers was a singing way of expressing things, and this I heard so very early that it became my own speech; that's the way

I write. I love spending money to talk to her on the phone in Texas an hour at a time because it's just as though the curtain that came down on an opera last night goes right up when I call her tonight. The aria goes right on; it's just wonderful.

PHILLIPS: What do you talk about?

GOYEN: About how Houston has grown, and how she wants to go back to the little town she left fifty years ago. I write her expressions down; I have to do that to understand what they really mean; it's almost another language. But she keeps breeding it. I mean, she's writing all the time. I may not be writing, but she is. She's alive. . . .

PHILLIPS: Do you carry a notebook with you to put these things in? Or keep a diary?

GOYEN: Oh yes, I always carry paper with me . . . something to write on, always. And I keep not so much a formal diary any longer, but, well, it's a notebook, and in it I keep most things.

PHILLIPS: What do you do with those ideas that strike you in the middle of Macy's, say, and you can't record them fully or easily? Are they often unrelated to what you currently are writing?

GOYEN: It's rarely unrelated. When one's really engaged deeply in a piece of work, truly writing it, it takes over almost everything else and you find you're thinking about it constantly and it's a part of everything that happens. Even the clerk in Macy's suddenly speaks out of the novel that you are writing, it seems, or is a character in it. All the people in the world are suddenly characters in the novel you are writing. Everything contributes. The created piece of work has suddenly replaced what is called real life . . . life as it really is, whatever *that* means . . . so that it's not surprising to have it come at one from all angles.

Therefore, I know that if I've been writing all morning and I've got to buy groceries at noon, I better take paper with me, because I'm going to *keep* writing as I go down the street; you can write on the sack that your groceries come in, and I have!

PHILLIPS: What about the six years you were an editor at McGraw-Hill? Were you able to write, or did this interfere with your work?

GOYEN: The whole McGraw-Hill period is one that I want to write about. I have been writing about it in my *Memoirs* (my next book). The writer in the world of publishing, and particularly *me* in the world of

118

publishing, who had been so disillusioned and embittered by publishers. . . .

PHILLIPS: You were disillusioned with your own publishers?

GOYEN: Not my own per se. Just publishing in general—the making of books and the life of the making of books. All these things seemed so dead-end to me, without meaning. In this great place, this huge publishing house, I was a special person, in that I was a special editor. I was brought there to concern myself with serious writers and with new writers and what would be called Good Books, "quality writing." I was so concerned with the writing of my own authors that I considered their books my own and I treated them as such. I entered into their creative process. Nevertheless, I was caught in the competitive crush and thrust of commercial publishing. There was no question of my own writing. I was relieved not to have to worry about my own writing. I scarcely grieved it, or mourned it. It had brought me so little—no more than itself.

I suddenly was not a man who I had known. I was on the phone . . . I hate phones, I really can't manage phones well. I won't answer it generally and if I do I can't talk very long; I just can't do it. But here I was having to live and negotiate on the phone. Editors live that way. With agents and all that. . . . Here I was doing this for the first two or three years. I was drawing up contracts and I never knew what a contract was; I didn't know what they were about.

But I began to fail after the fourth year. I got very disturbed for all kinds of reasons . . . publishing, that's a corrupt thing sometimes. I had my way for a while, but then pretty soon night must fall and I was back with the old budgets and best-selling books and a lot a crap.

PHILLIPS: I take it your interest in your own writing increased during those six years?

GOYEN: Yes, that was bound to happen. As years passed, I began to be hungry and I wasn't quite sure what that hunger was. Well, of course, it was that I was not writing, and the more I exhausted myself with other writers, the more hungry I became to do my own work. This is an exhausting thing, being an editor, and I had no time left for my own work, no matter how much I wanted it. The demands made on me were almost unbearable. And that was when I left McGraw-Hill— or was asked to do so by Albert Leventhal.

PHILLIPS: That was in the sixties. In the fifties you were teaching

Part 2

at the New School. Did you find teaching just as demanding? Or was this a more satisfactory way to earn an income while doing your own writing?

GOYEN: Teaching writing is draining too, of course. Especially the way I do it. You see, I believe that everybody can write. And in believing and teaching this, what happens, of course, is enormous productivity on the part of many students. One's students produce so much that he is followed down the street by the mass of stuff he's encouraged! I mean, he's overtaken by it. And there's that much more work to do and more conferences to hold, and it's a depleting and exhausting thing. Just as exhausting as editing.

PHILLIPS: Is there an ideal occupation for the writer, then? Other than teaching?

GOYEN: Probably teaching is ideal. Because there's a community of writers there, and because the writer is respected and understood as a writer in colleges now. He's brought there as a writer, so it's understood why he's behaving the way he does and what he's doing when he's not around; he's *expected* to write. It's well paid, now, too—universities are paying writers well. It's probably the best. It takes a lot a discipline for a writer to teach writing, though. But in the end, leading writing seminars and workshops is refreshing and exhilarating and creative and in touch with life. I consider teaching one of my callings.

PHILLIPS: What do you think of your students?

GOYEN: The young people I've been involved with in my classes seem to have no sense of place. It bewildered me at first and then it caused me no little alarm. We've talked about it and what they tell me is often what I've presumed . . that there isn't much of a place where they come from. I mean, every place looks like every other place. Even suburban places—around here or in Ohio or wherever—all look alike . . . a shopping center, a McDonald's, the bank with the frosted globes on the facade, you know, that's a given building. The repertory theatres all look alike. So that they really don't have a sense of place except through literature. But when they begin to write they can't write about Flaubert's place. So what they're writing about right now is the Princeton campus, and I've told them I don't want to hear about that. I ask them, But didn't you live somewhere before? Wasn't there a room somewhere, a house? A street? A tree? Can't you remember?

120

There was always a sense of belonging to a place in my childhood. The place. We called the house "the place." "Let's go back to the place," we'd say. I loved that. There was such a strong sense of family and generation and ancestors in it. It was like a monument . . . that's what my impression was and I wrote about it as that. It was a Parthenon to me . . . with that enduring monumentality to it. But these students . . . they've had terrible family problems—they are dissociated . . . they're so disoriented . . . divorce, my God, divorce is a way of life in these generations. I ask them, Don't you have a grandmother? Do you ever go to your grandmother's? Where does she live? Oh, they say, she lives with us; or she lives in an apartment; she lives in the condominium. These elegant old ladies, they don't live in places anymore, either.

PHILLIPS: To get back to your own work, do you feel that music is reflected in your writings?

GOYEN: It's an absolute, basic part of my work, there's no question, and I think of my writing as music, often; and of my stories as little songs.

PHILLIPS: "Little songs," of course, is the literal meaning of the word "sonnet." The Albondocani Press has just published an edition of your early poems, poems written before your first novel. What made you abandon poetry for fiction? Faulkner said that all short-story writers are failed poets. Do you feel this is so?

GOYEN: I think an awful lot of them are. I'm not a failed poet, I'm just a poet who made another choice, at a certain point, very clearly. Actually, I'm so taken by the dramatic form I'm really a playwright manqué! I still consider myself, after having written and seen produced four plays in the professional theatre, manqué in the theatre. And yet I continue to love the form, and fear it more than love it.

PHILLIPS: Do you think your playwriting has been beneficial to your fiction writing?

GOYEN: I think it has. I think it's made me care more about writing fiction, for one thing.

PHILLIPS: Do you feel a compromise in the collaborations between director and producer and writer?

GOYEN: No, no, that's welcome to me, all that. I need all the help I can get! I never accept playwriting as a solitary thing. Once you do, you're ruined: because from the beginning it's a collaborative affair, and the sooner you can get it on to a stage, the better. The more you write at the table on a play, alone, the farther away you're going to get from the play. So far as the theatre is concerned, it becomes a *literary* work the more you work on it. But writing for the theatre has made me understand plot. It's helped me with plot in fiction writing.

PHILLIPS: What European authors and what American authors have meant the most to you?

GOYEN: As for American authors, Hawthorne and Melville have meant a great deal. And Henry James. And two poets—Ezra Pound and T.S. Eliot—have influenced me.

PHILLIPS: In what ways? They seem odd choices for a Southwestern fiction writer. . . .

GOYEN: I still read, I still study, the *Cantos* of Pound. I found Pound in Texas when I was eighteen or nineteen through a young friend named William Hart. Hart was one of those prodigies, enfants terribles, that materialize in small towns, young men bearing a sense of art and poetry and life as naturally as others bore the instinct to compete and to copulate. He had a great deal to do with my early enlightenment and spiritual salvation in a lower-middle-class environment in an isolated (then) Texas town, where a boy's father considered him a sissy if he played the piano, as I've said, and questioned the sexual orientation of any youth who read poetry.

William Hart was a true pioneer; he brought me Pound, Eliot, and Auden. He was self-taught, finding things for himself out of hunger. He had a high-school education, barely, but afterwards he came and sat in my classes at Rice and listened. He knew more than the professors did sometimes—he really did . . . about Elizabethan drama, and medieval romances. He knew these things. He was a delicate boy, obviously, but not effete. He was French Cajun, from a poor family, and he was on the streets, and could have been in trouble a lot. But he ended up in the library. They felt they had a revolutionary in there. In the Houston Public Library at nineteen he would get up and speak about literature, and Archibald MacLeish, of all people. And oh, how this man Hart spoke. The whole library would turn and listen. He became that kind of town creature, one of those who go down in cities, unheralded . . . they go down into beds of ashes. Well, he brought me Pound.

Pound's *Cantos* hold for me madness and beauty, darkness and mystery, pain, heartbreak, nostalgia. Some of the most beautiful and most haunting were written as a prisoner. He made, above all, *songs*, and he told his stories lyrically, as I have felt driven to tell mine. By ordinary speech, ordinary people. I mean that it seems to me that Pound sometimes speaks from a sort of subtone in his poems like a con man, a back-street hustler, using pieces of several languages, bits of myth, literary quotations and mixed dialects and plain beguiling nonsense. There is a stream, flowing and broken, of *voices* in Pound, echoes, town speech, songs, that deeply brought to me my own predicament, in the home of my parents and in the town where I lived. He helped show me a way to sing about it—it was, as most influences have been for me, as much a *tone*, a sound, a quality, as anything else.

The same for T.S. Eliot. He seemed then so much more American than Pound—but then Pound has the Chinese calligraphy and the heavy Greek and Latin. Eliot's wan songs broken suddenly by a crude word or a street phrase directly influenced me as a way to tell *The House of Breath*; and doom cut through by caprice shocked me and helped me survive in my own place until I could escape; showed me a way of managing the powerful life that I felt tearing through me, and trying to kill me. I saw a way: "Cry, what shall I cry?"—the dark Biblical overtone of the great poem; "the voice of one calling Stetson!" Oh, Eliot got hold of me at that early age and helped me speak for my own place.

The story-telling method of Eliot and Pound—darting, elliptical, circular, repetitive, lyric, self-revealing, simple speech within grand cadence and hyperbole, educated me and showed me a way to be taken out of my place, away from my obsessing relations: saved me from locality, from "regionalism." I knew then that it was "style" that would save me. I saw Pound as the most elegant of poets and the most elemental. Both. His madness partakes of both (elegance and elementalness) and is a quality of his poetry: "Hast 'ou seen the rose in the steel dust / (or swansdown ever?) / so light is the urging, so ordered the dark / petals of iron / we who have passed over Lethe." That's Canto 74, from the *Pisan Cantos*.

PHILLIPS: What of the Europeans?

GOYEN: Balzac above all, if just for the sheer fullness of story in him, for the life-giving detail in his novels. The daily *stuff* and the *fact* of his writing helped me struggle against a tendency toward the ornate and fantastical and abstract. Then come Flaubert, Proust. Of the English, Milton—a curious choice, right? The minor poems of Milton, but *Paradise Lost* above all. Milton's richness and grandness—his *scope*. I had an *epic* sense of my story, my material, and he helped me see it. Then Dante—the *Inferno*. Heine's poems—their sweet-sadness. The beautiful lyric poems of Goethe. Thomas Mann's stories, especially "Disorder and Early Sorrow," and *Buddenbrooks*. And some of the lyrical poems of Wordsworth. Poetry has been a strong influence on me, you see. I read it as often as fiction.

PHILLIPS: You weren't influenced by Faulkner in any way?

GOYEN: No, not at all. His work is monumental, and extremely important to me, but not in any way an influence. It goes along beside me—*Light in August, Absalom, Absalom*—but not through me. I can't say why, but I know that that's true. Maybe he's too *Southern*. If that is a tradition . . . I'm not part of that. Thank God for my southwestern-ness . . . that Texan thing. My father, I'm afraid, is a Southerner, a Mississippian, but my mother and her family for generations were native Texas people . . . so that was a strong influence. I knew a lot of my father's family; they're the people I've really written about in *The House of Breath*. But something kept me away from those sicknesses and terrors that come from that Deep South.

PHILLIPS: *The House of Breath* came out at the same time as other celebrated works—Styron's, Capote's, Mailer's. Did you feel part of a writing generation?

GOYEN: I felt immensely apart. And most certainly did not belong to any "writing generation." I remember, indeed, saying in an interview with Harvey Breit in 1950 in the *New York Times*, that I felt excited about joining the company of those writers, but that I had not before that time been aware of any of them! I stayed off to myself. I read nothing of "the literary world" when writing *The House of Breath*.

PHILLIPS: Subsequently, did you ever do any reviews of your contemporaries?

GOYEN: I reviewed *Breakfast at Tiffany's* for the *New York Times Book Review*. Actually it was a fair review . . . but it was critical. . . . I called Capote a valentine maker and said I thought he was the last of the valentine makers. Well, this just seemed to shake his life for the longest time.

PHILLIPS: Do your contemporaries interest you now?

GOYEN: They really don't interest me very much. I still feel apart and, well, I *am* apart from my contemporaries. And they don't know what to do about me, or they ignore me. I am led to believe they ignore me.

PHILLIPS: Hasn't that perhaps something to do with your books having been out of print for a decade or more, until recently?

GOYEN: No, I don't think so. How could it? My books have been in libraries, on reading lists in universities. Somebody was always writing a thesis or a paper on my work and writing to me for my help.

But: if I am so full of the books of all these people—Doris Lessing and John Updike and X and Y and Z—how will I have a clear head for anything of my *own*? I'm really not very interested in contemporary fiction, anyway. I consider my fiction absolutely separate and apart from and unrelated to "contemporary American fiction."

PHILLIPS: You feel closer to the European literary tradition?

GOYEN: I do.

PHILLIPS: Your books continued to remain in print in European editions long after they were unavailable here. Do you have any notion why that is?

GOYEN: No, unless it was because my books were translated by such eminent translators—Ernst Robert Curtius and Elizabeth Schnack in Germany, Maurice Edgar Coindreau in France.

PHILLIPS: All your novels have a rather unique form: they do not follow a linear line, for one thing. Did *The House of Breath* ever take form as a straightforward narrative and then later get broken down into monologues?

GOYEN: No, no, no. The form of that novel is the way it was written. It was slow, although it poured from me and a whole lot of it was simply *given* to me, absolutely put into my mouth. There were great stretches when nothing came. Then it poured out . . . in pieces, if that's possible. So I thought of it as fragments . . . that was what established its form. I once called it *Cries Down a Well*, and then I called it *Six Elegies*. Later it was *Six American Portraits*. So it came in pieces, but I knew that they were linked.

Part 2

PHILLIPS: What do you have against the linear novel?

GOYEN: I always *intend* to write a linear novel when I begin. It's my greatest ambition to write a straightforward novel, and I always feel that I am, you know. I get very close. I thought *Come, the Restorer* was very close to being a linear novel. Then people laughed at me when I finished and said that's not true at all.

PHILLIPS: What people?

GOYEN: Friends or interviewers, I suppose. What I end up writing each time, you see, is a kind of opera. It's a series of arias and the form is musical, despite myself, and it is lyrical. The outcry is lyrical despite myself. These novels have come to me at their height, passages have come to me in exaltation. So that the gaps between have been my problem and the—I was going to say—*quieter* . . . spaces and moments . . . but I don't mean that, because there are *many* quiet spaces in these books. But the less *intense* spaces seem to be hard for me to manage, somehow. What seems meant for me to do is always to begin what's called the linear novel, and try and try and try. . . .

PHILLIPS: Going back to form: Do you think of the novel as a lot of short stories, or as one big story? Or does it depend upon the novel?

GOYEN: It might. But it seems to me that the unified novel, the organic entity that we call a novel, is a series of parts. How could it not be? I generally make parts the way you make those individual medallions that go into quilts. All separate and as perfect as I can make them, but knowing that my quilt becomes a whole when I have finished the parts. It is the *design* that's the hardest. Sometimes it takes me a long time to see, or discover, what the parts are to form or make.

PHILLIPS: Does the completion of one "medallion" lead to another?

GOYEN: No, the completion of one medallion does not usually lead to another. They seem to generate, or materialize, out of themselves and are self-sufficient, not coupled to, or, often, even related to, any other piece. That seems to be what my writing job is: to discover this relationship of parts. Madness, of course, comes from not being able to discover any connection, any relationship at all! And the most disastrous thing that can happen is to *make up*, to *fake*, connections. In a beautiful quilt it looks like the medallions really grow out of one another, organic, the way petals and leaves grow. The problem, then, is to graft the living pieces to one another so that they finally become a living whole. That is the way I've had to work, whatever it means.

126

PHILLIPS: Have you made medallions that did not fit into the final quilt?

GOYEN: There's rarely been anything left over, that is, medallions that didn't fit into the final quilt. If the pieces didn't all come together, the whole failed. It's really as though all the pieces were around, hidden, waiting to be discovered, and there were just enough for the design on hand. If, in rare cases, something was left over, one tried to use it as some sort of preamble or "postlude"—that sort of fussy thing. It never worked, even when one felt it was such "fine" writing that it should be kept in. It's this kind of exhibitionism of bad taste that's harmed some good work by good writers.

PHILLIPS: So you started writing under a quilt and you came out producing quilts.

GOYEN: Producing them is right.

PHILLIPS: How else would you describe your own writing, or your style?

GOYEN: As a kind of singing. I don't say this because others have said it. But we've spoken of my work as song, earlier, the musicality of my writing and its form. It's impossible for me not to write that way. I write in cadence—that could be very bad. Just as in the theatre, when an actor in rehearsal discovers that lines in a speech rhyme, he or the director is horrified. Someone in the back of the theatre will scream out, "Couplet! Couplet!," meaning, "It rhymes! It rhymes!"

Now, when I speak of writing in cadence, I obviously don't mean "Couplet! Couplet!" Nor am I concerned with alliteration or any kind of fancy language. But I am concerned with the *flow* of language (the influence of Proust). I think of my writing as having to do with singing people: people singing of their lives, generally, arias. The song is the human experience that attracts me and moves me to write.

PHILLIPS: Are you concentrating now on short stories or novels?

GOYEN: I have less an urge to write the short story, and more of a concern with writing The Book. It has nothing to do with anything but my own lack of a need for the very short form and a deep love for the book itself, for a longer piece of writing.

PHILLIPS: Some may say you achieved both in *Ghost and Flesh*—a book of short stories which, on rereading, seems a total book rather than a collection of pieces. Was it conceived as a book, or was it a true gathering?

Part 2

GOYEN: No, it was conceived as a book, it truly was. A sort of song cycle, really, that made up a single, unified work, a thematic unity like Schubert's *Die Winterreise* (which influenced *The House of Breath*—an early Marian Anderson recording. Frieda Lawrence first made it known to me, that is, the poem on which the songs were based).

Ghost and Flesh . . . you can see in those stories . . . wow . . . quite surreal and I loved those, and when that was finished and published, I kind of went off the beam. I think the book made me quite mad; writing it, the obsession of that book; but, on the other hand, *The House of Breath* did not. And that's an obsessed book, you see. It's hard to say these things but something always pulled me through. Of course my critics might say, He *should* have gone mad.

PHILLIPS: What sort of madness was it?

GOYEN: While I wasn't that sane, I knew that madness—that's the word I use but I don't know if it's quite right—that dangerous thing . . . that terror, and I knew that. I guess I knew when to let it alone.

It comes in a loss of reality. If we say madness that sounds funny. But let's say an other-worldness. It has to do with identity. I go through phases of not knowing my own history. It's amnesiac, almost. I've known this all my life; as a child I've known that. The loss of the sense of the world around me, of the reality. It means that I just have to isolate myself and then I'm okay.

Also, I found a very strong wife. So my choices must have been blessed. God knows, when I brought her home to Texas, people gathered to meet her and congratulate us and one woman came over to me who had known me all my life and said, "My God, I can't tell you how relieved we all are. We thought you were going to bring home some *poetess*!"

PHILLIPS: Is writing a work of nonfiction markedly different for you from writing fiction? Did you derive equal satisfaction from reconstructing the life of Jesus (in *A Book of Jesus*) as you do composing a novel?

GOYEN: Oh, yes. The excitement was tremendous in writing that book. There was no difference in feeling between that and what I felt when I had written fiction. It was as though I were creating a character in this man. A marvelous experience. Astonishing. A very real man began to live with me, of flesh and blood. He did the same work on me that He did on the people of the New Testament that He walked among: He won me over, enchanted and captured me, finally possessed me. I went rather crazy with the love from Him that I felt. I carried a little New Testament around with me in my pocket and would flip it open and read what He said, at cocktail parties or at dinner tables. A surprising reaction from my listeners generally followed: they were struck by the simplicity, wit, and beauty of what the man said to others, particularly to the wonderful woman at the well.

PHILLIPS: How do you react to the charges of being a regional writer?

GOYEN: For me, environment is all. Place—as I was saying about my students—is absolutely essential. I know the vogue for the non-place, the placeless place, á la Beckett, is very much an influence on writing these days. It has been said that places don't exist anymore. That everything looks alike. There is the same Howard Johnson on your turnpike in Kansas as there is in Miami and in the state of Washington. And the same kind of architecture dominates the new office buildings and the skyscraper. What is a writer to do? Free the "reality" of his environment? To lament loss of place, to search for it in memory? Because within place is culture, style. We speak of a lost way of life. In many of my books and stories, I've felt the need to re-create, to restore lost ways, lost places, lost styles of living.

PHILLIPS: Isn't this what Marietta did in *In a Farther Country?* And what was expected of Mr. De Persia, in *Come, the Restorer?*

GOYEN: Exactly. So to this extent, then, I *am* a regional writer. In that my writing begins by being of a region, of a real place. It begins with real people talking like people from that place, and looking like them. Very often regional reality ends there and these people become other people, and this place becomes another place. The tiny town of Charity, in *The House of Breath*, is really Trinity, Texas, truly, accurately described. Once described, however, it ceases to be Charity or Trinity and becomes . . . well, London or Rome. The pasture in front of the house in Charity where a cow name Roma grazed becomes the Elysian Fields, and Orpheus and Eurydice flee across it. The house itself becomes a kind of Parthenon, with friezes of ancient kin.

I think there are moments when I exceed myself as a human being, and become Ulysses, perhaps, or Zeus. It is the point of time at which the human exceeds himself, is transformed beyond himself, that I most care about writing about. This is the lyrical, the apocalyptic, the visionary, the fantastic, the symbolic, the metaphorical, the transfiguratory, transfigurational—all those terms which have been applied to my work.

Now, by "exceeding myself as a human being" I mean in *life*—epiphany moments in life—not in *writing*. I mean those moments when human beings experience an epiphany, a transfiguration (that's the word) are the moments that most excite me. I've seen it in supreme artists who sang or danced or acted, in people who've told me they loved me, in those whose souls have suddenly been reborn before my eyes. These are moments and people I most care about writing about, no matter how small the moment, how humble the person. "I seen the little lamp," the transfigured child said at the end of the Katherine Mansfield story.

PHILLIPS: Are your closest friends writers? Is talking to other writers helpful or harmful to your work?

GOYEN: My closest friends are theatre people. Painters were once closest to me. For some years I lived among painters. But that changed. Now it's either performers or directors. I love theatre people, they give me a great deal. I don't particularly like writers, and I am not prone to talk about writing. Since they're solitary workers, writers tend to *act out* in public, I believe. They seem to carry more hostility maybe because they are responsible to more people (their characters), to a whole world—like God—than painters or actors. Maybe it's because writers are caught in the English language, which sometimes seems like a sticky web you can't pull your antennae out of, like insects I've watched in webs, and are, in public and when they're with other people, still thrashing about in an invisible web. It is *enraging* to work in words, sometimes; no wonder writers are often nervous and crazy: paint seems to be a more benevolent, a more soothing and serene-making medium.

Musicians always want to play for you, which is wonderful and wordless; painters seem to want to talk only about sex or point out to you the hidden genital configurations in their canvas! Since the writer is truly a seminal person (he spits out his own web, as Yeats said, and then, as I just said, gets caught in it), the truly creative writer, I mean, he's full of the fear and the pride that a maker of *new* things feel. So it's seemed to me.

PHILLIPS: After one of your books is done, do you divorce yourself from the characters, or do you seem somehow to maintain a contact with them?

GOYEN: Oh, the characters in my first novel haunt me to this day! Actually *haunt* me. And characters like Oil King (from *Come, the Restorer*), who's been in my life a long, long time. I've lived with him and loved him and written about him for many, many years. They stay with me, yes indeed they do. They stay. They not only enter my life, but I begin to see them in life, here, there. I see Marietta McGee quite frequently, in several cities. I had not dreamt she was down in Ensenada, Mexico, until recently when I was there. They seem absolutely to exist in life, when I've seen some of them transferred to the stage: like Oil King in *The Diamond Rattler*—it's as though they read for the part and got it—read for their own role. And Swimma Starnes crops up a lot.

PHILLIPS: How much of a plan do you have before you begin a novel or a play?

GOYEN: I plan quite a bit. But I'm not too aware of it. That is, I've not got it all down, but I've got a good deal of it thought through or *felt* through, before I begin writing. So that the whole world of it is very much alive and urgent for me. I'm surrounded by it—almost like a saturating scent. I feel it like a heat. The world that I'm going to write has already been created, somehow, in physical sensation before I go about writing it, shaping it, organizing it. My writing begins physically, in *flesh* ways. The writing process, for me, is the business of taking it *from* the flesh state into the spiritual, the letter, the Word.

PHILLIPS: Do you see, from *The House of Breath* to your latest novel, a progression? Do you see any new directions forthcoming?

GOYEN: There *is* a progression. I'm much freer. And I see a liberation of certain obsessive concerns in my work, a liberation towards joy! I feel that I'm much freer to talk about certain aspects of human relationships than I once was. . . . What was the other question?

PHILLIPS: Do you see any new directions in your subjects or forms?

GOYEN: That's very hard to say. I'd find that only as I write on. I *do* want very much to write a heavily plotted novel, a melodramatic novel.

PHILLIPS: Finally, a last question: Why do you write?

GOYEN: And the easiest to answer! I can't imagine *not* writing. Writing simply is a way of life for me. The older I get, the more a way of life it is. At the beginning, it was totally a way of life excluding everything else. Now it's gathered to it marriage and children and other responsibilities. But still, it is simply a way of life before all other ways, a way to observe the world and to move through life, among human beings, and to record it all above all and to shape it, to give it sense, and to express something of myself in it. Writing is something I cannot imagine living without, nor scarcely would want to. Not to live daily as a writing person is inconceivable to me.

Interview, 1982

This interview was taped at Goyen's house in Los Angeles, the first three days of November 1982. We went once to his writing studio, also, in a shabby office building on the fabled corner of Hollywood and Vine—a location that delighted him. In the studio were a high, homely writing table and stool, a desk, and a filing cabinet containing many of Goyen's manuscripts, copies of which were also stacked on the desk. But in his house, in his study, which was a room with mock-adobe walls and even a round corner fireplace of the kind found in New Mexico adobe houses, Goyen had made himself at home—had "nested," as he liked to say.

The transcript cannot show the range of tones of voice that animated, punctuated, and emphasized Goyen's statements. Most to be missed in the printed version is his laughter. Unexpectedly, at moments of seriousness or in pondering somber subjects, Goyen would heartily, delightedly, laugh, as if with wonder, with an unselfconscious and entirely becoming sense of amazement at the complexity and mysteriousness of the things he was talking about. Perhaps such laughter came partly from what Flannery O'Connor characterized as a daze writers enter when they look longer and more fixedly at things others merely glance at. "The longer you look at an object, the more of the world you see in it," she said, echoing William Blake. But beyond that, Goyen's wonder seemed to me of the deep sort that Plato calls the source of philosophy and poetry—of theogony and myth. Given Goyen's last works, no other attitude could be more appropriate, for both his language and his material seem now to be aimed at shaping stories in which the mysterious course of human action and of human speech reveals the presence of compelling outer powers—whether it is the command of the "black-winged figure" over others in "Tongues of Men and of Angels" or the simple awareness that, as a storyteller speaks, another figure speaks through him.

Interview conducted by Reginald Gibbons in *TriQuarterly*, no. 56 (Winter 1983): *101–125*. © 1983 by *TriQuarterly*, a publication of Northwestern University. Reprinted by permission.

What I did not know when interviewing Goyen was that despite his apparent recovery from serious illness, he knew himself to be in mortal peril and was keeping this knowledge entirely to himself. It is likely that this knowledge was what spurred him to invite the interview, for he told me, when he suggested it, that there were certain things he wanted to record not by writing them down but by *saying* them: things about writing, style, and other matters. In light of his work and of the analysis offered in part 1, this intention can come as no surprise. Goyen's fascination with the *situation* of narration, of human intercourse through speech, permeated not only his fiction but also, as this interview evidences, his thinking about fiction.

> What starts you writing?
> It starts with trouble. You don't think it starts with peace,
>   do you?

GIBBONS: A passage from "Nests in a Stone Image" [*CS*] could serve as epigraph for all your work:

> He had come here out of some loss and bereavement and to sit
> and have back again, as it wanted to come back to him, with
> whatever face or feature, shape or name, what he had lost; to
> turn back into what had happened and let it speak to him and,
> out of his listening, make it all over again, this time, at least,
> to control it and keep it from chaos again, to give it its meaning
> that it waited for. . . . This was what claimed him.

GOYEN: I found a kind of statement for myself there, didn't I?— through real deep suffering. It's really meditation. It's kind of a salvation—a lot of those pieces are really my little salvation pieces: they represent my being rescued again from deep suffering.

GIBBONS: Rescued by what?

GOYEN: I felt that I was rescuing myself. I got a sense of myself, in a flash. It was a spiritual experience, of course. And with that clarification, I was able to move on out of what might have destroyed me. I don't know that I have ever felt that I have been lifted by a higher power—a god or anything. By divinity. It must have been art, then—

a sense of one's self suddenly frees him, at least for that time, and one is able then to go on.

GIBBONS: The story is quite free of what readers normally expect from a story—

GOYEN: God bless them!

GIBBONS: —it doesn't give them a plot or character development.

GOYEN: But I see that it was a form I found for myself, and used over and over again, in a whole body of work, without knowing that I was using it. I didn't put it up on the wall and say, "This is the form I will now follow." But it was deep pain, a feeling of utter isolation and removal from the community of human beings—that kind of lostness. And then, through an acuteness of feeling and an awareness of things around me, coming back to life, through life around me—in this case— in the story you quoted from, "Nests in a Stone Image"—people in the rooms around the speaker in the story. In his misery and isolation he was surrounded by human beings, all singing and making love and talking, and life was in those rooms around him, and then rising. It was always the rising action, that I felt, over and over again.

GIBBONS: That's what you mean by the sense of form?

GOYEN: Coming up, yes, from the bottom, rising to the top and then being freed of that pain and being *identified*, is surely what it was, wasn't it?

The form was new each time. But two things—it's about love, and total giving in love till there was nothing left, total faith in life and love; and then feeling destroyed and abandoned, and then finding again . . . through life going on. Despite my misery, life was just going on! Those were such great revelations, do you know that? Suddenly you heard people next door saying, "Well, do we need eggs? Well, let's see, we need eggs, bread. . ." They're making a list of groceries! And writing checks. That life was restored to me, so often not through great bursts of something, like St. Paul's revelation, but through just the trivial, which I still hold to, the everyday trivial detail. That has always pulled me through.

"Nests in a Stone Image" Katherine Anne [Porter] cared a great deal for, and I read it to her, I read her a lot of these stories, I was writing these stories when I was close to her, in the early fifties. She was not able to write at all, then; she was tremendously shut down. She wanted to hear, yet she was really—really she could have murdered me. She listened *murderously*. Once, when I finished reading a new story to her

135

(it was "Children of Old Somebody" [*CS*], which I've dedicated to her, for that reason), she stood and walked up and down the floor and cursed at me. She had all the feelings of a writer who couldn't realize her own work. I read a lot of newly finished work to her in those days in New York in the early fifties. I had never done this before with anyone. But Katherine Anne was so close to my work then and so impoverished and cut off, I hoped I could help her to work again. She, indeed, invited me to share my work with her.

GIBBONS: Do you remember having conversations with her about questions like this—the form that you felt was peculiar to your stories?

GOYEN: We discussed that a great deal. I told her I felt submerged in life, given love and work and vision—and that suddenly I felt drowned. It was always almost a water image, and then it was only when I was able to rise from the depths that I could go on. So that each time these memory pieces were being written—"People of Grass," that whole group of stories set in Rome—it's someone who has lost his way. *The House of Breath* is just the great mother-shape, isn't it? It begins with someone who has lost his way. His own name, even. Through the detail of people in life around me, through their simply saying, you know, "We've got hemorrhoids, and the peas in the garden are all burnt up"—it was the simple detail of everyday struggle—this character was always brought back in these stories to some realization. And then there was an apostrophe to something at the end, often in italics. It embarrassed me later but now I think it's O.K. A great utterance—he has lived to utterance, he can speak! As in *The House of Breath*, speech is found for what is not spoken.

GIBBONS: Why did you feel embarrassed by that?

GOYEN: I suppose I felt—you know, we go through periods of restraint. And now I'm very pleased that I got the pure feeling down on paper, but there was a time when I felt (probably in the sixties—those stories were written in the fifties) that I wanted to be more restrained. Burst at deeper depths. Not detonate right on the ground!

GIBBONS: You often mention "listening" in "Nests in a Stone Image," and I gather you listen when you work. But you told me you didn't entirely trust what Arcadio was saying, in your new novel.

GOYEN: I am responsible as the listener—the responsibility lies with the listener, the re-teller, not the teller, and my responsibility is to know when I'm hearing madness or to know how to give *on* what *I've* heard, because what I'm talking about is the continuity of listening, telling, listening. The listener needs a listener, then, when he now begins to tell the tale *on*. This is what everything I've ever written seems to be about. I see that now, yet if I sat down and thought that, when I wrote, I'd fall, like the centipede trying to count his own legs to see which moves when, over into the ditch.

So I'm telling *again*. "Twice-told tales," Hawthorne called them.

GIBBONS: The telling of the story, not its substance, is the meaning, then.

GOYEN: It has a spiritual significance. Someone wrote that about my work—that the liberating, therefore spiritual, significance of storytelling was in the very telling itself, a kind of a prayer or meditation or apotheosis of feeling, a dynamic spiritual action. So: the need to tell, on the part of a lot of characters I have written about, like Raymon Emmons ["Ghost and Flesh," *CS*].

But in some writers what one gets is diction more than voice. That is, it's *thick speech*, rather than voice. There's a great difference between speech and voice. "Correcting" the speech of my characters, as some copy editors wish to do, affects the voice. That's the pitfall of some writers, some of the Southern writers, who get hung up on diction and speech. Synge was in danger of that, too. There is a quality of voice that is, I guess, undefinable. I feel I know what that is, and I have to wait for it, and that determines my work: voice. I can't fake it, and I can't find it if it's not there. I have to hear it. This I know for myself. Sometimes the voice, the same voice, tells me a bunch of stories.

People in my life told me stories, and I sang. They had the speech, and I got the voice. And I place the burden for that difference on angels, good and bad. Some people seem to have a good angel, or a bad one (can there be bad angels?), and yet some have none at all.

GIBBONS: Still, you have to work at the art—the angel's not going to do the work for you, is it?

GOYEN: But it can put a tongue in my mouth for a little while ["Tongues of Men and of Angels," *HIHM*]. That's what happened to me.

When I first rode a bicycle, I couldn't ride it without my father pushing me, holding me there, and I said, "But what am I going to do? Don't let loose! Don't let loose!" (We had just a little hill.) He said, "Son, I wouldn't let you aloose, don't you worry." And one day, he *had*, and I was going right along! And I looked back, and he wasn't there, and I was doing it! From then on I rode the bicycle.

Now, when I'm really working, really writing, I have the feeling it's coming from outside of me, through me. An absolute submission, absolute surrender. It's being *had*, being possessed. I'm being used.

GIBBONS: Are you very curious to define that "it" that is using you?

GOYEN: No. I recognize it, and know when it's *not* there. It's like being in love, or being mad—all those radical emotions.

GIBBONS: Are you reluctant to talk about it?

GOYEN: There's something in me that shuts it off.

GIBBONS: Is it like that moment when Dante describes Virgil and Statius walking ahead, speaking of poetry, and Dante won't repeat what they said?

GOYEN: I'm not able to talk about it. St. Paul speaks of the inexpressible, what you *don't* repeat. There are some revelations I have, he said, that there are no words for, and why should I try? There is a reticence.

GIBBONS: In an interview with William Peden, you said "the storyteller is a blessed force in telling his story to a listener; a redemptive process occurs, and it's therefore a spiritual situation, and one cannot avoid that." What do you mean, "a spiritual situation"?

GOYEN: It has to do first of all with distinguishing simply between spiritual and material. It's not, "How much am I going to get for it?" And if it doesn't have to do with tangible rewards, then it has to do with intangible ones, with my spirit, with my own yearning toward something higher than I, something by definition divine, some outer higher power working through me, that I have no power over or at least did not create.

I remember Marian Anderson was my first experience with what truly was a spiritual moment. Suddenly when she sang she was purely an instrument for the spirit, pure spirit. Through her mouth, here was this blessed moment, the light and the fire were on *her*, way beyond her training or the song itself. I was sixteen; I identified thoroughly, purely, with her. "That's where I belong, I come from that," I said. "That's why I feel so alone, because I belong to whatever that was."

GIBBONS: You wrote some poems once. What is the difference between the fictional and poetic impulses, to your mind?

GOYEN: The poems aren't very good—they're not poems. I have no interest in the form of poetry, in the *lines*. I really care about the fiction and style and speech and form, and that seems to be wholly the way I wish to work. I'm refining that more and more, and I feel great control, most of the time, when I'm really down *on it*. I feel the weight of all those lines I've written. I know a lot more about that instrument. But the impulse is to tell *on*, to reveal, and to be absolutely *un-self-censoring*. Not to hold back because I feel it might be unseemly or offensive or whatever. I never did feel censored. But I spent some time wrestling to make a decision again, not to be censored. I don't any more. I trust the impulse now, or the vision of it. I may think I'm *mad* for a moment—so I wait. I do all the things an artist does; I wait. When revising I do whatever I can for the form of it, the art of it, the clarity of it. I have the sweep of the story from the beginning, and the imagery of it develops, astonishingly, almost like a bone structure. *Arcadio* is another kind of *aria*, though.

GIBBONS: Two sorts of stories in your work seem distinguished from each other by your presence in them, as narrator. Stories like "Old Wildwood" [*CS*] seem almost memoir, and very unlike "The White Rooster" [*CS*].

GOYEN: But I think the stories like "Nests in a Stone Image" are delivered beyond that. I was freed, myself, as the experiencer of things (as in "Old Wildwood") to see the revelation of stone and wood and the eternal city and a little town fading away.

GIBBONS: You don't seem to feel that a story *needs* to be cut loose from the writer, needs to be consciously taken away from autobiographical sources?

GOYEN: Katherine Anne [Porter] kept feeling that, she kept feeling that it had to be cut away finally, all strings cut away from the bearer of it, as if it were a bunch of balloons.

GIBBONS: Did she think it was terribly unsophisticated otherwise?

GOYEN: She did, yet she saw that her salvation was in *not* cutting herself free. And this is why she sat down and committed a fairly unseemly act in writing a novel called *Ship of Fools*. She cut some strings loose, and others not. Her prejudices and her bigotries were quite cut away; she was caught—holding a lot of things aloft, maybe balloons. The hand that is holding those strings is absolutely essential to the aloft-ness of the story. She says in the end, cut them all free, and the hand is gone that held them.

GIBBONS: Didn't Eliot and Pound, whom you count as useful influences on you, cut those things away and conceal the hand?

GOYEN: They held some strings more than we know. Who did cut away all of them? I was constantly told that that was naughty, to hold on that way, if my hand was visible. That was not desirable, for some reason. And I kept saying—Well, to hell with you, was about all I said, but not without worrying, "How will I get my hand free? How will I erase my own clutching hand?" Even in stories like "The White Rooster" I didn't *strive* to remove myself, and the body of my work is made up of both kinds of stories. Now you see the hand, and now you don't.

GIBBONS: In "Had I a Hundred Mouths" [*HIHM*] you reveal the hand at the beginning, in the presence of the two nephews, one of whom will tell this story again, later. But then Ben delivers the tale, and that listening presence, that nephew, who is the hand holding the strings, disappears, until the end, when with a startling effect the nephew's voice speaks, and there's the hand again.

GOYEN: That happens often in my stories—as in "The Faces of Blood Kindred" [*CS*].

GIBBONS: So if the invisible hand is the modern, or the sophisticated, then to hell with that?

GOYEN: Well, *yes!* All I ask is that living voice.

GIBBONS: What's the connection between this sense of the visible hand and what you call listening?

GOYEN: Finally, and foremost, we're speaking of the person, the personal. What clears the way for me is listening, finding the listener. In terms of craft, too. Often I begin by telling what I know, what I'm feeling, in terms of myself, but soon I know that that can't go very far, to my own satisfaction, that I'm caught in a web that is self-begetting. And that doesn't interest me. I have to be freed to let somebody tell *me* what I'm telling, and I know the voices, very often. It's often a woman's voice talking to me. It's someone who is trying to make it clear to me—you see, I'm not clear about what I'm telling: somebody else has to make it clear for me. I get all mixed up. And somebody keeps editing me, and saying, "That's not right, listen to me, what I'm trying to tell you is. . ." This helps me tell the story. I have to have help! It also removes me another step. I keep trying to step out of it, as the speaker—I don't want it to be my memoir, my reminiscence, it's much more than that, it's Rome, not Charity, Texas, finally. It's ancient ancient fossils in stone instead of a clapboard house ["Old Wildwood"].

GIBBONS: What's your sense of the occasion of a story? What starts you writing?

GOYEN: It starts with trouble. You don't think it starts with peace, do you? It's an occasion that brings a whole cluster of occasions together.

GIBBONS: You don't worry about the connections between them?

GOYEN: No. The bridges start forming. That's the fun sometimes, and the slavery too, in making the bridges. They are always implied, because they come of their own volition, I feel.

Trusting the connection *is* the process of work.

Everything I've written has been generated that way. I once spoke of medallions: when my mother made a quilt, she made what she called medallions first, a whole bunch of separate pieces. They don't do the whole quilt at once! When these were all together—till then, you don't see the connections, but it makes a whole.

GIBBONS: I think of your work as domestic in a similar sense.

GOYEN: I understand. One of those stories I saw as a kite—and we used to make our own kites. The idea of buying a kite! *Who* bought a kite? We made it out of stuff at home. String, newspaper—and it flew, it flew. But it was made domestically. That's what you call domestic invention. The cruder the better, sometimes. I think of writing as that very often. I'm most comfortable with things that happen at home.

Without art . . . would I just have been a kind of evangelist?

GOYEN: Style is, or has been, for me, the spiritual experience of my material.

GIBBONS: How do you mean, "spiritual"?

GOYEN: Well, people say craft, and I'm talking on the other side of craft. Of course, I know my craft, I know what I will let go and what I won't, and I know when it's not the best. More and more I know about the control of words. But I'm talking about the spiritual experience of Arthur Bond [*HIHM*]—to have experienced those characters and the world they have created around them through their own infirmities or . . . life in the world, has become a spiritual revelation of the human being that I would not have got by studying the work of other writers.

GIBBONS: What's the bridge between that experience and the words that make up the story?

GOYEN: The bridge is the transformation. An artist transforms. He can't just stay where life is as he finds it, not at just the *level of life*. Or so it is for me: the art of it becomes the transformation that must occur of that spiritual experience into the controlled craft so that the vision is tied down, is anchored everywhere, by craft. "Arthur Bond" had to be anchored in all kinds of detail, and mostly painterly detail—there was some yellow (the color came to me), the worm with the head of a doll: it all became very pictorial for me. But the man was caught in a spiritual wrestling. This was what I experienced first, his wrestling. "It is not his fall you see, but this man's wrestling," Shakespeare said about one of the kings.

GIBBONS: The word "spiritual" then doesn't mean "religious"?

GOYEN: Not at all. It has to do with a certain program of action. By that I mean I don't come into this experience to get my eyebrows longer, or my muscles stronger, or my belly flatter. So it is therefore *not physical*. O.K.? That's as clear as I can make it. Something else is involved beyond the corporeal. Shall we all start there? I can't define it any more than that. That's what I mean by my spirit. It is not my body. So let's go away from whatever we think of as physical and try to get into an area that is non-corporeal. Something happens to me which changes my attitude toward . . . you? What is that? It's not that you've given me a lot of money, or bought me a house, or given me a reward. What changed my attitude toward you? Something, I say, came from outside me. And I see as I say this that I tend to look up, because we've been told that heaven is above us, though it may not be at all, it may be quite lateral, I don't know. But it has come from beyond me somewhere, it is not anything I have learned, been taught, or even done. So that the *spirit* is involved in this change of feeling between me and you.

Style, then, is directly related to that experience. So that style is a spiritual manifestation of the experience of the story, for me. My stories *are* spiritual.

And yet there are an awful lot of *genitalia* in them.

GIBBONS: Why is that?

GOYEN: That's spiritual, too, I guess. "Ghost and Flesh," I wrote—one's expressed right through the other, for me.

GIBBONS: Is there some writing that, you feel, doesn't have this spiritual element?

GOYEN: I don't feel it's in most contemporary writers that I try to read. I feel that they really are too busy with repeating themselves, and repeating their own success, not necessarily material.

GIBBONS: But despite your artistic intransigence on this point, I know that as a person you have been extremely generous and helpful to many writers who haven't displayed much of the spiritual in this sense, at all, haven't reached that level of art.

GOYEN: I've tried to lead them toward it, I guess. That's all I can give them. An opening out. That's obviously why they have come to *me*. I'm not proselytizing and I'm not looking for disciples. I think that's my freedom as a teacher—I don't think people should write like me. I couldn't, by my nature, stay very long in a classroom, teaching. I've started out thinking, this is a class about craft, and that's what we'll be about. But halfway through it I soared into this other thing, we're off into another realm. I can't talk about writing very long without talking about seeing that *possible* transformation. And this is what I talk about a lot. There has to be a change, some change has to pass over what happens to me, what I experience. It seems to come from a deeper reality than a knowledge of what *literary device* I can use to bring the change.

So I like to talk about style that way, and maybe finally I will write about it a little. In the past few years I've had fresh experience with these things—style, image, and life-writing—in my work. Image brings a spiritual revelation of the very life-material itself.

GIBBONS: Do you mean both the small-scale image, the occasional thing—

GOYEN: No I mean the larger . . . I don't say Symbol because I mean a concrete image, and it is concrete. It comes abstractly to me, but then my problem is to transform it into the concrete. The drowned (in sand) diving figure in "Bridge of Music, River of Sand" [*CS*] is an example. I was haunted by that *image*, to begin with.

GIBBONS: "Had I a Hundred Mouths" seems to demonstrate something of what you mean by style as a spiritual transformation of the experience or the material. But the second part ["Tongues of Men and of Angels"] is very different, a flamboyant explosion and fragmentation of stories, so many different ones. How do you come to shape a piece like that?

GOYEN: It's odd that I chose to keep each little tombstone—is that what they are? That's what appears to be the peculiar form of the story, that it's in lives, in the shape of about five lives.

GIBBONS: As if you had set a little cemetery around Leander's empty grave, since we don't know where he is. Is he a kind of touchstone for the others, his tale—of being begotten by lust and condemning himself with it and being made to suffer for it—the origin of their stories?

GOYEN: You could see that the teller was preoccupied, at the beginning, with how some people just put down everything they have and go away from it. And how some do come back and how, if they do, some force has totally changed them. He's perplexed by that. *That's* what he has to tell.

GIBBONS: But it's not Ben who's telling the tale.

GOYEN: No, that's the point, the voice has changed, the voice is really the nephew. He's in a search. When I first wrote *The House of Breath*, and it was published in that very form, in *Accent*, it was called "Four American Portraits as Elegy." I wrote four lives: "Aunty," "Christy," "Swimma," and "Folner." *In a Farther Country* is written the same way. And so is *Come, the Restorer.* This too is style.

GIBBONS: It seems less style than shape.

GOYEN: It *is* shape. The design is the last thing that comes, for me, yet it is the first thing, as well as the last. But without it I'm lost. I get it early. But then I have to lose it, and the feeling is that I'll never get it back. But finally it's the design that I'm able to see, specifically, the architecture of it. The two parts of this new story were pretty much of a whole, and actually the second part is contained in the first few pages of the first. It is *there*. All these people seem to me to be out of some book of the accurst. They're evil figures. They're demonic figures. They frightened *me* to death, those three sisters! Or they're just spiteful figures, or just nuisance figures. But the horror of the Klan, the blackness of that, the evil of them, just pervaded that whole land. And there always seemed to be henchmen of it, and it seemed to be a nightmare of mutiny and banditry. This is the world I was in.

GIBBONS: At the end of "Had I a Hundred Mouths," the narrating nephew sees his cousin in white sheet and hood, with others. Then that Klan nephew is tormented and tortured by the Klan in the second part of the work, for having spoken of their doings.

GOYEN: Because he told their secrets. And what were they? That they had had children by black women, and that they had hanged black men for fucking white women. They had scapegoats. Those are horrors, horrors! A medieval world of terror. You know it *was* like that, to me; as a child I really felt that. I lived around all of that. There was a man preaching the salvation of my soul in a tent across the road from my house, but up on the hill beyond there the Ku Klux were burning their crosses and I saw them run tarred and feathered Negroes through the street. I saw them running like that, twice. Aflame. We stood and watched that.

GIBBONS: What sort of reactions were apparent in those around you?

GOYEN: They were terrified. Just as if you were a Jew and those were Nazis. Most of them simply lived in terror and hid. It was that kind of world, as I saw it. And it could only have to do later with the brutality that I wrote about and also with salvation. It was also full of the erotic and the sensual and all that, for me, too. It was a maelstrom, it was a cauldron.

GIBBONS: Does that world seem another universe now, as if you were writing about something you could present only emblematically, that sort of horror?

GOYEN: How is it another universe? It seems very contemporary. If they murdered how many hundreds in those camps in Beirut . . . the terrorism around us. . . . Hollywood is a town of absolute terroristic violence. It's a cursed place. It's full of a violence that comes out of a whole lot of things, but out of abuse, and persecution. . . .
   But the town, the environment, which for me was the river and the fields, and the wonderful things that bloomed, that are so much in my stories, was still stalked by some horror all around it. And the tale I heard—a whole lot of that is stated in "The Icebound Hothouse" [*HIHM*]. That story comes to be about that. And at the end there is an apotheosis, again, to say, "Why did I ever think that that house, that door, where I'd like to go home, that promised hospitality to the one who was arriving—why did I think that there were all sunny stories of joy and laughter?" The door is a dark door. Who chose that door?

Who is the dark presence in that house? This is a culmination for me of the *House of Breath* metaphor, all these years later—this is what I came upon in finishing this story. So it is a precious door again [*HIHM*].

And now as I grow older and I go through these experiences—of almost dying, and changes of place, as from the East to the West, here—I keep getting closer to those images of terror and horror, as well as of the sublime pastoral garden.

GIBBONS: So there's a way to redeem that experience?

GOYEN: Yes, and it's art and the holy spirit, which are one for me, more and more. Without art, without the process of memory, which is the process of art, and the spiritual experience of it, which for me is style, what else would I do about it? Would I be an addict? Would I be dead from alcoholism and addictions of one kind or another? Would I just have been a kind of evangelist?

GIBBONS: Are you saying holy spirit with small h and small s?

GOYEN: Well, you know, I tend to capitalize where other people always strike things down to l.c. That means that I'm elevating it, somewhere, that's what it means in my head, and I insist on keeping that, because it is somehow elevating it beyond the pedestrian lower case.

I think there's no such thing as meaningless suffering, and this is spoken by someone who sees the terror of life. You know, there's a recent book called *The Horror of Life?* Of course, I bought that faster than I'd buy something called *Days in My Garden*. And it's the lives of five people who all view life as horrible. Their life-view was one of horror and fear. Baudelaire, De Maupassant, Flaubert, Jules de Goncourt, Daudet. It turned out that they were all syphilitic and had a horrible disease. I'm not talking about that. I'm not talking about the horror of life. But the horrible and the terrible element in life. Why would I endure life if I thought *life* was horrible? What good would I gain by enduring? Enduring is a hopeful action.

GIBBONS: Flannery O'Connor said in answer to those who criticized the apparently despairing content or material of modern novels, that people without hope don't write novels.

GOYEN: Of course it's an act of hope, and faith. Art is redeeming, and art is an affirmation. There's no other way. The creation, the result, may not be very wonderful in some cases, or even very good, but I'm given joy and faith again through watching people's impulse to make something, and their energy in making it, their willingness to make something.

GIBBONS: You also seem to agree with Lowell, however, that poetry is *not* a craft. Do you think that the craft-mentality of the writing schools is all right? Does craft drive out art?

GOYEN: I don't think that's possible. Art won't have it. There's no way possible to substitute anything for art. I believe in the absolute hegemony of art, and craft can't hurt it.

GIBBONS: You have said that "elegance in fiction frightens me, and exquisiteness." Even if you were speaking there of style, I suspect that "elegance" applies also to the impulse to wrap things up a little too neatly. *You* certainly leave a lot of things just flapping their wings in the air. That can seem to mean something in itself. Do you worry about being too symbolic?

GOYEN: No. I don't have any worry about being symbolic, I don't think I'm symbolic. Arcadio *has* got two genitals—

GIBBONS: But you take a figure like Leander, and you castrate him. He is de-sexed; he is half white, half black. He was a man and is no longer a man; Arcadio is half man and half woman: these things are emblematic. Not that I can put a ready meaning to them, but you seem to be interested in more than the shape of a man, you're interested in the significance of the shape of a man.

GOYEN: And yet, you know, how emblematic is a woman with one breast? I saw a great photograph yesterday in a bookstore, a huge life-size photograph of a very beautiful woman with a wonderful breast, and on the other side was a tattoo of roses across no breast at all. She had had one removed, and yet the photographer was saying, "This is all right. This is beautiful. Don't be horrified. She *has* one breast!" But it was a *creature:* it seemed almost like Leander. I said, "What a defamation of a beautiful thing!" I heard myself say that. "How *defaming* to take a breast off her! How they slaughter women in the name of cancer." But I was with a woman, and she said, "But look how beautiful, it's all right." So I caught myself. It was kind of a wreath of roses tattooed. So that is very emblematic—that's what I'm talking about: there's a breast, I could *suck* that breast! That's very exciting. On the other hand, there's a kind of monster.

GIBBONS: And a kind of symbol? Not a real rose, but the picture of a rose?

147

GOYEN: No, a woman, who is saying, "I am a woman, and I am beautiful still."

GIBBONS: Is it the physically grotesque that interests you?

GOYEN: I really mean more of a spiritual deformity. Of course, dwarves, and humpbacks, and harelips, and so forth. That's only the beginning for me. I can't linger on that very long but it delivers me from the boring reality of realistic reporting. Since I am *not* writing Zola-istic realism, then everyday reality, the detail of it, is obviously not going to sustain itself for me, forever. I'm not Dreiser, I'm not interested in that at all. I'm aware that there is no everyday trivia in itself; that beneath it, or going on within it, there's always some slight deformity of thought or action. It's the hidden life I'm talking about.

I'm not writing within the vogue for the bizarre. My insights are deeper and deeper into what we're talking about, and the revelations that are coming to me make me more and more aware of an overwhelming imagery of the crude and the violent, but I mean more than that. I suppose it's always been with me, and I can see it back in *The House of Breath*, my earliest work. It really has more to do with tenderness, rather than less. It's not hardness of heart that is happening. I see more and more brutality, and the metaphor that exists in brutality. It may be that in my earlier work I gentled that, but I see it more now. It begins in the latter half of *Arcadio*, for me, and continues on through Leander's story ["Had I a Hundred Mouths"] and the last I've written ["Tongues of Men and of Angels"].

GIBBONS: Far from the sorrow and the wonder and gratefulness that surround the erotic in "Ghost and Flesh," you've moved to consider it a dark power.

GOYEN: True.

GIBBONS: A dark power over men, not a mystery in their lives that is constructive or renewing.

GOYEN: Yes. It *was* a great power, that's true. I'm really astonished by all that, myself, it's still new for me, I have no hypothesis about it yet. Where I am in this work—and it's leading me more and more—there's a tenderness, always, at the core. "Had I a Hundred Mouths" is a tender story—the love of that man, and the love of the black man: those people have a tenderness that is almost old-fashioned. But what I really see is that within that tenderness is a brutality and a striking violence of feeling and action. It has nothing to do with disillusionment—I was never more spiritual in my life. It has nothing to do with losing faith, or any of those clichés. It's that the light is on *that* now, I *see* that: I see lust as demonic. I have never known it to be anything else! Have you? Good Lord! The lust is the very devil working, a demon in me—*my* lust. I don't know about anybody else's. I've had a demon in me.

GIBBONS: How can *la Santa Biblia* and that lust inhabit the same creature, as they do in Arcadio?

GOYEN: It's the human arrangement, it's just our very nature, I think. It created people like St. Paul, but oddly enough it didn't create a man like Jesus, did it? We don't think of Jesus as a lustful man, but it's very possible that Paul was—he's so angry against women, against marriage, against sex.

GIBBONS: Is that fruitful anger?

GOYEN: Fruitful in his case—he did a lot of good work, and he did walk among real violent, lustful characters—all those Romans! I think lust is a very rare feeling, and one of the grand emotions. Arcadio is a grand figure of lust and tenderness, I think.

GIBBONS: With a Bible in his hand?

GOYEN: Sure. Redemption is what he was looking for. And the Bible is the handbook of redemption. It's the song at the end of a life, he's an old man, in his seventies. And he seems a bit deranged, too— I don't know *what* he is! He's gone a bit mad. I'm not sure how much is true and how much is false of what he's telling me at the end. He's now such a fabricator that he's one of the *great* fabricators.

GIBBONS: Near the end of an interview, in French, you mentioned St. Francis, and the sense that certain saints had of sexuality, of the erotic and the sensual. I think the popular image of St. Francis is of someone feeding the birds from his open hand, and not of him as a sensual creature.

GOYEN: Have you ever fed a bird? It's very exciting. These holy people were walking around with the same impulses that I have, or else they wouldn't be able to reach me. They had the same equipment that I have, if they were men, the same desire, man or woman. Those desires were not submerged; they exist; the Pope perhaps wakes with a hard-on.

I think there is an inevitable confrontation with the spiritual in every human life at some time or other.

GIBBONS: Right in the most sensual experience? Eating?

GOYEN: Coming. Absolutely. Certainly all the nailing, and the Penitente things, are sensuous. No: sensual.

GIBBONS: You want the word that seems more animal?

GOYEN: Yes. The French *sensuelle* is the word that applies to all those almost genital actions. St. Francis to my mind was a genital human being. St. Theresa was—she no doubt menstruated. This is what I mean—this helps me to find purity and holiness. It's even there in the act of hiding away: like that woman in my story, Inez Melendrez McNamara, who went into that convent ["Tongues of Men and of Angels"]. Her hair became more and more sexual. Her body itself became more voluptuous.

GIBBONS: At the same time, *Arcadio*, like Leander's story, leads to genital horrors.

GOYEN: I see people who have emasculated each other. I see people who have been made Leanders of, by wives and husbands, by lovers. My God, the brutality of love-relationships! A mastectomy would be more benevolent than what men do to women's bodies sometimes, making them loathe their bodies or abusing them or hating them or whatever. That's why that picture of that woman with one breast, and one scar, was such an *affirmation:* She said "I am beautiful." So that in a way Leander means that to *me*—as much as all the other abuses of whites upon blacks, and so on. People render each other sexless, finally; they can castrate each other, and the denial can close up the genitals of a woman and she can grow together. She's been denied that, or it's been abused.

A lot of that is in Leander.

GIBBONS: And in *Arcadio*, especially in characters like Arcadio's father and Johna, the whore who is with him when he dies.

GOYEN: *Those* people live for their genitals *only*. She had a *máquina* between her legs, that was an absolute machine, and they were *purely* genital, and that's death.

> I feel everything of mine is on the ground, now, but not gathered. There are still some things on the tree, that have to get ripe, but the great body of my work is on the ground, but not gathered.

GIBBONS: You have prepared a new selection of your stories, and you seem to want a larger audience for this book in particular—not that any writer doesn't want the largest audience possible.

GOYEN: I've been thinking about the curious kind of recognition that I have experienced, a curious misreading or misjudging of my work, I think. Or misplacing! I suppose I don't need an explanation for it, and the reason I may seem to be asking for one is that I don't understand it when people say my work has been ignored in Texas or the country as a whole, and it has such an audience in Europe. I used to get sick over that, to suffer over it, and something seemed wrong. I was turning out work, and it seemed worthy of being recognized, I mean of being *acknowledged*, at least. Acknowledgment of my existence as an American writer: neither praise, not dispraise, but, "Here!"— with my hand up. "Present!"

GIBBONS: I think this has partly to do with a climate of expectation among readers who are more used to what I'll call "writing" than to what I'll call "art." A literary climate formed by trivial or superficial or inconsequential or over-intellectualized or journalistic work may leave readers disabled in the presence of powerful feeling.

GOYEN: But who disables them? Where is that perpetuated? This is probably the bafflement of my life. But I could either let it obsess me and take the place of my work, which is what many people do . . . or I can keep working.

GIBBONS: What's the particular forcefulness of your work? It is quite different from much contemporary fiction, which seems emotionally barren by comparison, though the other is also, by that token, not as emotionally exhausting as your work, either, especially your recent work.

GOYEN: Well, "Had I a Hundred Mouths" is an exhausting story. I just know about my own work, not that of others. Somebody asked Tallulah Bankhead, "What makes you so sexy? Can you give us an idea?" She went around in a mink coat without anything under it, things like that. "You're a naturally sexy woman, what makes you so sexy?" they'd ask. "I don't know," she said. "I don't do a *thing*." I don't know why I'm exhausting. I don't know what other writers do, I only know what I do.

GIBBONS: I think the simple answer to the question, "What do you ask of your reader?" is: a lot. More than many other writers ask.

GOYEN: But you see, *those writers* ask too much of *me*. They ask me to bog down in boring tale-telling that is not new anywhere. They're asking me to listen to warmed-over tales of lives that have already been handled. They're not startling me into experiencing freshly what they're giving me. I want life made clean again. I want it brushed up clean so I can *see* it again. Some writers give the reader what they think he can handle, because he has handled it before. Like your mother putting down the same goddamned meat loaf a lot of nights, and you said, "But I'm tired of it." "But you *like* it," she said, "this is what you *like!* You told me how you *love* it." So she just settles down for what I like. Stops all enterprising; no longer surprises.

I'll do something else if I have just to repeat the old images. Everybody is slightly knocked in the head and benumbed by the beginning of a boring story. And so they read through kind of stupefied.

I don't know why *I* know this but it's sure not a stand I'm taking, and I'm not a revolutionary, I don't have a thesis, "The trouble with writing is. . . !" I don't have answers. Writing can be benumbed by attitudes like that.

GIBBONS: Were there some writers whose influence you felt you had to reject or throw off?

GOYEN: Oh sure. I had to work through them. Because a lot of them are standing in the way. We have to go through their legs or get around them or really just kind of *have* them, in order to be free of them, or let them have us. Thomas Wolfe. Singing people. Whitman. Early Saroyan. I had to find out whether I could do it or not, and since I didn't have anything to replace it with yet—I tell students this: since you don't have anything to offer yet, then *take* what they have to offer, and spend it. If somebody wants you to make love to them that badly, then go ahead and do it. Just go ahead and do it, get out, get through it! Never James—though he astonished me. The same as Proust: those were abundances, flowerings. They confirmed me.

GIBBONS: Why is a minor writer like Saroyan more of a problem than a writer like James or Proust?

GOYEN: Saroyan speaks very much to young people. That great freedom—"I'm leaving, I'm going to do what I have to do, get out of my way, let me fly!" But his spiritual transformation was not mine; his style, finally, was not one that I could graft onto me as my own. It was *his* spirit.

GIBBONS: Did you read Sherwood Anderson?

GOYEN: He didn't attract me. I didn't know what Ohio was. I hardly knew what Texas was, but I was determined to find out. I did find stories that knocked the hell out of me, and made me want to write—but write my own stories. Flaubert's "Saint Julien, l'Hospitalier"; Thomas Mann's "Tonio Kröger." I suddenly found literature through classes at college. I had been cutting classes trying to learn how to compose music, and hiding out in vaudeville theaters, and trying to say something through *performing.* I hadn't found the *word* yet. I settled for that, really, when my father told me that I couldn't perform, that I was not *allowed* to, and almost at the same time in my life I came upon writing, and the whole thing burst open for me. I was reading French and Spanish, and German, too, early—languages were easy for me and I was studying them. *Lazarillo de Tormes!* Poetry: Goethe's lyrics. Heine's. Rimbaud. Blake.

The American writing around me seemed to all just hang at that level of life that I spoke about, just at whatever tide there was—there was Hemingway, whom I couldn't abide. Fitzgerald, totally foreign to me. I didn't know about that world, the swell life. Or even Fitzgerald's own transformations. Hemingway seemed to me to be like the brutes that I knew that I wanted to escape from, in Texas. That physical bravado, that leanness of style, that was anathema to me. Why would I not use three adjectives? Why not? I was a rhapsodist, why would I cut down on my adjectives? What was Hemingway trying to tell me, what was he hiding?

So those people were around me, and I chose Whitman, and Saroyan, and Wolfe.

GIBBONS: But you chose them as enemies, did you not?

GOYEN: No, I had to go through them. Then I went into people who had a profound influence on me—like Milton, Chaucer, Dante.

GIBBONS: It was a long time between 1937, graduating from Rice, and 1950, when you published *The House of Breath.* Were those figures riding with you all that time?

GOYEN: All that time. They rode with me on a godforsaken aircraft carrier, for five years. I got into the ship in 1939 and I got out of it in nineteen fucking forty-five, at the end of the war. *That's* where *I* was. I had to study ballistics, command a battery of anti-aircraft guns. But I was carrying these people with me. I was shooting off in my bunk when I should have been in love affairs of all kinds, I should have been in *life,* breaking my heart. That's a forced monastic living—since I'm a late bloomer, that's something to think about. I can see the deprivation of that; but I can see too that it probably added years to my life because I was physically in good shape. I realize as I talk now the extent of a residing anger in me, resentment, bitterness, about that. I've never really assessed that time. It did free me from all the crippling influences in my life, the crippling circumstances—family dependence, Texas, and probably from excessive study and scholarly isolation. I have never really realized the madness of those years. I went quite mad at the end of the fourth year of it, quite crazy, I had to be under morphine on the ship. I became so enraged at the war that my rage couldn't be contained by my body or quietened by one thousand men. We were near the coast of Japan. When would it end? It was all right for a while, but will this go on!? I was a captive. I felt punished. For what? What had *I* done? I recall these maniac feelings. I was a wild man on the ship, a rebel, an outlaw. My poetic and voluptuous youth, I felt, was dying and passing away a mile a minute in the China Sea in 1944.

> He thought how he had always wanted to belong to a landscape, yet it seemed his destiny to be only a figure riding through many landscapes, drawn to places and faces, bodies and minds, drawing these to him, disappearing and vanishing. Sitting in public places in his own country, returned, listening, he had thought how strange and outlandish he was, as though he were a ghost that was revisiting his native place and was never seen, never spoken to.
>
> —"Nests in a Stone Image"

GIBBONS: One could divide your stories into those in which uprootedness is central, and those others in which for a moment that homelessness is conquered and there is a sense of getting back.

GOYEN: I had a sense of myself—which has lessened a bit, but is still an underlying sense of myself—as a *passager*, as someone passing through. So many of my stories were almost ballads—saying that I'm on my way, I'm just passing through, I've sung my song, now I'm going on, I just stopped by here. That came out of my feeling that I couldn't live in Texas, that I couldn't live among my own, that something alienated me, that I was drawn apart. And that was a heartbreak for me. I accepted it as a kind of destiny and often as a curse. I couldn't be there, whatever those reasons were, and that led me to an immense home-sickness, a longing for where I couldn't be. It's an exile. I don't know what the exiling factors or forces were, may never know.

GIBBONS: Were they personal more than artistic?

GOYEN: An artist moves, goes out, comes back and then leaves again.

GIBBONS: You're not speaking about a cultural question, about the writer who goes to New York because there is no one to read him in Texas?

GOYEN: No, of course not. When I went back, it was almost—just a death, one of my deaths. I couldn't get over waking and hearing Texans. I couldn't believe their speech! At once I thought, "This is where I belong! I'm here, I'm home here!" And then my second feeling, on the heels of that, was that they would never let me become a part of them. I talk like that, that's my speech, and those are all my people, but why is it I can't be a part of them? Why am I here in this room alone, isolated and exiled from them, just outside my door?

I still feel that when I go home.

GIBBONS: Is that relationship something you expect to find, or aren't surprised to find, in other people's work, or do you feel it's peculiar to you?

GOYEN: It seemed to be so deep in me that I thought, if I read it somewhere else, I felt confirmed, or affirmed. I didn't associate it with Joyce and with the classic exile of Joyce, because I felt that Joyce's was much more planned, reasonable, he was much less bewildered by the forces upon him, at him, and he was dealing with a whole huge culture, a literary and an ethnic culture, the whole Celtic renaissance. My case seemed a very personal thing, almost demonic—a curse: dark. Therefore the meditational quality, a prayer-like quality, almost "Help me, Save me, Deliver me."

GIBBONS: Given the italicized passages we spoke of, rising at the ends of some stories, it seems to me that prayer was addressed to the language itself.

GOYEN: True.

GIBBONS: And you have called them songs, those stories, as well.

GOYEN: They always came like anthems, or serenades. And they were sung, finally; it was an anthem, a joyous hymnal-feeling I had, even in "Arthur Bond," that late. The language is always a principal

155

character in the story for me; I suppose that's why I can't read so many other writers. They feel they're giving me whole characters and they probably are but the characters don't interest me if I can't hear them speak or identify them with *words*, by which they are delivered to me.

GIBBONS: Your literary mode, your literary consciousness, your artistic devices, and your gypsy experience, have all been extremely cosmopolitan, but even when you start on West Twenty-third Street with Marietta Chavez McGee [*In a Farther Country*], you always go back to that rural reality, in your work, more a different place in the mind than a geographical place, a world of fewer emblems and more powerful ones, which we seem to say is rural, mostly. A good example is "Old Wildwood," which begins in Rome, but goes back to the funny little motel cabin on the shore of the Gulf of Mexico.

GOYEN: That saves me each time, though, because it's the detail of the small scope that keeps me from being lost in the Rome of it, or in the New York City of it, because I am not really writing about Rome, or I would have to find the detail of Rome.

GIBBONS: *That* sort of fictional texture doesn't interest you, does it?

GOYEN: No. The *house*, therefore. I look for containment. I see this now, and I guess I do at a certain point know when I'm engulfed by too much, and then I really try to get into some little manageable harbor, get anchored somewhere, and it's in simple and homely detail, and often in bizarre detail. An absolutely recognizable detail, that seems trivial. I have to be contained by a house, or a place. I'm then free to do what I want.

GIBBONS: And yet, if sometimes you suggest containment, at other times you suggest freedom of a roaming, wandering sort.

GOYEN: Sometimes people just go, and you never hear from them again. Or they come back very different from what they were when they left. What makes them come back? Or changes them—if some force took that demon out of them and put it into swine? Later I'd like to talk about the swine! Somebody was exorcised through me, I took over people's demons and I went on off with those demons, a lot of the time. *They* went off pure and fine. They flew on off, like angels, and I was cursed! I was the pig. The cliff by the sea beckoned me.

The bizarre, and the supernatural, that we were talking about—I thought sometimes I was the receiver of a cursedness. I felt often that I was a carrier: that image. I've written about the carrier, in *The House of Breath.* That image of myself, carrying, benignly walking through and infecting others, or receiving what others put onto me. . . .

GIBBONS: You describe Lois Fuchs [*In a Farther Country*] falling in love at thirty-five with a seventeen-year-old boy, who then dies, as if she has cursed or infected him.

GOYEN: That's what I'm talking about. But I can't account for these people—not Leander either. I'm not responsible for *accounting* for Uncle Ben ["Had I a Hundred Mouths"], although it seems I'm his creator. I'm therefore held, it seems, accountable. But I don't believe the artist is held accountable. Is he, maybe? Morally, we feel that he is. Do we just abandon characters to the destiny that life has for them? Do we let them go into life out of the art we have made? Or do we hold them within our art and try to account for them totally through art? I don't think so. Leander was restored to life, I guess—he had to take his chances out there maybe. I was done with him, in a way. I came upon my own redemption in the streets somewhere, as creator-narrator, and looked upon my own flesh and felt my own reality in Leander now at large from my own creation.

GIBBONS: In the French interview [*Masques*, Summer 1982] you were asked if all your characters weren't either waiting for something or wounded. Is that waiting a kind of disablement like the physical disablement that afflicts some of them?

GOYEN: I think they're waiting for miracles, for wonderful visitations—they're waiting for the marvelous.

GIBBONS: Is the marvelous that important?

GIBBONS: I'm not didactic—it's just surprise, waiting for the wonderful surprise. It's probably waiting for the Second Coming, underneath. I'm sure that's all I've ever been writing about. Salvation, redemption, freedom from bondage, complete release. All those people from those little towns, that's what they were brought up to wait for: the end of the world, when the trumpets would sound, and they'd be free of all this daily labor. That's the whole black southern thing. Rebirth, a new life, heaven—freedom from pain, bondage, travail.

Those characters in my stories all *are* waiting. They're really kind of hopeful people, expecting more. They're open to something. They are forerunners. They've lost place—a lot of them are displaced, that's their sorrow.

"But there's a better place I know," don't you know that's what they say? "I accept that I've lost my place, my home, my town, my river—a whole river is gone!" When Jessy comes back to her mother, in *The House of Breath*, she says to her, "Life is loss, Mama." Her mother is just waiting, sitting in a chair. She had closed the blinds, and the wind played memory through them. Jessy says, "Life is loss, don't you know that? I know that, and I'm only ten years old."

GIBBONS: How do you feel now that you have adjusted to living in southern California, after several years?

GOYEN: I feel exhilarated, it's encouraging and hospitable to me, for my work, because I *am* in a foreign country. This is the way I've been able to accept it. The people are foreigners to me and I am in a strange land. I'm at home in a strange land—always my image of home was of someplace where I would put down the deepest roots and build a permanent place and I would never stray from that. But of course that was pure fallacy, pure idiocy, a fake way of thinking about my life, that was never possible, I would never allow that, anyway. It's not anything I really would care about!

Beckett said this for me at a time when I was looking for the statement, that the artist lives *nowhere*. *"L'artiste qui joue son être est de nulle part. Et il n'a pas des frères."*

GIBBONS: Who would have guessed this of a writer as concerned with such specific speech and with exile's return?

GOYEN: But that place has become a language, now, for me. That's a language of its own; I've created a language, as I did for Arcadio, that was never spoken there. That's become my *style*, for me.

GIBBONS: You're not reproducing a speech?

GOYEN: Not at all, not the way those Southerners do. I'm not a "Texas writer" or a "regional" one. I'm not interested in that, I never really was. I was making a *language* out of *speech*. If you harm that language, you're harming the life of that work, and you're harming the character himself. You're re-dressing him. You're saying, "No, he wouldn't have this kind of a hat on, he wouldn't have that color eyes." It's a violation. The language has become paint, as for a painter—the quality of the paint, the texture. A Cézanne local mountain is *paint*.

GIBBONS: What's special to you about Arcadio speaking Spanish? Why does he speak it? Why isn't he just a *redneck* . . . hermaphrodite?

GOYEN: He is a Mexican. That is his speech. That's his mother— she has a real hard time with English. His father is an East Texan, but his mother is a strange, foreign thing, jumping around, and she don't belong nowhere, she can't stay still!

That's his language too and what you get out of him finally is his struggle to speak, any way he can. He can't use his father's language, or the *speech* he hears around him, and he knows his own. Again, he's trying to *tell*.

GIBBONS: Bilingual, and split sensual/spiritual, male/female—schizoid?

GOYEN: He becomes quite crazy at times. . . . And what son can tell you about his father?! I think the son-father relationship is as enigmatic as can be. . . . That's a wild nightmare there, though, that was given to me. And I feel I just have to let it alone. There's no such thing as clarification of it. I'm interested in what other people say about it, but it's almost like "Tongues of Men and of Angels"—that's the way that tree grows. And either further work will clarify it, will straighten that tree up, or . . .

GIBBONS: You revise and revise, though, so it's not your spontaneous early drafts that you seem to be protecting in this way.

GOYEN: But something is never changed. And that's what I know not to change. I can't say that it's words: it's the vision, and it is never changed. There are no "revisions" for me, in that sense. I'm really in trouble if I try to change that. But it's not as if my first *draft* were holier than any other.

GIBBONS: Your attitude is nothing like that of the Beats, then, for whom the spontaneous composition was sacred?

GOYEN: Those states were induced, those visionary states. Now, in the last five years, I've read the Beats, and I've found there's something there. But at that time, the fifties, they were crazy, and I was trying to be sane. My God, I *started* by being crazy, why would I want to induce insanity? And writing kept making me sane, at least tying me down somewhere. So I couldn't hear any of that, then. They scared me, too. *Wild* people . . . I find that when I get a little depressed or morbid I want to stop talking. It's probably that I've just used it up. That's a good sign, to me.

GIBBONS: A clear signal, you mean?

GOYEN: Yes, I think it is, to let it alone. So that I don't get into
other feelings—fear. And the kind of memory that is not creative.
There *is* a destructive memory, too, that has nothing to do with recreating life, and I know when it is, more and more. I used to brood on it,
and use it, and think it was a part of my creativity—it really was demonic. It came when it came. I was a prey to it. I drank to stop that,
obsessed and on the verge of insanity. I'm through that. I was afraid of
those things of *mind*, and I just joined the ranks of many others. The
destructive memory was all that would come to me then, and you have
to learn through the destruction—if you survive—when it is creative,
when it is a building thing. I think some poets never knew that. I
thought at that time that the idea of insanity in poets was somewhat
hallowed. And there was such a false feeling about that. There still is.
I have not much patience with it now, I just consider them ill, people
who need help. And once they are restored, then their process goes on
again. But the madness of the poet, and the poetry that came out of
madness and suicide and all that—it impresses me less and less. Too
much destructive memory. And I feel that a lot of poets begin to use
that as a way of life, a pattern of behavior, even as a creative pattern.

GIBBONS: How do you distinguish between the creative and destructive memory?

GOYEN: Through surviving it. And through knowing when to let it
alone. This is why I am physical, thank God. I *am* physical. I would
use sex. I would go digging—I dug whole *arroyos*, irrigation ditches
where there was no water, in New Mexico. I made adobes, and lifted,
and built.
   This was healing, I thought—to go into the detail of everyday life
again. That was my survival, that's why I'm here. I knew that. Because
basically I wanted health, I wanted an art that was healthy and healing,
that had life-force in it, life-*strength*. When it got into this darkness, I
knew more and more to let it alone. If I was in a relationship, a love-
relationship, that was dark, and was caught in it, with no way to escape
from that, then it was very very dangerous for me. Or if I went *home*—
often I would go home thinking that would restore me, but I found
that black angel there, though home was a great source of restoration
and healing for me, I *thought*. This was when I was not writing. But if
there were traps that I couldn't escape—I won't stay where that black
angel is—then that's a dangerous time for me. And it looked to me that

California might be the final trap for me. And it seemed that that dark angel, that bad angel, that I wrote about, was here.

I came here thinking: sunshine, the flowers, and a new way of life, from New York apartment living—and I never *have* been able to live in New York, really. Ever! I've done it, but only happily in my own place, my own rooms, a nest—a life-giving place.

GIBBONS: Not in the *city*, only in your nest there?

GOYEN: That's right. As my present self, I'm not able to handle the place now.

GIBBONS: But when you go home, aren't you wiser and stronger than before?

GOYEN: But what I'm shown is that I'm *not*, and that's the last straw! I come there vulnerable. I have come there out of seeking, and to seek is to be vulnerable, I guess. I have come there seeking, saying, "Well, *that* will save me," and already now I'm open to any kind of force that can get me down, destroy me. Also I suppose that wisdom reveals that often there was a dark angel where we thought there was a bright one. I said, "Those people sitting on the porch, and singing together at night, and those stories they told, in the twilight . . . who was the dark figure in that house? Who among them chose that front door pane with that forbidding figure that says 'Don't come in this house—Who are you?—don't enter here—you're not welcome here.'" When I'd come with my suitcase, saying, "I'm here!" I'd see that figure on that horse saying "Come in!" and yet "Don't! It's just pain and darkness."

That house is still there, and so far as I know, that door is still there. A very precious, suspicious, dangerous door.

Part 3

THE CRITICS

Introduction

Most of the critical attention devoted to William Goyen has been directed to his first novel, *The House of Breath*. Many important critics and writers, including Gaston Bachelard, Ernst Robert Curtius, Anaïs Nin, Ihab Hassan, Christopher Isherwood, Stephen Spender, Katherine Anne Porter, Northrop Frye, Edwin Muir, and Robert Shattuck, have commented—at least in passing and often more substantially—on that remarkable novel. But even this impressive roster of critics includes no one who has devoted a book-length study to Goyen's work. In fact, Goyen's work has not yet had anything like the critical attention it merits, and this point is especially true of his short fiction. Attention has been more capable, more responsive, abroad. As the foregoing list of names suggests, several of the most important essays on Goyen are in German and French, and the best study of *The House of Breath*, by Patrice Repusseau, is available only in French. Most of the individual published articles and essays in the United States represent only the first stages of critical appreciation, when an author's work is, for the most part, summarized and examined for themes and correspondences to biographical facts. There has been little critical sophistication—literary, historical, or psychological—in the majority of these articles; nor has much notice been taken, except in passing by Robert Phillips (the author of the only other book-length study of Goyen in English), of the potent political implications in some of Goyen's work.

Repusseau's study, while it makes many references to Goyen's short fiction and offers a great deal of comment on some individual stories or themes in that fiction, is not easily excerpted. Readers of Goyen who command French will find Repusseau's book (which was his doctoral thesis) the starting point for many avenues of thought about Goyen's short fiction.

This state of affairs is very much related to American literary fashion, about which there is some comment in the preface to this volume. Literary fashion is an extraordinarily powerful force and, of course, arbitrarily so. Goyen's work suffered while he was alive—and continues to suffer—from the present and most assuredly temporary blindness of received critical opinion and evaluation. Therefore, the critical selections that follow are not as extensive as they might be with regard to another author of Goyen's generation and his stature; but in the excellent remarks by Joyce Carol Oates, Robert Phillips, Lyman Grant, and James Korges readers will find the general lines of an understanding of Goyen's work by his contemporaries, as well as suggestions for the direction of future criticism.

Joyce Carol Oates

William Goyen has always been the most mysterious of writers. He is poet, singer, musician as well as storyteller; he is a seer; a troubled visionary; a spiritual presence in a national literature largely deprived of the spiritual. Yet there is something driven and demonic—"accursed" Goyen would say—about his art. The extraordinary cadences of the language exert a hypnotic power that the events of the fiction roughly dispel; the reader is confronted by beauty, and ugliness; then again beauty and ugliness in the same instant, housed in the same image. Arthur Bond's curse is a worm buried in "the sweetest part of the thigh" but we also understand that Arthur Bond *is* his curse; the worm is his soul, his very being. The fantastic diver of "Bridge of Music, River of Sand" is both a suicide and a redeemer. In "Figure over the Town" Flagpole Moody absorbs all the projections of the town yet remains a symbol of the artist—stubborn, isolated, precarious, triumphant. The hermaphrodite hero of the novel *Arcadio* is probably Goyen's most powerful symbol of this inexplicable doubleness—the physical expression of a paradox that is primarily spiritual. All serious art celebrates mystery, perhaps, but Goyen's comes close to embodying it.

A story by William Goyen is always immediately recognizable as a story by William Goyen. He is not boasting when he says in the interview with Reginald Gibbons . . . that people in his life (his family and relatives in East Texas) had the speech, and he inherited the voice. Speech and voice are distinctive—the one natural, the other refined, calibrated. So seemingly fluid and artless are the stories they give the impression of being "merely" narratives of memory. The voice of the unconscious, the surreal, is most seductive when its cadences are colloquial, as in these masterful openings: "I started out to tell about what became of two cousins and their uncle who loved them, according to what the older cousin told me. But some of their kinfolks' lives would

From the introduction to William Goyen, *Had I a Hundred Mouths: New and Selected Stories 1947–1983* (New York: Clarkson N. Potter, 1985), *vii–xii.* © Copyright 1985 by Joyce Carol Oates. Reprinted by permission.

have to be told if . . ." ("Tongues of Men and of Angels"); "Now this is about the lives of Old Mrs. Woman, Sister Sammye, and Little Pigeon, and how they formed a household; but first . . ." ("The Letter in the Cedarchest"); and my own favorite, "Do you remember the bridge that we crossed over the river to get to Riverside? And if you looked over yonder you saw the railroad trestle? High and narrow? Well, that's what he jumped off of. Into a nothing river. 'River'! I could laugh. I can spit more than runs in that dry bed . . ." ("Bridge of Music, River of Sand"). So fluid is the voice the stories seem to tell themselves, each story distinctive yet part of a large communal narrative, like a broad river fed by numberless tributaries. And Goyen's characters too, when one comes to know them, are frequently kin—"blood kin"—whose stories and lives reflect and help to define one another. All are caught up in the fundamental mystery of life, all are compelled to speak of the "trouble" that occasions their tales. ("It starts with trouble," Goyen says in his interview. "You don't think it starts with peace, do you?")

These are tales of vanishings and hauntings, love-making and rape, mutilation, murder, abandonment, rediscovery. In "The Faces of Blood Kindred," a story that seems more autobiographical than most, the young protagonist has left his home and has become distinguished (as a writer, perhaps?) yet his most powerful revelation has to do not with his own individuality or uniqueness but with his kinship with a cousin to whom he does not speak when they happen to meet—years after an unfortunate incident of betrayal. The young man is alone, estranged from his kinsman, yet a single glance confirms their blood tie: "struck like a blow against ancestral countenance . . . leaving a scar of resemblance, ancient and unchanging through the generations, on the faces of the grandmother, of the aunts, the cousins, his own father and his father's father; and would mark his own face longer than the stamp of any stranger's honor. . . ." The doubleness that is both curse and blessing in Goyen's imagination is resolved in such moments of dramatic epiphany.

Though Goyens's art is carefully revised and refined, its impetus is unconscious, intuitive, "passional" as D.H. Lawrence would say, springing from blood- rather than mind-consciousness. Hence the mesmerizing quality of such stories as "In the Icebound Hothouse" and "Old Wildwood" and the dream-like incantatory "Children of Old Somebody" in which language itself is active; a character, or a focus of vision, by way of words. Goyen has said that when he is deeply immersed in his writing ". . . I have the feeling it's coming from outside of me, through me. An absolute submission, absolute surrender. It's being *had*, possessed. I'm being used." The storyteller uncle of "Had I a Hundred Mouths" is a nurturing, even a maternal presence; his is the power of seduction—"the surrender of listener to teller, almost a kind of love-making, of sensual possession, yet within innocence and purity." Thus, even when we read Goyen's stories silently we *hear* them: they are, as Goyen rightly says, ballads, serenades, anthems, even hymns of universal loneliness and salvation, the same powerful themes struck again and again in different keys, by way of different characters. Language *is* character here, but it too is always changing.

Reginald Gibbons shrewdly points out that Goyen is interested in more than "the shape of a man"—he is interested in "the significance of the shape of a man"—hence the emblematic nature of the fiction which is symbolic rather than allegorical, haunting and provocative rather than didactic. An early story like "The White Rooster" suggests the D.H. Lawrence of "The Escaped Cock" and has an ending that is dramatically logical, emotionally inevitable, yet it differs from Goyen's more mature—and typically Goyenesque—work in that it *has* so emphatic an ending. Elsewhere, Goyen's stories are not resolved in any conventional way; nor do they simply trail off into silence. Image-centered, as our dreams are image-centered, each story is a unique cluster of (often contradictory) occasions—a field of contending forces, one might say—like the numerous medallions Goyen recalls his mother sewing, one by one, before quilting them together into a whole. The wholeness is present in the imagination (or in the unconscious) but it must be *quilted* into being by way of the artist's craft. It must be discovered or, better yet, uncovered. Hence the visionary writer trusts to his yet-unarticulated vision to guide him and to provide him with the necessary voice. When I say that a story by William Goyen is always recognizable as a story by William Goyen this is not to say that the voice is always the same voice—far from it. The canny, funny narrators of "The Texas Principessa" and "Where's Esther?" bear no kinship whatsoever to the distraught narrator of "In the Icebound Hothouse." Yet the cluster of occasions of "The Texas Principessa" includes a nightmare image—the deadly spider at the heart of a peach innocently eaten—and the exiles of Horty Solomon (heiress to a Texas Jewish fortune in drygoods!) and Esther Haverton ("How could we know *that* was what it was? That we were losing a whole person?") are not so radically different from the exile of the speechless narrator of the icebound hothouse, the poet compelled to write to assuage the violence of his interior vision.

Goyen has said that he felt at times he was "the receiver of a cursedness": the carrier or bearer of images denied by his kinfolk and neighbors in East Texas. The Ku Klux Klan, for instance, appears frequently in his stories, even in so relatively benign a story as "Figure over the Town" where no one is terrorized or lynched. (Goyen was born in Trinity, Texas, in 1915, and spent his childhood in a house very like the large crowded disorderly house of the grandmother central to some of the stories in the "Blood Kindred" section of this book.) Images of physical mutilation and malformation recur in Goyen's fiction as the outward expression, I would suggest, of the unacknowledged evil of his world, which the artist is accursed (and blessed) to acknowledge. Like many another writer Goyen chose exile of a sort while passionately retaining his childhood's experiences. He could not remain in Texas, "couldn't live among my own," he knew himself estranged, alienated, yet his destiny was to focus his creative powers upon the very world he'd left—hence the doubleness of many of his emblematic heroes. His case, Goyen said, seemed "a very personal thing, almost demonic—a curse: dark. Therefore the meditational quality, a prayer-like quality, almost 'Help me, Save me, Deliver me.' " If there was an evangelical minister preaching the salvation of the soul in Goyen's childhood there was also the Ku Klux Klan tarring and feathering Negroes, setting them ablaze to run in the streets. ("I saw them running like that, twice.") How ironic it is, that the artist/writer/poet who *sees* and *feels* the horror of such events is so frequently denounced by kinsman and his fellow citizens as mad, or wicked, or spuriously "muckraking"—as if the measure of sanity were the capacity to assimilate horrors without comment. Goyen's bouts with madness—of which he briefly speaks—are the very emblems of the fissures of consciousness accommodated by his kinsmen and neighbors back home.

But the stories are not finally stories of alienation, violence, or madness. The most startling images—the naked diver of "Bridge of Music, River of Sand," for instance—give way to a narrative meditation that roots the stories in the familiar human framework of exile and return, loss and redisovery, death and redemption. The image of two brothers—one dead—on a door floating in a Texas flood gives way to a curious sort of harmony. The split tongue is an angel's tongue—perhaps! It has been said of Goyen's fiction that its spiritual significance resides in the very telling itself, in the voice given body and form by way of the writer's vision: and it might be said that the reader, in reading, in *hearing* this unique voice, completes the spiritual event. My suggestion is that William Goyen's stories be read slowly, no more than one at a sitting, perhaps, and that the reader suspend his expectations of what the "normal" should be no less than the "conventional" in terms of the short story. Simply allow the words to sound, and to resound. Words too are physical—rhythms and cadences spring from the body. This is an art of healing and the process cannot be forced.

Robert Phillips

If *The House of Breath* presents, among other themes, the necessity for a young man to break with the past, Goyen's second book, *Ghost and Flesh*, is an eight-part work depicting the ceaseless conflict between past and present, invisible and visible. A group of eight extraordinary stories, obviously written as a book with a common theme and unique symbols, rather than having merely been "collected," *Ghost and Flesh* deals with simple, compassionate people, men and women, each driven by a need to reach beyond and outside themselves to find in life some sort of absolute truth. As the critic William Peden states, the characters "are dominated or victimized by what the author seems to consider the tyrannies of the past, of tradition, of sex, and of an all-encompassing, nameless fear. They search for a means of effecting some kind of satisfactory compromise between past and present; they struggle to believe that life and death, the visible and the invisible, are factors in a continuous chain of being which is existence."[1]

Another major theme of the book is the failure to communicate. (In one story a message at the end of a kite breaks loose and flies away to wherever its words are unseen!) In story after story, one sign of man's isolation from himself and from others is the ghost. Goyen's use of the ghost often corresponds with the idea of the ghost or revenant—some shade of a lost culture or a guilt appearing out of the past—as often found in Irish literature. Ghosts also serve as symbols for all we have lost which demand recognition still. Story after story records a great struggle for wholeness, what Jung would call individuation. Goyen's characters' waking and dream lives create a meandering pattern in which individual strands become visible, then vanish, then return again. A meandering design of dust and water, ghost and flesh, dismemberment and wholeness, mechanical and human, lost and found, ultimately reveal in the characters a process of psychic growth—the process of individuation.

"Ghost and Flesh: William Goyen's Patterns of the Invisible and of the Visible," *Delta*, no. 9 (1979): *173–185*. © 1979 by Robert Phillips. Reprinted by permission of the author.

172

As related as their themes and symbols may be, the stories reveal widely varying styles, from the very straightforward narrative of "The White Rooster" to the shifting focuses in "Pore Perrie." The latter is an example of Goyen's point of view which might be called multiple refraction,[2] a technique which further serves to reveal the isolation of the individual.

The first story in this first book of Goyen's stories is still one of his most famous. "The White Rooster" is frequently anthologized and was even made into an experimental film. The late Frederick J. Hoffman, in *The Art of Southern Fiction*, cited it for its "fineness of comic perception and a precision that place it very high on an already distinguished list of short fiction in Southern literature."[3]

Numerous other critics have discussed the story as well, but all seem to miss the point. Peden, for instance, has called it "essentially realistic,"[4] and Louise Y. Gossett interprets "The White Rooster" as a dramatization of "the conflict of generations." She sees Grandpa Samuels' orgy of violence at the conclusion as "a startling comment on the fury of age. It is as if the past, feeling itself threatened, turned in an insane rage to demolish the present."[5]

But "The White Rooster" is not a realistic story, but rather a Western tall tale on one level, and an allegory on another. Mrs. Gossett's interpretation of the allegory as the battle of the generations is incorrect. It is, rather, the battle of the sexes that Goyen dramatizes. Mrs. Marcy Samuels is the author's prototype of the emasculating female. Described from essentially a misogynist's point of view, she is "a terrible sight to any barnyard creature, her hair like a big bush and her terrible bosom heaving and falling, her hands thrashing the air."[6] Later she is described with "her full-blown buttocks protruding like a monstrous flower in bud." Marcy already has rendered her husband, Watson, ineffectual and cowardly, and at the time of the story he is reduced to a "slow, patient little man."

Having conquered Watson, Marcy turns her ambitions toward Grandpa Samuels and, by extension, the white rooster: in her obsession the two figures have become one. The rooster, of course, is a traditional male symbol. Now, with tired body and torn feathers, it is a figure of the pursued male. When the rooster violates Marcy's pansy patch, it is the violation of her feminine psyche by the male. And when Grandpa Samuels defends the rooster, he is defending the honor and the supremacy of his sex: "Don't you know there's something in a rooster that won't be downed? Don't you know there's some creatures won't be dead easily?" But Marcy, determined, replies: "All you have to do is wring their necks."

Goyen then, has staged his battle of the sexes on the symbolic level, in the conflict between the rooster and Marcy, as well as on the literal level, between Grandpa Samuels and Marcy. To reinforce his theme, moreover, he has borrowed heavily, I suggest, from the Biblical legend of Samson and Delilah as a controlling framework for his story. (Goyen appropriates archetypal figures from world literature to underscore the point of certain other of his stories as well. Son Wanger in "Pore Perrie," whose dark complexion, rumored Semitic blood, and unfulfilled quest, recalls the figure of The Wandering Jew; and George Kurunus, the freak in the midst of beauty who crowns himself King of the May in "The Grasshopper's Burden," recalls the Hunchback of Notre Dame, both in his symbolic deformity and in his symbolic act.)

Grandpa Samuels, of course, is the Samson figure, his last name one clue to his legendary role. He is the figure of the incapacitated male at the mercy of a female in league with the Philistines. Like the Biblical Samson, Grandpa Samuels has been a wanderer and is at times capable of great displays of physical stamina, but intellectually and morally is weak. Like Samson when he entered Delilah's life, Grandpa Samuels is in good health when he came to live with Marcy, and "would probably live long." Yet before the second year is over, he "fell thin." Goyen does not give us a cause for Grandpa Samuels' fast falling; yet within the context of the story, we can assume it is due to the corrupting influence of Marcy herself.

When Marcy lies in wait to torment Grandpa Samuels and to strangle the white rooster, she is like the Gazites lying in wait for Samson. Grandpa Samuels' repeated recoveries are Samson's repeated victories over the enemy. When Marcy sets a trap for the rooster, she is Delilah setting a trap for Samson secretly shearing his hair in the night, an act of symbolic emasculation. When Grandpa Samuels is finally subdued, he becomes the figure of Samson eyeless in Gaza—physically as well as symbolically violated—grinding in the prison house. He restlessly wheels his chair from room to room in Marcy's home, and his confinement to a wheel chair is a symbolic statement of his impotence. The Philistines have captured him at least.

Grandpa Samuels is to have his Samsonian revenge, however. Just as Samson brought down the temple on all his enemies in revenge for his blindness, so too Grandpa Samuels destroys Marcy and her home. Goyen even describes the day of the act in the language of a legend:

"All through the home, in every room, there was darkness and doom, the air of horror, slaughter, and utter finish." When Grandpa Samuels destroys the house, he relives the Samson legend and simultaneously exorcises his fear of the tyranny of the female:

> And then he wheeled wildly away through the rooms of Marcy Samuels' house, feeling a madness all within him, being liberated, running free. He howled with laughter and rumbled like a runaway carriage through room and room, sometimes coughing in paroxysms. He rolled here and there in every room, destroying everything he could reach, he threw up pots and pans in the kitchen, was in the flour and sugar like a whirlwind, overturned chairs and ripped the upholstery in the living room until the stuffing flew in the air; and covered with straw and flour, white like a demented ghost, he flayed the bedroom wallpaper into hanging shreds; coughing and howling, he lashed and wrecked and razed until he thought he was bringing the very house down upon himself.

The phrase "bringing the very house down upon himself" affirms the probability that Goyen consciously or subconsciously evoked the figure of doomed Samson when he created Samuels.

The Samson legend is fulfilled when Grandpa Samuels himself dies in the destruction of the house. Death through the compulsive act is preferable to living incapacitated and tormented by the female Philistine. The story concludes with the ineffectual Watson standing dumbfounded in the ruins, incapable of the revolt that was the salvation of Samuels' soul, helpless even to understand it, much less to tell others its meaning. Watson is the ultimate victim of Goyen's battle royal of the sexes.

"The Letter in the Cedarchest" concerns Lucille—one of the many orphans in the book, and a lady whose husband has left her—and Little Pigeon, a crazy woman whose sister has left *her*. The two are opposites: Lucille has nothing, and lives in an unfurnished house. Little Pigeon, while having no mind, has a house full of material things. Together the two of them come together to create a world of their own in Little Pigeon's house: "The room was so full of decorations and stuff that there wasn't enough space left in it to cuss a cat in. There were hanging paper lanterns, paper streamers streaming from the ceiling, paper balls and paper stars. They had made a fairyland playhouse out of Little Pigeon's spotless living room."

There is a parallel here with the "Spain" which Marietta McGee-Chavez creates in her apartment on West 23rd Street in New York City, in Goyen's second novel, *In a Farther Country*. There is in much of his work a design on the part of characters to reshape their environments into their own images, or into the images of their origins. As the third character in "The Letter in the Cedarchest," Sammye, says: "All we want, I guess, is a household that will let us be the way we are." That desire forms the basis of some of Goyen's best stories. Certainly it is also the theme of "The Tenant in the Garden," a tale in which a gentle man desires to live in a tiny playhouse, but will not be left alone to do it by meddlers. The theme also predominates in "Figure over the Town," in which a flagpole sitter figures as a symbol of the artist and the non-conformist.

In "The Letter in the Cedarchest" Sammye functions as the protesting majority. To Little Pigeon, she is nothing more real than a ghost come to vex her once in a while. But to Sammye, Little Pigeon is a total preoccupation. Sammye is the outsider who cannot tolerate such individuality. The life of the imagination is not to be endured.

"Pore Perrie" is a simple tale, but one containing the seeds of a large theme which was to concern Goyen for decades: that is, the multiple problems of another man's son, when the search for identity, the knowledge of one's true roots, and the acceptance of responsibilities becomes a preoccupation. (As late as 1974 Goyen was immersed in these same themes; indeed, the working title of his novel, *Come, the Restorer*, originally was "Another Man's Son," and the phrase motivates his *Book of Jesus*.)

In "Pore Perrie" we are given Son, an adopted foundling, at the time he learns he is an adopted bastard. Upon receiving this knowledge, he sexually mutilates himself (as does Boney Benson, later in the volume, in the story "A Shape of Light.") It is the ultimate act of rejection of the flesh. Son becomes the eternally homeless, the disinherited, the unsatisfied spiritual seeker. He is not unlike Old Somebody, in the later story "Children of Old Somebody," who also roams the earth searching peace; or even the above-mentioned Boney Benson, forever chasing after his chimera; and both can be related to the ghost of Raymon Emmons, in the story "Ghost and Flesh, Water and Dirt," forever revisiting his wife in search of a separate peace. In all these stories Goyen is continually attempting to explore variations on a theme, the impossible quest for unity of the spirit with the flesh.

"Ghost and Flesh, Water and Dirt," is a soliloquy, in colloquialisms,

176

of Margy Emmons, who at seventeen married a thirty-year-old railroad man who later committed suicide just after their daughter and only child died of a riding accident. The principle theme of the story is that one never knows what one possesses until after one has lost it. All of life, Goyen explicitly says here, is a sharing of flesh and ghosts, of present and past, and each of us is composed as much of the past as we are of the present, and that part which lasts the longest is the past. Moreover, Goyen here insists that there is a world of the spirit as well as of the flesh, and tells us we must accept the spirits (ghosts) as easily as we do the flesh. One supplements the other make a full life, and it is the full life which is the life worth living, let alone contemplating.

"Ghost and Flesh, Water and Dirt," is written in a language which deliberately attempts to approximate the word as spoken in the South-west. As Goyen wrote of it in the "Author's Preface" to his *Collected Stories:*[7]

> . . . Since the people of the region where most of my stories ema-nate—or hover over—(they do, I believe, move in and through the great world) are natural talkers and use their speech with gusto and almost operatic delivery; and since the language of their place is rich with phrases and expressions out of the Bible, the Negro imagina-tion, the Mexican fantasy, Deep South Evangelism, the jargon of cottonfield and cotton gin, of oil field, railroad and sawmill, I, com-ing up among them, had at my ears a glorious sound, and in my hands a marvelous instrument of language, *given* to me. I worked at this instrument as though it were a fiddle or a cello, to get the music out of it; and I was finally able to hear it almost as a foreign language; and in several of my stories (most notably "Ghost and Flesh, Water and Dirt"), I have wanted to record as closely as possible the speech as *heard*—as though I were notating music.

A "skulled building of stone," in reality a schoolhouse, is a central symbol in "The Grasshopper's Burden," the stone building seeming to the writer not only a microcosm for the world, but a symbol of the skull beneath the flesh. It is a tale of Beauty (the girl Quella) and the Beast (the deformed George Kurunus). Quella represents the egocen-tric, non-thinking norm. George, with a face "like a grasshopper's face," is all the others are not. A sensitive human, he is seen by the others as no better than an insect: "If the school house burned it would burn him like a cricket in it." Yet George is symbol of the artist.

Given such prejudice, it is only by disrupting the given order of

177

things (during a fire drill) that the nonconformist can prevail. With all the others out of the schoolhouse, George Kurunus crowns himself King of the May, much as did Quasimodo. And Quella, one of the May Day Royal Princesses, sees George and notes that during the surreptitious act he is crying. She at last perceives his humanity and unhappiness. In the end, when all the handsome and conforming students reenter the building, all "the lean ball-players, the agile jitterbuggers, the leaping perch of yell-leaders, the golden-tongued winners of the declamation contests, Princes and Princesses, Duchesses and Kings," at least simple-minded Quella knows one more thing than the rest. The artist must crown himself in this world, must "create his own glory, in the face of opposition and conformity. The grasshopper's burden is that he must be considered a plague rather than a useful part of life."

"Children of Old Somebody" is the first of three difficult stories which conclude the volume. Ostensibly it is the tale of a child disowned by his elderly parents and left at first to grow up in a log. Later the child is removed, but too late: already it is unfit to live in society, having grown up amongst wild things. The sin committed against this child is our own heritage and ancestry, Goyen seems to be saying. The disowned son roams the world, knocking on every door, to remind us of our sins. Indeed, Goyen, titled the story not "Child of Old Somebody," but "Children of Old Somebody," enlargening the implications and referring to us all. The innocent figure roaming the world and knocking on doors asking for our repentance surely is a Christ figure as well, reminding us of the famous painting of Christ at the door by the Pre-Raphaelite, Holman Hunt. Christlike, the babe in the log represents perfect innocence. As Goyen tells us, "there was no hostility between its world and creatures' world, that hostility is learnt."

The babe in the log is also a Childe Percival figure. Indeed, Goyen's story relates to a special phenomenology of the child archetype, that of the abandonment of the child. Abandonment, exposure, and danger are all elaborations of the child's insignificant beginnings (in Christ's case, in a manger) and of its mysterious and miraculous birth (in Goyen's child's case, not an immaculate conception, but a conception between elderly parents). The child is a symbolic content, manifestly separated from its background (the mother), but sometimes including the mother in its perilous situation (as when she comes to nurse it). In Jungian terms, the child would be that third thing of an irrational nature which the unconscious psyche creates during a collision of opposites: "The new configuration is a nascent whole; it is on the way to wholeness, at least in so far as it excels in 'wholeness' the conscious mind when torn by opposites and surpasses it in completeness. For this reason all uniting symbols have a redemptive significance."[8]

And redemption is clearly Goyen's theme here. The "child" of the story is a symbol of the self's evolution toward independence. In order to achieve this, it must detach itself from its origins. Abandonment is therefore a necessary condition, and not just a concomitant symptom. The conflict is not to be overcome by the conscious mind remaining caught between the opposites, and for this very reason it needs a symbol to point out the necessity of detaching itself from its origins. As Jung says of the psychic situation, "because the symbol of the 'child' fascinates and grips the conscious mind, its redemptive effect passes over into consciousness and brings about that separation from the conflict situation which the conscious mind by itself was unable to achieve."[9] The symbol anticipates a nascent state of consciousness: so long as it is not actually in being, the "child" remains a mythological projection, and one requiring renewal by ritual. As the Bible says, unless ye become as little children, you cannot enter the Kingdom of Heaven.

Goyen's baby here is as isolated in its environment as was Boy in *The House of Breath* and Son in "Pore Perrie." And all three, the baby, Boy and Son, must detach themselves to achieve true selfhood. Consciously or unconsciously, Goyen in "Children of Old Somebody" has hit upon a timeless archetypal situation. The fact that the child is delivered helpless unto the dangers of nature, but is endowed with superior powers to pull through, represents the strongest and most ineluctable urge in every being, namely, the urge to realize itself. The archetype of the child expresses man's wholeness. Jung has said it best: "The 'child' is all that is abandoned and exposed and at the same time divinely powerful; the insignificant, dubious beginning, and the triumphal end. The 'eternal child' in man is an indescribable experience, an incongruity, a handicap, and a divine prerogative; an imponderable that determines the ultimate worth or worthlessness of a personality."[10]

"Nests in a Stone Image" consists of one man's ruminations in a hotel room on the eve of Easter. The hotel, like the high school in "The Grasshopper's Burden," is stony and skull-like. The man's flesh

and vulnerability are contrasted sharply with the coldness and permanence of the building and city in which it is situated. He sees himself
perched like some bird in the stone mouth of some stone image.

During the course of the story all manner of human connections—
social, spiritual, sexual—are overheard by him in the hotel. He alone
seems to be alone. Yet by the story's end we see that he is alone by
choice, having renounced someone younger than himself, someone he
loved but would rather abandon than see corrupted by their difference
in age (and, possibly, their sameness of sex).

This suggestion that the renounced beloved might be of the same
sex arises from the scene in which the protagonist is made love to by a
woman, and finds himself unable to respond and, even, is unmanned.
That the story occurs on Easter Eve and is resolved on Easter morning
is perhaps meant to be significant: the impotent member shall rise,
with glory, again.

The final story in the book, "A Shape of Light," ostensibly is the
story of one Boney Benson, who lost both his wife and his unborn
child, and consequently disfigured himself in guilt and expiation, bury-
ing his dismembered organ in the same grave as his loved ones. There-
after his unborn child rose like a light to haunt him, a ghostly gesture
of the inexpressible. As a total, the story is a meditation on the quest
for the unanswerable, the unnamable, the unseen.

Boney's name of course indicates his mortality, and his seeking after
the shape of light he sees in the dark is a Grail quest. He is a wise man
following a strange star, that "gentle and curious light," which is no
ordinary fireball or lantern, but a source of light which consequently
becomes a source of spiritual strength. To become illumed is to become aware, As Goyen writes,

> This radiant object shed the most delicate and pure clear illumina-
> tion on little things in its path and along both sides; so that what it
> showed us who followed was the smallest detail of the world, the
> frail eternal life of the ground, the whiskers of a fieldmouse, the
> linked bones in the jointed feet of a hidden sleeping bird, a clean
> still white tincture of dew hanging like a fallen star on a blade of
> grass, a hairy worm on a stem like one lost eyebrow, the hued cres-
> cent of the shale of a sloughed snake like a small pale fallen rainbow.

Clearly, to follow the light is to be in greater communion with the
things of this earth. To follow the light is to follow Christ ("I am the

light and the way." "I am the resurrection and the light.") To follow the light is to follow the spirit. Thus, Boney's unread message, which he sends heavenward on a kite (". . . send up a message!") is the emblem of our need to communicate with that power beyond us all. And though the kite falls, becomes, like Boney, a mere skeleton, the message sails on. Through Goyen's story, the lost message is risen and reclaimed "and fixed forever in the light of so much darkness and of so many meanings."

As in "Children of Old Somebody," Goyen here works with archetypal material. As pointed out, in Christianity Jesus was a light shining in the dark. As Jung says of Jesus, "Whether he lit the light with his own strength, or whether he was the victim of the universal longing for light and broke down under it, are questions which, for lack of reliable information, only faith can decide."[11] In another tradition, within the Tibetan Book of the Great Liberation, we read that those "fettered by desires cannot perceive the Clear Light." Here the clear light refers to the One Mind. Boney's withdrawing from the conscious world is a quest for the healing power.

In most of the numerous forms of mysticism, in fact, the central mystical experience of enlightenment is appropriately symbolized by light. And, as Jung says,

> It is a curious paradox that the approach to a region which seems to us the way into utter darkness should yield the light of illumination as its fruit. . . . Many initiation ceremonies stage a descent into the cave, a diving down into the depths of the baptismal waters, or a return to the womb of rebirth. Rebirth symbolism simply describes the union of opposites—conscious and unconscious—by means of concretistic analogies. Underlying all rebirth symbolism is the transcendent function. Since this function results in an increase of consciousness (the previous condition augmented by the addition of formerly unconscious contents), the new condition carries more insight, which is symbolised by more light. It is therefore a more enlightened state compared with the relative darkness of the previous state. In many cases the light even appears in the form of a vision.[12]

This would seem to be the case with Goyen's Boney Benson.

In addition, there is even an historical precedent for Goyen's light-seeking hermit, an actual person he may or may not have read about. I refer to the visions of the Blessed Brother Klaus. In 1947 Nicholas of Flüe, called "Bruder Klaus," was canonized by Pope Pius XII and declared the patron saint of Switzerland. During his lifetime (1417–1487), he abandoned his wife and children to live in a hermitage in Unterwalden. The single most significant event in Nicholas' life was the apparition of light, of surpassing intensity, in the form of a human face. The oldest extant account of Nicholas' life is a biography by Heinrich Wolflin (b.1470), who wrote:

> All who came to him were filled with terror at the first glance. As to the cause of this, he himself used to say that he had seen a piercing light resembling a human face. At the sight of it he feared that his heart would burst into little pieces. Overcome with terror, he instantly turned his face away and fell to the ground. And that was the reason why his face was now terrible to others.

Goyen's Boney Benson is a modern Nicholas, a real spiritual anchorite with a singular inner life, experiences for which no merely natural grounds can be adduced. In his unearthly quest, he is a figure central to a moving and disturbing book.

Notes

1. *The American Short Story: Front line in the National Defense of Literature.* Boston: Houghton Mifflin, 1964, pp. 122–123.
2. The term is Louise Y. Gossett's, used in her excellent chapter on Goyen, "The Voices of Distance," in her *Violence in Recent Southern Fiction.* Durham: Duke University Press, 1965, pp. 131–145.
3. *The Art of Southern Fiction.* Carbondale: Southern Illinois University Press, 1967, p.129.
4. *The American Short Story,* p. 122.
5. *Violence in Recent Fiction,* p.136.
6. *Ghost and Flesh.* Stories and Tales by William Goyen. New York: Random House, 1952.
7. "Author's Preface," *Collected Stories of William Goyen.* Garden City: Doubleday & Co., 1972, p. x–xi.
8. *Psychology and Religion: West and East,* Vol. XXI of the *Collected Works of C.G. Jung.* Princeton University Press, 1969, p. 441.
9. *Ibid.*
10. *Ibid.*
11. *Psychology and Religion: West and East,* p. 508.
12. Quoted by Jung in *Psychology and Religion: West and East,* p. 319.

Lyman Grant

I was getting myself ready for the world, to tell tales, la grandeza *is what I wanted,* la extrañeza, la belleza, *you wan hear?*

Contando, compadre. Canto. *But there was a long time when I didn't sing no song. I am at large. Which is how they called me on the radio when I was found missing. At large. There is no Mexican word for it.* Cantor soy. *I think of myself as a singer at large.*

—from *Arcadio*

Ten years ago William Goyen and his readers could have been celebrating. After ten years he was finally publishing again. True, *A Book of Jesus* was not a novel, but for a writer who had begun with so much promise, after ten years anything was welcome. Before the appearance of *A Book of Jesus* all of Goyen's books had gone out of print. In the following two years Goyen's work, old and new, was everywhere. Random House issued the *Selected Writings of William Goyen,* containing passages from Goyen's novels and short story collections, and a twenty-fifth anniversary edition of *The House of Breath.* Doubleday published *Come, the Restorer,* a new novel, to some appreciative reviews, and *The Collected Stories,* which was praised by almost everyone. William Goyen had returned—or so it seemed.

But until now, after an eight-year period that saw all but two books again out of print, we had not seen any new novels. (Palaemon Press did publish 100 copies of a children's tale, *Wonderful Plant,* in 1980.) Word had been out that Goyen had completed a novel called *Arcadio,* for which he was seeking a publisher. Pieces of the novel had appeared in *The Southwest Review* and *TriQuarterly.* And Goyen had talked about the book in a 1979 interview. His descriptions whetted my anticipation. "It is so outlandish that I can't believe it," he told Patrick Bennett in *Talking with Texas Writers.* "I'm up every morning at four-thirty or

This article appeared after Goyen's death in the 9 December 1983 *Texas Observer.* © 1983 by the *Texas Observer.* Reprinted by permission.

183

five to write this outrageous thing that I'm writing. But I truly love it, and I'm just about through. . . . Arcadio is a Texas Mexican. He just tells his story. He is something like Mr. de Persia in *Come, the Restorer*, except I believe he has gone him one even better. . . . He's escaped from a sideshow; he's at large, so at large he tells his story. I'll just tell you that little bit. I've never talked so much about it, but I'm full of it this morning, or of Arcadio. He got me. He's got me."

Now, almost four years after that interview, *Arcadio* is published and the story is wilder than Goyen let on. It is outlandish and outrageous, a large story told at large. If William Goyen had not died of leukemia one month before its publication, we would certainly be celebrating this time.

Like many of Goyen's works, *Arcadio* is a memory piece, a story within a story. It is, first, the story of a man who remembers as a child sitting in his yard one hot summer night with his family listening to his uncle's tale about a person, a hermaphrodite called Arcadio, whom he saw gently and lovingly bathing itself in the Trinity River. The nephew also remembers the dream—he calls it a vision—he had that night after listening to his uncle's story. The bulk of the novel is the boy's vision of Arcadio, and the story Arcadio tells of himself. The young boy meets Arcadio beneath an old train trestle over a dried-out river, and with little prompting Arcadio begins to tell his story.

Besides being of mixed gender, Arcadio is of mixed blood, the child of a white man, Hombre, and a Mexican woman, Chupa. Arcadio's story is one of his attempts to reconcile his torn body, his torn soul. His mother leaves him soon after his birth, and his father raises him in a whorehouse. When he is older he runs away and becomes a sideshow attraction. There someone gives him a small white Bible (*la Biblia Blanca*) and from it he reads the stories of *Jesucristo* and of the importance of faith and hospitality. His mother finds him there, and he escapes the sideshow with her but later loses her, thus becoming a fugitive, "at large." He then begins a series of odd adventures, searching for his mother and a half-brother, along the way picking up others who are trying to find out who they are and to make peace with their pasts.

I avoid describing these people and their journey for two reasons. First, much of the fun of reading this novel is meeting each character and experiencing the fertility of Goyen's imagination. Second, Goyen's novels have never lent themselves to summary. From the beginning

Goyen shunned the traditional plot, and each novel is increasingly sur-real and fantastic. He has not totally abandoned narrative, but he tells his tales as the subconscious might. In the preface to his *Collected Stories*, Goyen wrote, "I've not been interested in simply reproducing a big slice of life off the streets or from the Stock Exchange or Con-gress. I've most cared about the world in one person's head."

Over the years he became more explicit in his depiction of the sexual act, and beginning with *The Fair Sister*, more humorous. *Arcadio* is the culmination of Goyen's development. All the promise he began with, all the experiments since, have come together in a sexual, humorous, philosophical allegory of man's search to become one with himself and with God.

Readers who have become wary of Goyen, especially since the wild, disjointed, and highly symbolic *Come, the Restorer*, will welcome *Arcadio*. The difference lies in the title character: though Arcadio, as a hermaphrodite, is not a character with whom we naturally identify, he quickly becomes one we like and care for. He is less a freak of nature than he is a human being damned twice by his own humanity, an object of lust for both sexes, and an object possessed by his own double lust. He is twice the attraction with twice the desire. Another reason for the success is Goyen's continuing ability to capture the voice of his story tellers. We sit with Arcadio beneath the train trestle, and once Goyen puts us under Arcadio's spell, Goyen never cracks, never breaks char-acter. Arcadio's idiosyncratic English touched with Spanish sings in our ears.

As Goyen has often stated, he is most interested in the teller-listener situation. "Somebody is telling something to somebody: an event!" In *Arcadio*, Goyen has written a rhapsody in praise of tellers and listeners, for it is in telling our tales that we learn who we were, who we are, and who we will be. The taciturn uncle decides after many years to tell of his seeing a hermaphrodite bathing in the Trinity River and of the effect it had on him. He finally tells the story not only to communicate and commune with his listeners, but also to keep his story and all that it holds for him alive for future listeners. He says, "Twas—well, just a feeling I never had before and not again since, I guess, until just now when I've told it, more than I could ever find a word for. . . . But now somebody else will know its story cause I've told it, and I'm glad."

And when Arcadio finishes telling his story in the young boy's vision, he says, "And so goodbye to you, *Oyente* patient listener I feel half in love with you. When you sing your songs so close to someone for so long a time and they listen, you feel them listening with love you feel close to that *Oyente* listener. *Oyente* there in the dark I have sung you my own very life please to not forget me."

So the nephew becomes twice listener and only after many years does he tell the tales again. Therein lies the magic. The teller and listener become one, literally, as the listener retells the story, and figuratively, in the act of communicating. The teller also communicates with the past, retrieving the tale, and the future, passing on the tale. He lives eternally, becomes his whole self—his past, present, and future.

Arcadio ends with the nephew, grown up, having told both stories and aware of the meaning of having become a listener and teller. "Uncle Ben! I have today given you back your darling creature; Arcadio! your creator Ben has come to you through me. And I, both teller and listener, solitary maker, grand and absurd and homesick, who am I? what is life? why are we all here where is God?" For the uncle, for Arcadio, for the nephew, and, too, for Goyen and perhaps for us, telling and listening become the means by which we find ourselves, make ourselves whole, find God.

Perhaps more than anything, *Arcadio* leaves us with a William Goyen reconciled with himself and the world. Although Robert Phillips warns us against viewing Goyen's works as autobiographical, I think we can look at *Arcadio* as symbolically autobiographical. Goyen was a torn man, highly sexual with a deep religious sense, torn by not knowing who he was in a family that didn't understand him and even rejected him. He was a homesick outcast, an unwilling exile, a solitary maker. yet, he, too, was a man who survived, who found peace in the telling.

Early in Goyen's writing career, Christopher Isherwood warned him that he would never survive "with that kind of sensibility unless you change, get some armor on yourself." But he didn't, and because he never wrote mainstream fiction, he found himself painfully pulled in the tug-of-war of contemporary criticism. After *The House of Breath*, he was hailed as one of America's brightest young writers and damned as just another southern homosexual. Even in Texas, Lon Tinkle would call Goyen the best lyric talent since Thomas Wolfe, and Tinkle would conclude that *The Fair Sister* was a "minor triumph." A.C. Greene labeled the same novel "phoney, phoney." *The Faces of Blood Kindred*, Greene suggested, was "all somewhat like eating cotton candy made from unsweetened sugar." The effect of this on Goyen is summed up by Anaïs Nin in her diary. "Another fatality in the world of publishing. His books, though much admired and respected, did not sell enough so most of them are now out of print. Another wounded writer."

Then after *The Fair Sister* in 1963, William Goyen quit writing. Making sure he could not write, he became a fiction editor at McGraw-Hill. Of his writing he said, "I was relieved not to have to worry about my writing. I scarcely grieved it, or mourned it. It had brought me so little—no more than itself." But life grew worse and Goyen began sinking. "You drink and it kills you," he told Elizabeth Bennett of the *Houston Post.* "Can't tell a joke—sex is no good—there's no way out."

Like Arcadio in the sideshow, there to be watched but not allowed to speak, Goyen found his voice in *la Biblia Blanca.* On several occasions he described how he carried with him a small copy of the *New Testament* and even read from it at cocktail parties. With the inspiration of Jesus' words, Goyen began writing again, this time a life of Jesus. His Jesus, however, was not just a healer but also a fugitive, a man at large, not understood by his enemies or friends.

So in 1973 Goyen began publishing again, and for the next two years he saw his name in the major reviews. He could have been celebrating, and he may have been, but he has also called 1975 an awful year, and, in an excerpt about Margo Jones (of the Dallas Theater Center) from his memoirs, he writes about what may have been his lowest period. It was 1976 and he and his wife had moved to California. "And I, too, fell to my own floor in that beach hotel in California," Goyen writes, "saw in the haze of my sinking away, shining on my hands, my feet, my naked body, red, green, purple, yellow. And the miracle that drew like a siphon that deadly color out of me, those countless pills soaked in gin, and saved me there, has kept me here to speak to you now, has given me mind to remember, vision to see some meanings, tongue to speak amends of love."

Since that time Goyen had been writing and publishing, especially short fiction tucked away in little journals with small circulations. Although some of this work will appear later expanded and collected in a novel and a collection of short stories, *Arcadio* is the book that tells us that Goyen reconciled the parts of his warring soul.

Goyen, therefore, left us with a body of work, whole, complete, and meaningful. It tells us that one can remain a solitary maker, a fugitive, at large from the current trends, that one can experiment, be knocked about because of it, and survive with one's talent, vitality, and vision intact. This lesson is important for all of us no matter what we do, especially for writers who happen to be from Texas.

From the beginning, critics tried to label Goyen a Southern writer, which he resisted, saying he was Southwestern instead. Of course we in Texas claimed him, more than we had any right to. In a recent essay, A.C. Greene recalled the last time he spoke with Goyen. "He was a Texas writer by birth and circumstance, and the very last words I heard him pronounce were, proudly, 'I've never been anything else,' when I beseeched him not to forget."

That Goyen was proud of his Texas roots is undeniable. He loved the East Texas language that was given to him, that he heard in his mind all his life, despite leaving Texas in his twenties. He was even grateful for the heritage that the old Texas writers, Bedichek, Dobie, and Webb, had left him. However, Goyen was in no way overwhelmed with Texas; at no time did he think Texas was big enough. He would not be limited by his roots. He may have admired the old three but he had no desire to be Texas' literary master. Goyen saw himself as a writer, not as an arbiter of taste.

Goyen took his legacy, his Texas heritage, and left the state to become more than a Texas writer. And he made it, not by offering a slice of life, not by recording his experiences, not by remaining regional. He made it by going beyond the East Texas language into the many single human voices of his characters, their subconscious voices made to speak, the voices they use to explain and understand themselves. In so doing, he has, as in *Arcadio*, taken late night conversations on a lawn and their resulting visions and turned them into "an event," encouraging us all to become listeners and tellers, reconciled and at large.

James Korges

Like the work of Flannery O'Connor, John Hawkes, and the later Mailer, Goyen's fiction is deliberately outside the realist traditions. Virginia Woolf in a review of Dorothy Richardson's *Revolving Lights* pointed out that Richardson was concerned "with states of being and not with states of doing." The violent activity in these writers' stories is often the outward sign for psychic states, so that Mailer in *An American Dream* seems finally uninterested in the murder, but rather more interested in the states of being of his characters—something quite different from Dreiser's treatment of the murder in *An American Tragedy*. Whether concerned with religion, sex, or politics the works are Romance. Hawthorne, after all, defined the word "Romance" at the beginning of *The House of the Seven Gables*—and despite Hemingway's brave assertion in *Green Hills of Africa* that all American literature comes from Twain's *Huckleberry Finn*, it is apparent that almost all major American novels can, in their theoretical basis, be traced back to Hawthorne's preface to his novel. William Goyen and a few other contemporary American novelists have taken the process a step further with their increasing reliance on a poetic prose to evoke deep psychic states, and their increasing abandonment of traditional realist themes and strategies: these novels are closer to *Cymbeline* and *A Winter's Tale* than to *Tom Jones* or *Bleak House*.

This particular sort of Romance has been distinguished in Ralph Freedman's important study *The Lyrical Novel*. The lyrical novel he defines as "concentration on the inner life and on its distillation in spiritual or aesthetic forms. The passive hero, recreating his perceptions symbolically, dominates the world of images for whose existence he is responsible." Further, "the lyrical novel assumes a unique form which transcends the causal and temporal movement of narrative within the framework of fiction." Though Freedman centers his examination on European writers of "the lyrical novel" (Rilke, Hesse, Woolf, Gide),

From the entry on William Goyen in *Contemporary Novelists*, ed. James Vinson (New York: St. Martin's Press, 1982), *265–67*. © 1982 by St. Martin's Press. Reprinted by permission.

that examination might be extended to Anaïs Nin, John Hawkes, Flannery O'Connor, and William Goyen. I have labored this theoretical point because Goyen's work has been constantly overlooked or even dismissed, since its aim and strategies have been overlooked or mistaken by critics and other readers.

Faces of Blood Kindred, for example, is a collection of brilliant "lyrical" stories, in Freedman's sense of the word. In many of them nothing much happens in the sense of external "doing." Yet states of being are evoked, or explored. The stories bear down on moments of revelation, when ties of family or kinship are revealed, usually by chance incidents. The consequences of the revelation or discovery seem less important than the moment of perception itself: in a 19th century English novel, a boy might discover who his parents were, and he would automatically fit into a family structure; but in Goyen's work, the old stable family units have broken down, so that kinship tends to be spiritual rather than social, tends to an archetypal relationship beyond the social world.

To many readers, expecting a different sort of fiction, the stories seem vague, seeking to evoke more than they say, something beyond language at which language can only offer hints and guesses. "There are, indeed, things that cannot be put into words. They *make themselves manifest.* They are what is mystical." These words are not Goyen's but Wittgenstein's in his supposedly "positivist" *Tractatus* (6.522).

Like Carson McCullers, whose stories are also often ostensibly violent yet internalized, Goyen is a true extension of the Transcendental strain in American fiction. The rude, scarred, outcast people of the stories are manifestations of spiritual conditions. In his second novel, *In a Farther Country,* the narrator says: "Here, again, was the frail artifice built by the world that dreamt the solid other, the marriage and mixture of dream and circumstance that breeds back daily the pure race. . . ." His novels and stories are collections of voices (compare Wallace Stevens's great line in "The Woman That Had More Babies Than That": "The self is a cloister full of remembered sounds") each trying to tell of some hidden sort of Platonic other-world of forms or ideal states, or the truth of a life.

The stories and tales collected in *Ghost and Flesh* all concern characters whose telling of their lives, as in conversation, lead Goyen to deal with intermediate states, to the struggles between body and soul, ghost and flesh, the frustrated search of each for the other in a total communion that can at best be only momentary. The intermediacy is also temporal; for as in *House of Breath* the narrator recounts stories that do not happen in the present, yet are not entirely in the past: they are part of what the narrator thinks he might blow away (the house, or family, of the book is, after all, the creation of the telling, the boy-man's breath) yet cannot since it all exists like "a fresco on the wall of [his] skull." The permanence of the fleeting moment, in altered lives as in a single man's memory, constitutes one of the recurring themes. Yet reality always seems to lie elsewhere, somewhere toward which the tensions between ghost and flesh may lead. It is strange to hear Mailer apparently so different from Goyen, now saying in *Maidstone* (1971): "You can't say that this is real now, what we're doing. You can't say what we were doing last night is real; the only thing you can say is that the reality exists somewhere in the extraordinary tension between the extremes."

This questioning of reality is one of the central themes in Goyen's books. *The Fair Sister*, for example, is a shrewd, witty, and revealing study of religious feeling. The first person narrator, Ruby Drew, tells (or seems to tell) about the Light of the World Holiness Church, her fair sister Savata, and Canaan Johnson who tempted and won. The story of two sisters, one dark and one light, gives us the struggle of ugliness (self-concealed) and devotion (self-congratulated), of holiness and sensuality, cast in the diction and rhythms of a revivalism which is finally ambiguous: who can say what is being revived, or what the truth of the situation is? Or another example from *In a Farther Country*, the setting in Woolworth's to which the central character returns "every day to smell and touch" the things of this world within the other world of New York City. "She seemed unhurried, unenthusiastic. She asked the same question every day, 'Where is the lunch counter?' as though Woolworth's were a vast uncharted country. . . ." When she gains entry to the store at night, she asks, "But where is Woolworth's?" The counters have been covered with dustcloths, so that the store of the nightwatchman is not the same as the store of the salesgirls. The eccentric behaviour of the woman and her apparently simple questions raise issues of appearance and reality which become central in later chapters, as each character in his telling of his life arrives at some moment of communal insight: "Confusion seeks confusion to clarify itself before falling to confusion again." And the novel rises to a visionary denouement.

I have not dealt with Goyen's superb first novel, *House of Breath*, since it has received ample critical commentary already; nor with his classic stories, "The White Rooster" and "Letter in the Cedarchest," well known through anthologies. For it seems to me crucial that we begin to see the work of this fine literary artist not in terms of the southern gothic novel of violence and race, but in larger terms.

Chronology

The information herein is derived from the following sources: Goyen's introduction to the twenty-fifth-anniversary edition of *The House of Breath* (New York: Random House/Bookworks, 1975); the chronology by Robert Phillips in *William Goyen* (Boston: Twayne, 1979); published interviews with Goyen; Patrice Repusseau's *The House of Breath dans L'oeuvre de William Goyen* (Lille, France: Atelier Nationale de Reproduction des Thèses, 1980); and personal conversations with Goyen.

1915   Charles William Goyen, first of three children, born 24 April in Trinity, Texas, to Mary Inez Trow and Charles Provine Goyen.

1923   After Charles Provine Goyen moves the family to Shreveport, Louisiana, for a few months, he takes them on to Houston. They live at 614 Merrill Street for all of Goyen's childhood and youth. From the third grade on, Goyen attends public schools in Houston. In his high school years, he becomes interested in music and drama, as well as in writing.

1932–1937   Attends Rice Institute and receives a B.A. in literature and languages, reading works in French and German as well as English literature.

1939   Receives an M.A. in comparative literature from Rice. Enrolls in a Ph.D. program at the University of Iowa but quits after three months and returns to Houston, where he begins teaching at the University of Houston. Is drafted but enlists in the U.S. Navy.

1940   First serves in a navy recruitment office in Houston and is then sent to midshipmen's school at Columbia University in New York. Serves for several years at sea in the Pacific but suffers from migraines and seasickness. Works on early drafts of material that will become *The House of Breath*.

1945   After a brief return home to Houston, he leaves with his friend from the navy, Walter Berns, for California by car but stops in Taos, New Mexico, where he meets Frieda Lawrence. She gives him three acres of her land at El Prado, and, with Berns, he builds a small adobe house. (For the next ten years he returns to this house off and on.) Works on short fiction and his novel. Frieda Lawrence introduces him to Dorothy Brett, Mabel Dodge, Stephen Spender, and others who will influence him in one way or another in years to come.

1947   The first acceptance for publication of Goyen's work comes from James Laughlin, who accepts "A Parable of Perez" for a future issue of *New Directions in Prose and Poetry* but does not publish it until 1949; in the meantime, Goyen's first published story, "The White Rooster," appears in *Mademoiselle* (although in a version drastically edited by the magazine). A few months later, the first of his several works to be published in *Southwest Review*, "River's Procession," appears. Goyen travels to California with Walter Berns, on his way to taking up a teaching post at Reed College. He seeks out and meets Katherine Anne Porter.

1948   Goyen's stint at Reed is extremely brief; he receives a literary fellowship from the *Southwest Review* (whose editors Allen Maxwell and Margaret Hartley will, over the years, publish many of his stories). Works not only on his novel but also on a translation from the French of *Les Faneants* (*The Lazy Ones*), by Albert Cossery.

1949   Travels to London, where he lives off and on for a year in a room in Stephen Spender's house; visits Paris. Finishes *The House of Breath*.

1950   After the publication of *The House of Breath*, wins the MacMurray Award for the best first novel by a Texan (the book is reviewed prominently in the *New York Times Book Review* by Katherine Anne Porter). Lives briefly in New York, then Chicago, Houston, and various points in Texas and New Mexico, while finishing *Ghost and Flesh* in 1950–1951.

1952 Publishes his first collection of short stories, *Ghost and Flesh*, and afterward wins a Guggenheim fellowship. Returns to El Prado and works on a stage adaptation of *The House of Breath*. Maurice Coindreau's French translation of the novel is published and wins the French Halperin-Kaminsky Prize. (The novel is also translated into German by Ernst Robert Curtius, eminent scholar and translator of other American masterpieces, most notably T.S. Eliot's *The Waste Land*.) "Her Breath on the Windowpane," a part of *The House of Breath*, is selected for *Best American Short Stories of 1950*. Goyen's translation of Cossery is published by New Directions.

1954 Goyen's stage version of his first novel is produced off-Broadway. With a second Guggenheim fellowship, he now goes to Rome for a year.

1955 Second novel, *In a Farther Country*, is published, and he lives in New York. Over the next several years, travels back and forth from New York to New Mexico while continuing his involvement in the theater world: a film version of his short story "The White Rooster" is produced; he revises the screenplay and writes song lyrics for the film *The Left-handed Gun*; a new play, *The Diamond Rattler* (1960), is produced at the Charles Playhouse in Boston; and a television play, "A Possibility of Oil," is produced (1961). Meanwhile, some of his stories are published in German translation (1956). Between 1955 and 1960, teaches creative writing at the New School for Social Research in New York.

1956 Frieda Lawrence dies. Goyen sells the house in El Prado and definitively leaves New Mexico.

1960 Second book of short stories, *The Faces of Blood Kindred*, is published.

1961 "A Tale of Inheritance" is selected for *Best American Short Stories of 1961*. Goyen travels to Germany.

1963 Returns to the United States, and his fourth play, *Christy*, is produced in New York. Meets actress Doris Roberts, who is in the cast, and they are married. His third novel,

The Fair Sister, is published. Receives a grant for theater writing from the Ford Foundation to work with the Lincoln Center Repertory Company.

1964   In Germany, where the translation of *The Fair Sister* had been published the year before, a translation of a collection of Goyen's short stories is also published. "Figure over the Town" is selected for *Best American Short Stories of 1964.* During the 1964–1965 school year, teaches at Columbia University.

1966   Takes a job as editor at McGraw-Hill, in New York; stays in this position until 1971. During this period writes very little but continues to involve himself in the theater: he is playwright-in-residence at the Trinity Square Repertory Company in New York, and a new stage version of *The House of Breath,* entitled *The House of Breath, Black/White,* is produced in Providence, Rhode Island.

1970   Teaches in the writing program at Brown University.

1973   Nonfiction book, *A Book of Jesus*—the first work completed after his resignation from McGraw-Hill in 1971— is published.

1974   Publishes fourth novel, *Come, the Restorer;* his musical, *Aimee!,* based on the life of Aimee Semple McPherson, is produced. Publishes *Selected Writings of William Goyen.* Martha Graham's dance company presents a new work, "Holy Jungle," based on *The House of Breath.* During the 1974–1975 school year, teaches at Brown University.

1975   Publishes a twenty-fifth-anniversary edition of *The House of Breath* and *The Collected Stories,* which is nominated for the Pulitzer Prize (and which includes a number of new stories). Begins to split his residency between New York and Los Angeles, where Doris Roberts has moved to work in television and films. Robert Phillips conducts a detailed interview on Goyen's life and work.

1976   A limited edition of *Nine Poems by William Goyen* is published; "Bridge of Music, River of Sand" is selected for O. Henry Prize stories anthology. Beginning in the fall, Goyen teaches creative writing at Princeton University. Writes his first new story in several years, "Precious

Door," beginning the burst of creative energy of the last phase of his work (and fittingly, the story is published in *Southwest Review* [vol. 66, no. 1, Winter 1981]. Robert Phillips's interview with Goyen is published in *Paris Review*. Begins teaching at Princeton University (he will continue until 1978).

1977　Receives the Distinguished Alumni Award from Rice University. Over time, is spending more and more of the year in Los Angeles and by 1980 has effectively moved there. In Los Angeles, he rents an office to use as a writing studio in a building on the corner of Hollywood and Vine and works on a new collection of stories. In 1979 the French magazine *Delta* publishes a special issue on his work. Having suffered increasing medical problems, is diagnosed in 1982 as having lymphoma. Works to complete the collection of stories, tentatively entitled *Precious Door,* and a new novel, *Arcadio.*

1982　Is hospitalized and released and enjoys a recovery. Gives substantial interview on his writings and aesthetic ideas; the interview is published in *TriQuarterly* magazine in 1983, along with a large sampling of his work in progress, including short stories and excerpts from *Arcadio* and the unfinished autobiographical work, *Six Women.* Finishes *Arcadio.*

1983　At New York University in April, delivers the lecture "Recovering," on the act of writing and his experience of physical health and illness. In the summer is hospitalized in Los Angeles again, interrupting his final work on the collection of short stories and on a new novel that was to be based on two of the recent stories and tentatively entitled "Leander." Dies in the hospital on 30 August. Shortly after his death, *Arcadio* is published to triumphant reviews, and the lecture, "Recovering," is published in *TriQuarterly.*

1985　*Had I a Hundred Mouths: New and Selected Stories 1947–1983,* incorporating most of the new stories Goyen had prepared for book publication, as well as stories from his earlier collections, is published.

Selected Bibliography

A complete bibliography of William Goyen's works and of works in which his fiction is analyzed or cited would occupy many more pages than are available here. What follows is a bibliography of all his published books, other principal primary works, and a selection of critical sources having mostly to do with his short fiction. For more complete bibliographical details, see the "Bibliographies" section of the listings that follow.

Primary Works

Short Fiction Collections

The Collected Stories of William Goyen. New York; Doubleday, 1975. Contents: Preface by Goyen; all the stories from *Ghost and Flesh* (1952) and *The Faces of Blood Kindred* (1960), in the same order (the only change being the new title "Zamour, a Tale of Inheritance"); plus previously uncollected stories: "Tenant in the Garden," "The Thief Coyote," "The Enchanted Nurse," "The Rescue," "Tapioca Surprise," "Bridge of Music, River of Sand," and "Figure over the Town."

The Faces of Blood Kindred: A Novella and Ten Stories. New York: Random House, 1960. Contents: "Savata, My Fair Sister," "The Faces of Blood Kindred," "Old Wildwood," "The Moss Rose," "The Armadillo Basket," "Rhody's Path," "A People of Grass," "A Tale of Inheritance: *A Novella*," "The Geranium," "The Horse and the Day Moth," and "There Are Ravens to Feed us."

Ghost and Flesh. New York: Random House, 1952. Contents: "The White Rooster," "The Letter in the Cedarchest," "Pore Perrie," "Ghost and Flesh, Water and Dirt," "The Grasshopper's Burden," "Children of Old Somebody," "Nests in a Stone Image," and "A Shape of Light."

Had I a Hundred Mouths: New and Selected Stories 1947–1983. New York: Clarkson N. Potter, 1985; posthumous edition prepared by Reginald Gibbons, with an introduction by Joyce Carol Oates. Reprint. New York: Persea Books, 1986. Contents: "Introduction"; *Last Stories, 1976–1982*: "Had I a Hundred Mouths," "The Texas Principessa," "Arthur Bond," "Where's

Esther?" "Precious Door," "In the Icebound Hothouse," "Tongues of
Men and of Angels"; *Ghost and Flesh, 1947–1952*: "The White Rooster,"
"The Letter in the Cedarchest," "Pore Perrie," "Ghost and Flesh, Water
and Dirt," "The Grasshopper's Burden," "Children of Old Somebody";
Blood Kindred, 1952–1975: "The Faces of Blood Kindred," "Old Wild-
wood," " Rhody's Path," "Zamour, or A Tale of Inheritance," "Bridge of
Music, River of Sand," "Figure over the Town"; *Interview, 1982*: "An
Interview with William Goyen."
Selected Writings of William Goyen. New York: Random House, 1974. Contents:
Preface by Goyen; excerpts from *The House of Breath, In a Farther Country*,
and *The Fair Sister*; plus "The White Rooster," "Ghost and Flesh, Water
and Dirt," "Old Wildwood," "A People of Grass," and "Figure over the
Town."

Uncollected stories

"A Parable of Perez." In *New Directions in Prose and Poetry*, no. 11, 240–43.
New York: New Directions, 1949.
"Black Cotton." *Ontario Review*, no. 17 (1982–83): 80–86.
"Right Here at Christmas." *Redbook*, December 1977, 77–78.
"Simon's Castle." [Written in 1941 but published only in Germany.] In *Simons
Burg und andere Erzahlungen* (bilingual edition), translated by E. Schnack,
80–92. Munchen: Deutscher Taschenbuch Verlag, 1978.
"The Seadown's Bible." *Delta*, no.9 (November 1979): 113–19; also in *Red-
book*, December 1982, 56 ff.
"The Storm Doll." *Ontario Review*, no. 7 (1977–78): 28–34.

Novels

Arcadio. New York: Clarkson N. Potter, 1983. Reprint. New York: Obelisk,
1984. Published in England under the same title. London: Serpent's Tail,
1989.
Come, the Restorer. Garden City: Doubleday, 1975.
The Fair Sister. Garden City: Doubleday, 1963. Published in England as
Savata, My Fair Sister. London: Peter Owen, 1963.
The House of Breath. New York: Random House, 1950. Republished in a
twenty-fifth-anniversary edition, in cloth and paper. New York: Random
House/Bookworks, 1975. Reprint. New York: Persea Books, 1986.
In a Farther Country: A Romance. New York: Random House, 1955. Published
in England under the same title. London: Peter Owen, 1955.

Poetry

Nine Poems by William Goyen. New York: Albondocani Press, 1976.

Limited Editions

Arthur Bond. Winston-Salem, N.C.: Paleamon Press, 1976. Story.
New Work and Work in Progress. Reprinted pages from *TriQuarterly* special feature, Winter 1983. Winston-Salem, N.C.: Paleamon Press and Evanston, Ill: *TriQuarterly*, 1983. Contents: "The Texas Principessa," "*Arcadio* (Excerpt)," "Margo (from *Six Women*)," "Tongues of Men and of Angels (from Work in Progress)," "Where's Esther?" and "An Interview with William Goyen."
Precious Door. With wood engravings by John DePol. New York: Red Ozier Press, 1981. Story.
Wonderful Plant. Winston-Salem, N.C.: Paleamon Press, 1980. Story.

Dramatic Works

"A Possibility of Oil." Produced on CBS television, General Electric Theatre, 1961. Teleplay.
Aimee! Books and lyrics by William Goyen; music by Worth Gardner. Produced in Providence, R.I., Trinity Square Repertory Company, 1973. Musical play.
Christy. Produced in New York, American Place Theatre, 1964. Play.
The Diamond Rattler. Produced in Boston, Charles Playhouse, 1960. Play.
The House of Breath, A Ballad for the Theatre in Four Scenes. Produced in New York, Circle-in-the-Square Theatre, 1957. Play.
The House of Breath, Black/White. Produced in Providence, R.I., Trinity Square Repertory Company, 1969. Play.
The Left-handed Gun. Warner Bros., 1956. Film. Goyen revised the screenplay and wrote the lyrics of the ballad.
"The Mind." Produced on ABC television, 1961. Teleplay.

Nonfiction

A Book of Jesus. Garden City, N.Y.: Doubleday, 1973. Reprint. New York: Signet Books, 1974.
My Antonia: A Critical Commentary. New York: American R.D.M. Corp., 1966.
Ralph Ellison's Invisible Man: A Critical Commentary. New York: American R.D.M. Corp., 1966.

Uncollected Nonfiction

"Autobiography in Fiction." *The Texas Observer,* 29 October 1982, 1, 8–9, 11–12.
"Recovering." *TriQuarterly,* no. 58 (Fall 1983): 126–32.
"While You Were Away (Houston Seen and Unseen, 1923–1978): A Letter to

Charles Provine Goyen, Distinguished Early Citizen of that City." Houston, Tex.: Houston Public Library, 1978.

Correspondence

"Like a Buoy: Letters from William Goyen to John Igo 1952–1983." Introduction and notes by John Igo. *Pax* 3, nos. 1 and 2 (1985–1986): 41–59.
"Letters to Zoe Leger," "Letters to Maurice Coindreau." *Delta*, no. 9 (November 1979): 49–99.

Translation

The Lazy Ones [*Les Faneants*], by Albert Cossery. New York: New Directions, 1950; London: Peter Owen, 1952.

Unpublished or Uncompleted

"A Vision of St. Eustace." Novella.
"Half a Look of Cain." Novel.
"Leander." Short Novel.
"Six Women." Goyen's autobiographical work, on which he had worked for many years, and which was to treat Frieda Lawrence, Margo Jones, Mabel Dodge Luhan, Dorothy Brett, Katherine Anne Porter, and Millicent Rogers.
"The Well." Novella.

Works to be Published

Selected Letters, edited by Robert Phillips.
The Complete Stories, edited by Reginald Gibbons.

Secondary Works

Interviews and Autobiographical Statements

"The Art of Fiction LXIII." Robert Phillips. *Paris Review*, no. 68 (Winter 1976): 58–100. Reprinted in *Writers at Work: The Paris Review Interviews, Sixth Series*, edited by George Plimpton, introduction by Frank Kermode, 169–204. New York: Viking, 1984.
"CA Interview." *Contemporary Authors*, New Revision Series, vol. 6, 194–96. Detroit: Gale Research, 1982.

"An Interview with William Goyen." Reginald Gibbons. *TriQuarterly*, no. 56 (Winter 1983): 97–125.

"Interview with William Goyen." Rolande Ballorain. *Delta*, no. 9 (November 1979): 7–45.

"Learning to See Simply: An Interview with William Goyen." John Igo. *Southwest Review* 65 (Summer 1980): 267–84.

"Portrait of the Artist as a Young Texan: An Interview with 1977 Distinguished Alumnus William Goyen." *Sallyport* [Rice University] 32, no. 5 (June 1977): 6–8.

"PW Interviews: William Goyen." John F. Baker. *Publishers Weekly*, 5 August 1983, 94–95.

"Talk with William Goyen." Harvey Breit. *New York Times Book Review*, 10 September 1950, 12.

"William Goyen." James Korges. *Contemporary Novelists*, edited by James Vinson, 507–11. New York: St. Martin's Press, 1972; also 1982 (3d ed.), 265–67.

"William Goyen: A Poet Telling Stories." In *Talking with Texas Writers: Twelve Interviews*, by Patrick Bennett. College Station: Texas A&M University Press, 1980.

Books and Parts of Books

Bachelard, Gaston. In *The Poetics of Space*, translated by Maria Jolas, 58–59. New York: Orion Press. Boston: Beacon Press, 1964.

Coindreau, Maurice Edgar. Preface to *The House of Breath*, edited by G.M. Reeves. In *The Times of William Faulkner: A French View of Modern American Fiction*, 132–40. Columbia: University of South Carolina Press, 1971.

Curtius, Ernst Robert. In *Essays on European Literature*, translated by Michael Kowal, 456–64. Princeton, N.J.: Princeton University Press, 1973.

Dasher, Thomas E. "William Goyen." In *Dictionary of Literary Biography: Post World War II American Novelists*, vol. 2, 202–8. Detroit: Bruccoli-Clark/ Gale Research, 1978.

———. "William Goyen." In *Dictionary of Literary Biography Yearbook: 1983*, 106–12. Detroit: Gale Research, 1983. [Includes tributes to Goyen after his death, by George Garrett, William Peden, Robert Phillips, and others.]

Duncan, Erika. "William Goyen." In *Unless Soul Clap its Hands*, 17–30. New York: Schocken Books, 1984.

Givner, Joan. "Katherine Anne Porter: The Old Order and the New." In *The Texas Tradition*, edited by Don Graham et al., 58–68. Austin: College of Liberal Arts, University of Texas, 1983.

Gossett, Louise Y. "The Voices of Distance: William Goyen." In *Violence in Recent Southern Fiction*, 131–45. Durham, N.C.: Duke University Press, 1965.

Selected Bibliography

Hoffman, Frederick J. "Varieties of Fantasy." In *The Art of Southern Fiction*, 124–29. Carbondale: Southern Illinois University Press, 1976.
Korges, James. "William Goyen." In *Contemporary Novelists*, edited by James Vinson, 265–67. New York: St. Martin's Press, 1982.
Lucazeau, Michel. *Surrealism in William Goyen*. Diplome d'Etudes Superieures, Faculté des Lettres et Sciences Humaines de Bordeaux, 1963.
Nin, Anaïs. In *The Novel of the Future*, 115, 166, 172, 181–82. New York: Macmillan, 1968. Reprint. New York: Collier Books, 1968, 1976.
Oates, Joyce Carol. Introduction to *Had I a Hundred Mouths*, by William Goyen, vii–xii. New York: Clarkson N. Potter, 1985.
Peden, William. In *The American Short Story*, 20, 122–23, 172. Boston: Houghton Mifflin, 1975.
Phillips, Robert. *William Goyen*. Boston: Twayne Publishers, 1979.
Repusseau, Patrice. *An Approach to William Goyen's The House of Breath*. Paris: Memoire de Maitrise, Institut d'Anglais Charles V, Université Paris VII, 1971.
———. *The House of Breath dans L'oeuvre de William Goyen*. Lille, France: Atelier Nationale de Reproduction des Thèses, 1980.
———, ed. "William Goyen." *Delta*, no. 9 (November 1979): 1–250. Montpelier, France: Université Paul Valéry.
Stern, Daniel. "On William Goyen's *The House of Breath*." In *Rediscoveries: Informal Essays in which Well-known Novelists Rediscover Neglected Works of Fiction by One of their Favorite Authors*, Edited by David Madden, 256–61. New York: Crown, 1971.
Taube, Eva. In *Alienated Man: Literature of Estrangement, Dissent and Revolt*, 38–48. New York: Hayden, 1972.

Articles and Reviews

Ashley, Leonard. " 'Tightly-Wound Little Bombs of Truth': Biblical References in the Fiction of William Goyen." *Literary Onomastics Studies* 8 (1981): 147–65.
Bourjailly, Vance. "Words for a World." *New York Times Book Review*, 9 June 1985, 28–29.
Gibbons, Reginald. "Redeemed in the Telling." *New York Times Book Review*, 6 November 1983, 14, 36.
Grant, Lyman. "With *Arcadio*, Goyen Is a Writer Reconciled." *Texas Observer*, 9 December 1983, 12–14.
Hartley, M.L. Review of *Faces of Blood Kindred*. *Southwest Review* 45 (Autumn 1960): 360–62.
Hendrick, George. "Goyen's World." *The Texas Observer*, 29 October 1982, 9–10.
McKendrick, Louis. Review of *Collected Stories*. *Ontario Review*, no. 4 (Spring–Summer 1976): 97–103.

Merle, Gabriel. "Les Liens du sang et les liens du temps dans *The Faces of Blood Kindred*," *Delta*, no. 9 (November 1979): 187–94.

Paul, Jay S. "Marvellous Reciprocity: The Fiction of William Goyen." *Critique* (1977): 77–91.

———. "Nests in a Stone Image: Goyen's Surreal Gethsemane." *Studies in Short Fiction* 15 (Fall 1978): 415–20.

Phillips, Robert. "*Ghost and Flesh*: William Goyen's Patterns of the Invisible and of the Visible." *Delta*, no. 9 (November 1979): 173–85.

Porter, Katherine Anne. "This Strange World." [Review of *The House of Breath.*] *New York Times Book Review*, 20 August 1950, 5, 17.

Oates, Joyce Carol. Review of Goyen's *Collected Stories*. *New York Times Book Review*, 16 November 1975, 4, 14.

Rechy, John. "The Last Literary Magic of William Goyen." *Dallas Times Herald*, 23 October 1983, "Books," 4K.

Repusseau, Patrice. "The Concentrated Writing of William Goyen: Reflections on *Come, the Restorer.*" *Delta*, no. 9 (November 1979): 197–216.

Spender, Stephen. "The Situation of the American Writer." *Horizon*, 19, no. 111 (March 1949): 162–79.

Vauthier, Simone. "The True Story: A Reading of William Goyen's 'Pore Perrie.'" *Les Cahiers de la nouvelle: Journal of the Short Story in English* 1 (1983): 139–58.

Weir, Allen. "William Goyen: Speech for What Is Not Spoken." *Black Warrior Review* 10, no. 1 (Fall 1983): 160–64.

Young, Vernon. Review of *Ghost and Flesh*. *New Mexico Quarterly* 22 (1952): 327–29.

Bibliographies

Grimm, Clyde L., Jr. "William Goyen: A Bibliographic Chronicle." *Bulletin of Bibliography* 35, no. 3 (1978): 123–31.

———, and Patrice Repusseau. "Oeuvres de William Goyen." *Delta*, no. 9 (November 1979): 219–50.

Phillips, Robert. "Selected Bibliography." In *William Goyen*, 145–53. Boston: Twayne Publishers, 1979.

Repusseau, Patrice. "Bibliographie." In *The House of Breath dans l'oeuvre de William Goyen*, 462–510. Lille, France: Atelier Nationale de Reproduction des Théses, 1980.

Index

Index

GOYEN William, continued
  teaching, 119–21, 143, 152, 194,
    196
  and the theatre, 5, 7, 11, 23, 34–
    35, 106, 121–22, 130, 153, 193,
    195, 196. *See also* theatre
  in World War Two, 8, 69, 107,
    108–109, 153–54, 193

WORKS:
Aimee!, 196
Arcadio, xii, 4, 11, 12, 19, 20, 33,
  41, 49, 53, 55, 56, 58, 59, 60,
  61, 62, 63, 64, 71, 74, 79, 80,
  86, 93, 136, 139, 147, 148, 149,
  150, 158–59, 167, 183–86, 187,
  197
"Armadillo Basket, The," 52
"Arthur Bond," xii, 16, 23, 24, 25,
  26, 34, 40, 41, 54, 56, 80, 86–
  87, 89, 91, 93, 142, 167
Book of Jesus, A, 60, 80, 128–29,
  176, 183, 196
"Bridge of Music, River of Sand,"
  4, 9, 16, 40, 52, 53, 64, 73, 143,
  167, 168, 170, 196
"Children of Old Somebody," 30,
  40, 53, 66, 67, 136, 168, 176,
  178–79, 181
Christy, 195
Collected Stories of William Goyen,
  11, 19, 31, 37, 64, 73–78, 97,
  101, 177, 183, 185, 196
Come, the Restorer, xi, 11, 19, 80,
  126, 129, 131, 144, 176, 183,
  184, 185, 196
Diamond Rattler, The, 131, 195
"Enchanted Nurse, The," 40, 56
Face of Blood Kindred, The, 10, 19,
  70–73, 101, 186–87, 190, 195
"Faces of Blood Kindred, The,"
  16, 21, 39, 51, 64, 140, 168
Fair Sister, The, xi, 19, 185, 186,
  187, 191, 196
"Figure over the Town," 16, 40,
  55, 59, 62, 75–78, 167, 170,
  176, 196
"Geranium, The," 40, 53, 64

Ghost and Flesh, 3, 9, 19, 21, 27,
  30, 51–52, 65–70, 75, 80, 101,
  127–28, 172–75, 190–91, 194,
  195
"Ghost and Flesh, Water and
  Dirt," xii, 8, 9, 15, 16, 23, 24,
  26, 33, 40, 54, 55, 56, 61, 66,
  68–70, 86, 102, 137, 143, 148,
  176–77
"Grasshopper's Burden, The," 16,
  40, 56, 58, 66, 67, 174, 177–78,
  179
Had I a Hundred Mouths, 11, 197
"Had I a Hundred Mouths, 19,
  16, 25, 26, 33, 40, 41, 42–43,
  45–48, 49, 50, 51, 53, 54, 55,
  56, 57, 58, 59, 60, 61, 62–63,
  64, 65, 79–80, 82, 86, 90, 91,
  140, 143, 145, 148, 151, 157,
  169
Half a Look of Cain, 12, 40, 75, 89
"Her Breath on the Windowpane,"
  195
"Horse and the Day Moth, The,"
  10, 22, 34–37, 38, 40, 41, 42,
  53, 66
House of Breath, The, xi, xii, 3, 8,
  9, 10, 19, 21, 22, 26, 31, 38, 42,
  51, 54, 55, 56, 61, 63, 64, 65,
  66, 68, 71, 73–74, 85, 92, 97,
  103, 105, 106, 107, 109, 111,
  113, 114, 123, 124, 125, 128,
  129, 131, 136, 144, 146, 153,
  158, 165, 172, 179, 183, 186,
  191, 192, 193, 194, 195, 196
In a Farther Country, xi, 19, 129,
  144, 148, 156, 157, 176, 190,
  191, 195
"In the Ice-Bound Hothouse," 24,
  50, 53, 61, 64, 80, 86, 87–91,
  168, 169–70
Leander, 11, 20, 49, 80, 197
"Left-handed Gun, The," 195
"Letter in the Cedarchest, The,"
  15, 39–40, 60, 66, 168, 175,
  176, 192
Memoirs, 118. See also *Six Women*
"Moss Rose, The," 40, 64

206

Index

language, continued
  158, 167, 168, 174–75, 177,
  188, 190
Laughlin, James, 113, 194
Lawrence, D. H., 8, 107, 109, 110–
  11, 168, 169
Lawrence, Frieda, 8, 9, 108, 110–11,
  112, 128, 194, 195
Lessing, Doris, 125
Linscott, Bob, 103, 114, 115, 116
listener, 15, 25–26, 31, 32, 33, 39,
  42, 44, 45, 49, 66, 71, 74, 80,
  92, 98, 102, 136–37, 138, 140,
  169, 186, 188. *See also* teller-
  listener situation
London, 9, 10, 112–13, 114, 129,
  194
Los Angeles, 54, 133, 158, 196, 197
Lowell, Robert, 147
Luhan, Mabel Dodge, 9, 110, 11,
  194

Macauley, Rose, 112
McCullers, Carson, 10, 60, 115–17,
  190
McGarth, Thomas, 31
McGraw Hill, 118–19, 187, 196
Mademoiselle, 101, 117, 194
Mailer, Norman, 124, 189, 191
Mann, Thomas, 124, 153
Mansfield, Katherine, 117, 130
Maxwell, Allen, 101, 194
"medallions," xi, 37, 80, 126–27,
  141, 169
meditation, 16, 90, 98, 134, 137,
  155, 170; meditative story, 19,
  21, 22, 24, 30–38, 49, 71, 75,
  87, 180
Melville, Herman, 100, 122
memory, 21–22, 30, 31, 32, 34, 35,
  36, 41, 46, 49, 68, 70, 71, 73,
  74, 77, 81–82, 83, 90–91, 93,
  97, 140–41, 146, 160, 167, 184,
  191. *See also* Themes: the past
Milton, John, 100, 124, 153
Molière, 38
Murray, Oswyn, 23, 43

music, xii, 6–7, 27, 30, 32, 34, 37,
  38, 41, 68, 74, 99, 102, 105–
  106, 121, 126, 127, 130, 153,
  177

narrative voice. *See* voice
New Mexico, 8, 9, 10, 63, 100, 107,
  108, 109, 133, 160, 194, 195
New York City, 10, 11, 33, 54, 107,
  114, 136, 155, 156, 161, 176,
  191, 194, 195, 196
Nietzsche, Friederich, 52
Nin, Anaïs, 13, 165, 187, 190

Oates, Joyce Carol, 166, 167
O'Connor, Flannery, 13, 60, 117,
  133, 146, 189, 190
O'Connor, Frank, 15
oil industry, 5, 33
Ong, Walter J., 60
orality, 23, 24–26, 30, 43, 44, 45, 60,
  61, 71, 73, 94n
orphan(s). *See* Themes: difference
outcasts. *See* Themes: difference

Paris Review, 97, 197
performance. *See* theatre; William
  Goyen and the theatre
Phillips, Robert, xiii, 18, 20, 93n,
  105–32, 165, 172, 186, 193, 196,
  197
Philoctetes, 11, 57–58
Plato, 133
plot, 41, 69, 71, 73, 77–78, 92, 122,
  135, 185
Porter, Katherine Ann, 10, 11, 135–
  36, 139, 165, 194
Pound, Ezra, 122–23, 140
prayer. *See* meditation
Proust, Marcel, 14, 61, 124, 127, 152
Purdy, James, 101

quilt, metaphor of the, xi, 41, 126,
  127, 141. *See also* "medallions"

race, racism, 61, 62–63, 65, 76, 150,
  192

208

The Author

Reginald Gibbons is a poet, fiction writer, translator, and critic whose works include *The Ruined Motel*, *Saints*, *Selected Poems of Luis Cernuda*, *The Poet's Work*, and *The Writer in Our World*. He has been awarded poetry fellowships from the John Simon Guggenheim Memorial Foundation, the National Endowment for the Arts, and the Illinois Arts Council and has also won the Denver Quarterly Translation Award and the Texas Institute of Letters Short Story Award. Born in Texas and educated at Princeton and Stanford, Gibbons is the editor of the literary magazine *TriQuarterly* and teaches English at Northwestern University.

The Editor

Gordon Weaver earned his Ph.D in English and creative writing at the University of Denver in 1970. He is professor of English at Oklahoma State University. He is the author of several novels, including *Count a Lonely Cadence, Give Him a Stone, Circling Byzantium,* and most recently *The Eight Corners of the World.* His short stories are collected in *The Entombed Man of Thule, Such Waltzing Was Not Easy, Getting Serious, Morality Play,* and *A World Quite Round.* Recognition of his fiction includes the St. Lawrence Award for Fiction (1973), two National Endowment for the Arts fellowships (1974 and 1989), and the O. Henry First Prize (1979). He edited *The American Short Story, 1945-1980: A Critical History* and is currently editor of the *Cimarron Review.* Married and the father of three daughters, he lives in Stillwater, Oklahoma.